HOOKED
A HURLING LIFE

HOOKED
A HURLING LIFE

Justin McCarthy

with Kieran Shannon

GILL & MACMILLAN

Gill & Macmillan Ltd
Hume Avenue, Park West, Dublin 12
with associated companies throughout the world
www.gillmacmillan.ie
© Justin McCarthy 2002
0 7171 3339 7
Print origination by Linda Kelly
Printed by ColourBooks Ltd, Dublin

This book is typeset in 10.5/12 Berkeley Book.

The paper used in this book comes from the wood pulp of managed forests. For every tree felled, at least one tree is planted, thereby renewing natural resources.

A CIP catalogue record for this book is available from the British Library.

1 3 5 4 2

1

GLORY IN ARDEE

It's easy to be a hurler in Tipperary. You can walk out with your stick and bag to training; your county has a chance of winning an All-Ireland. But the lad in the Short Strand in Belfast is in a different position. His county has only an outside chance of glory; he won't be able to carry his GAA bag. Carrying a hurl out of a place like that is a statement. You're telling everybody what you are and who you are. There are towns and areas where you just don't do it. You'd be killed.

Terence 'Sambo' McNaughton, *All or Nothing*

My body was stretched out flat along the ground. My lip was bleeding, my jaw was throbbing and my eyes were seeing stars. And yet, when I looked up, some of the people gathered around were in stitches laughing. The thought ran through my dazed head. 'McCarthy, how in the name of God did you get yourself into this, boy?'

I suppose it had a lot to do with something that had happened six years earlier. In 1970, a man called Frank Smyth, and his colleagues on the Antrim hurling board, were desperate to see their county win its first-ever All-Ireland title. They were looking for a coach from the south to go up and polish their hurling before their intermediate quarter-final against Galway. I was twenty-five at the time and the Troubles had just started, but it was also only a year after the Accident. I went up and together we won that All-Ireland.

Now, in March 1976, Frank and Antrim were desperate again. They were playing Westmeath in a Division Two relegation play-off in Ardee, County Louth. For Frank, Division Three hurling was unthinkable after all the progress Antrim had made in the early seventies. The Monday before the match, I received a letter from him pleading that I go up, talk to the team and help them on the line on the day. On the Thursday, he followed it up with a phone call.

I told him I wouldn't be there. I didn't want to be there. Cork to Ardee was over 200 miles. That was an awful long way up. A Division

Two relegation play-off was an awful long way *down* from coaching Cork in a Munster final. I had helped out Antrim a few times since 1970 but there was only so much I could do on the day of a game. Besides, I didn't know the younger players. 'I've played my part, Frank,' I said. 'What more can I do?'

Frank phoned again on the Saturday morning. The players were expecting me to be there. It would give them a huge lift if I'd be there. I *had* to be there. And, as normally happens when there's a real plea from the heart, I caved in. Frank told me the man who would be collecting me at Heuston Station in Dublin and driving me to Ardee would be the team's goalkeeper, Jim Corr.

Jim was Frank Corr's son. Frank Corr was one of the nicest and greatest hurling men I had met. He had gone out of his way for me and for hurling before. When I coached the team in '70, Frank was secretary of the South Antrim board and would collect me at the train station in Belfast before bringing me to Frank Smyth's house on the Glen Road. In 1972, he came all the way down to Thurles to see me play in the league final for Cork. After we won, he came onto the field to congratulate me, knowing all I had gone through to play on such a stage again. Later that summer, Frank made another long trip in the name of hurling. Galway had to go up to Ballycastle to play Antrim in an All-Ireland senior quarter-final and were anxious about how they'd get there after the spate of sectarian killings that had been committed in the previous six months. Frank met them in Monaghan, jumped onto their team coach and showed them a safe route to the venue. Then after the game, he made the journey in reverse and collected the car. That round trip was 400 miles. Five days later, Frank Smyth called me with some news that blew me back. The previous night, Frank Corr had been stopped by loyalist extremists in Belfast on his way home from work. He was tortured and killed and his car was set on fire. Frank had jet-black hair. When his body was found, his hair was snow white from shock. Frank was non-political. His crime was to have a hurley in the back of his car.

Four years later and his son was still carrying hurleys in his van. The question was whether it would be carrying me up to Ardee. I thought hard of what hurling meant to men like Frank Corr and Frank Smyth, of how much it would hurt them to see Antrim fall back into Division Three. I said I'd be in Ardee.

The game was to start at quarter past two. My train was due in Heuston at half-twelve. It didn't arrive until half-one, thanks to the cattle on the line outside Thurles. When I stepped off the train, Jim was there. We sprinted to his van and then he drove like the hammers of hell for Ardee; it wasn't as if we had a mobile phone and could call someone to delay the match. When we got into the field, the game was more than ten minutes old and Antrim were trailing by a few points. Jim sprinted to the dressing room while I tried to locate where the team's dugout was. Just as I spotted that it was over on the stand side, an Antrim player went down injured right in front of me. There was no one else around to help him, so I ran over to help him. I had just started to rub his leg though when, the next second, another Antrim player, thinking I was a Westmeath mentor meddling with one of his team-mates, came running out of nowhere and landed this massive haymaker on the side of my face …

So there I was on the flat of my back in Ardee, on a misty, windy Sunday in March, 200 miles away from my home and warm fire, at a Division Two relegation play-off, after breaking every red light between Dublin and Ardee. All because I was trying to help the fella who was just after flattening me. And yet some of his team-mates were laughing over me.

It was hard not to blame them. They had realised what had happened. The Antrim player who had hit me hadn't been around in '70 and had no idea that I was involved with Antrim. They were laughing even more furiously seconds later. Frank Smyth ran over to the commotion, went in to see what everyone had gathered around, and then went, 'Jesus, that's Justin McCarthy!' Then he turned to the fella who had lamped me. 'You! You're coming off! Selectors! Take him off!' I was still on the ground, but I tried to reach out to Frank. 'God, don't take him off, Frank!' I said, holding my jaw; as far as I was concerned, that player had exactly the kind of fighting spirit Antrim needed.

By half-time, that player was still on and had been joined on the field by Jim Corr. Antrim though were losing by a few points having played with the wind. When that whistle went, they huddled together on the pitch but I told Frank to bring them into the dressing room. In that half-time talk, I gave some instructions to every line of the field. The biggest thing I did though was to lay it on the line to them. 'Lads, I've seen good days with Antrim hurling, I've seen them win All-Irelands. But the way ye're going out there, ye probably should be in Division Three. Ye have to make up your minds now. Do ye want to be playing in Division Three? If ye slip into it, ye might never get out of it. Antrim hurling will be finished. Today is a day of reckoning.

'Let me tell you – actually I won't tell you – what I went through to get here today. Let's just say I went through a lot. And it wasn't for the crack. It wasn't to see ye lose. That's just me. What about this man here, Frank Smyth, who has given his life to hurling? And what about yerselves? Do ye want to play serious hurling or do ye want to be passers-by? Well, then, why am I seeing fellas making half-hearted tackles out there? How come I'm not seeing ye chasing down and blocking and hooking? Lads, I know Antrim hurling better than most. That's not Antrim hurling out there. Give us it out there now in that second half – and everything else ye've got.'

Antrim played like men inspired in that second half, especially Jim Corr. They won by three points. At the final whistle, you'd swear they had won the All-Ireland. About ten minutes later, while everyone was slapping everyone's back, mine included, this man came into the dressing room. 'You're Justin McCarthy?' he said.

'That's right.'

'Listen, I'm with the Down team. We're playing now in the Division Three promotion play-off. Will you come in and say a few words to us?'

So I went in to them. And again at half-time. And they won as well.

That evening, Jim Corr and myself headed back to Dublin in his van. We were held up by customs for ten minutes before being allowed move on. My jaw was still sore. And yet we were as happy as could be. Because the lads on their way home up north were too.

That's why I coach. The cynics in Cork say I coach for money but there's no money in days like Ardee.

There's glory in them though.

That's why I spread the word.

2

THREE WALLS AND THE TRUTH

'Why did you practise so much?' he was asked in an interview in '83.
'I had to,' Ben Hogan replied. 'My swing was so bad.'
'Is that all?'
'No,' he allowed. 'I loved it.'

Curt Sampson, *Hogan*

You can't hide in here.

When Liam Griffin coached Wexford, he would ask his players to look in the mirror because they couldn't fool the man they'd see there. There's a lot of truth in that but I ask my Waterford players to face something else. A wall. A hurler can't bluff the Alley. The Alley is truth. It will tell whether you're fit to hurl or not.

It's okay if you struggle at first. Some of the best players to play this game have served a racquetball against that front wall. Tom Cashman has been here, Charlie McCarthy, Seamus Durack, Pat Hartnett, Ger Cunningham, Tony O'Sullivan too. If you had asked them to stand behind the outside line and hit the ball six times off that top wall sixty feet away, allowing only one hop each time, they couldn't do it starting off; the pace of the ball would have been too much. Eventually though, they adjusted to its pace. And began to discover what a forum of self-discovery the Alley can be.

There's a problem if you're still missing the ball after a while. That tells you you're lacking hurling fitness. It could be a temporary thing. Maybe your eye isn't in, maybe your timing is off because you've overtrained. Jimmy Barry-Murphy would have realised that if he had come to Rochestown the week before the 1982 All-Ireland. I was a selector to Gerald McCarthy that year and fixed the players' hurleys. Jimmy never trained as hard as he did that year. Twenty minutes into training the Monday before the final, Jimmy came over and said, 'Justin, that hurley you gave me is a bit heavy. Can you give me the other one?' Now both hurleys weighed the same as Jimmy liked them to weigh but I said nothing and gave him the second hurley. At the end of the session, he came over again and said, 'I don't think this one is right either.' I said, 'Jimmy, your problem isn't the hurley. Your problem is you're tired. You have to rest. You're overdoing it.' Jimmy said, 'How can I rest, Justin? I'm the captain this year. I have to set the pace, show the way.' The following Sunday, Croke Park told him exactly what the Alley would have concluded a week or so earlier. That he wasn't fresh, that he wasn't hurling fit.

I know because it was the same for me ten years earlier. The week leading up to that 1972 All-Ireland was probably the only week in my entire career that I avoided the Alley; I was exerting enough energy as it was with the team in the Park. We trained like soldiers for that final and with twenty minutes to go it seemed certain we'd win. But we had nothing in the tank. It wasn't just our legs that went; so did our touch. And when your touch goes, your confidence goes. If I had gone to the Alley that week, I wouldn't have lasted twenty minutes in there; I wouldn't have had the freshness to return the ball. And as Kilkenny's coach, Father Tommy Maher, later told me, 'In Croke Park, Justin, freshness is more important than fitness.'

More often than not though the ball will beat you because there's something more fundamentally wrong with your game. Maybe you're one-sided. Maybe your *strong* side is too weak. Maybe your balance and footwork is poor. Maybe your anticipation isn't that great. Or your stamina. Or your concentration.

The Alley is here to help, not humiliate, though. Here you can develop your game more than you ever could on the field. On the field, the ball doesn't come back as fast or as often; you're waiting and waiting and it's boring. You get five shots in the Alley for every one on the field. You can work on a wider range of shots too. When that ball comes back, you have to hit it first time whichever way it comes.

I was recognised as a stylish hurler. When you hear that someone was a stylish hurler, you tend to assume that such a hurler was born, not made. Not true. I was stylish because I had good technique and I had good technique because I worked so hard on my game.

I wanted to be a good hurler. A good hurler must first be a good striker of a ball. Then he should strive to be a consistently good and *accurate* striker. The Alley helps you become that. If that ball is to keep coming back, you can't be pulling your shot; you need to have a true, direct shot all the time. You also need to be balanced. The Alley has props to help you. Keeping your shoulders parallel to the sidewall is a good start. If you do that and are still pulling your shot, that means you have to adjust your footwork. Listen for the sound of ball meeting wall too. The louder and quicker that *swoosh!* is, the better. That's a gauge of the speed and power in your shot.

The power comes from the quickness of your stroke though, not the strength of it. Most fellas come in here and try and break the ball and end up half-hitting it without any direction. Again, the power comes from the quickness. And that quickness should come from the wrists, not the arms. Think to yourself, 'Wristy Christy'. I've been blessed to coach some very good arm-action players like Ger Loughnane and Seán Óg Ó hAilpín but I found they couldn't get the same length as Con Roche could, because they weren't able to connect with the ball at the same speed as a wrist player like Con. The same with the points Tommy Dunne scored in the 2001 All-Ireland final. Ger and Seán Óg wouldn't have had the speed in their hands to get those shots off in time; they'd have been hooked because they'd have had to bring their hurley further back. The Alley is like Croke Park – the better wristwork you have, the better chance you have of doing well there. If you're an arm-action player in the Alley, you might be able to hit that ball back at your own pace, but what happens when you're playing a game with a skilful, alert wrist player? If he nicks that ball off the sidewall, you'll need a wristy shot to counter it; you won't have the time or the room for an effective arm stroke. Just like situations that arise in Croke Park.

It's easy for an inter-county player not to bother with the Alley, of course. He can live off the shots he has, point to his medals and say, 'Sure I don't need the Alley.' You'll also get people claiming that it's too late to iron out the bad habits of adult players. That attitude is a cop-out. My neighbour and friend, Martin O'Donoghue, played minor for Cork. When he was forty-six, he decided to go back to the Alley. Martin had a weak left-sided shot so when we'd be playing games in here, I'd play it to that side every time. He'd swipe at it and the ball would bounce off the ground, fifteen feet short of that front wall. I won a lot of points that way. Within a few months I wasn't. Through sheer practice, Martin became as good off his left as off his right. If a 46-year-old can do that, then a 26-year-old county player can.

Ger Cunningham was the only player I've coached that maximised his full potential. Ger practised as often as he could. That meant he'd come regularly to Rochestown. That took great humility. It was only in 1997 that he first beat me in a game. Ger was still playing for Cork then; I was fifty-two. But Ger always realised that the Alley and myself were there to help him. In those battles in the Alley,

Ger learned to think and hurl faster. His wristwork and footwork improved. When I'd play a ball that would hop within a foot of the outside line, Ger would have to go back on one leg to play his shot. Just like he sometimes would to clear his lines in Thurles.

I've been coming to the Alley in Rochestown College for nearly fifty years now. It's only a few hundred yards from where I live with my wife Pat and the kids. Next door to our house is where I was born. Whether those houses or the Alley is home is hard to say but the Alley feels like home. I don't think I'll ever be able to thank the Capuchin Fathers enough for building it. When I was a player, I'd often come here in the morning and then come back up after tea. Even now, at fifty-six, the sound of that *swoosh!* turns me on. I'm a man of simple tastes. I don't drink or spend hours in the clubhouse after a match. I prefer to take the dog for a walk through the fields, take some photographs, see the sun go down on Cork, call to a friend. Or come here, to the Alley. Here I can express myself. Here I can lose all track of time. Here I can escape the pressures of being regional manager of Tedcastles Oil. Here is simplicity.

There's no politics here either. I've had my share of politics. When I was five, all I dreamt about was playing for Cork. By the time I was twenty-five, I had notions of some day coaching Cork. A month before the 1975 championship began, that dream came true. The team I inherited had not won a championship match in three years. In the next three months, we won the Munster championship, winning every game by at least ten points. Then we lost to Galway and I was kicked out. People were stunned by how I had been treated but they wouldn't have known the politics. That summer I made four basic requests concerning the team's preparations. Frank Murphy, the county board secretary, initially turned them all down. Some were eventually granted, others weren't. When I asked why he couldn't give me new sliotars for every session the fortnight before the Galway game, Frank told me that I was costing the board enough.

Seven years later, we were at loggerheads again when I returned to the county set-up as a selector. One night, five of us were picking a team for a league game when I proposed that Seanie O'Leary be brought back onto the panel and team. Gerald McCarthy agreed. Frank didn't. He felt O'Leary was a bad influence on the team. Now Seanie might have been a prankster in the dressing room and was carrying some weight, but I knew of no better goal poacher in or outside the county. We argued the

O'Leary issue for about fifteen minutes when Tim Mullane declared that Seanie should be recalled. That third vote meant O'Leary was in. Frank said that if O'Leary was on for Sunday, he was walking out of the meeting. We thought he was joking but when we moved on to pick the next spot, Frank insisted he wasn't going to be a party to the meeting any longer.

I said, 'Frank, sorry, but it's a majority decision. Let's get on with the team.'

Frank stormed out. Our other selector, Denis Hurley, was about to go after him but I told Denis not to bother.

'But what if he doesn't show on Sunday?' Denis asked.

'He'll be there on Sunday,' I said.

Frank was there that Sunday. And that July, when O'Leary scored four goals in the Munster final.

A few months after that 1982 Munster final, Gerald and myself were voted out for losing the All-Ireland to Kilkenny. Within a year I was voted back in. Frank and Johnny Clifford weren't. I had put my name forward only hours before the vote was taken because a very prominent GAA official had urged me to do my bit to ensure Cork won the Centenary All-Ireland. Shortly afterwards, the county board executive was informed that the team's selection committee had decided I would be coaching the side.

The following week the five of us were called before a special section of the county board called the General Purposes Committee. That night in Páirc Uí Chaoimh, Frank Murphy and Denis Conroy asked us to do something no other selection committee in the history of Cork GAA had been asked to do. We were told to reverse our decision and appoint Johnny Clifford as team coach. We refused to back down.

The following week there was another twist. The county board sanctioned my appointment – as the team's joint coach. And if you look at the history books, they'll say that Father Michael O'Brien and Justin McCarthy were joint coaches to the Centenary All-Ireland champions. But Father O'Brien never deviated from what the five-man selection committee had decided prior to that GPC meeting and never interfered with the tasks of the team coach.

For you'll be amazed who nominated that team coach.

Even after we delivered that historic All-Ireland and retained our Munster title in '85, the politics continued. There was the Interview, the Photograph; I had enough of it all. After our last championship match that summer, I knew I'd never coach Cork again. I was only forty then. The thing was, Frank was even younger.

I've been lucky in this life though. When one door has closed, another has opened. That's why I'm not bitter about anything or anyone. After The Accident, I could have hated God but instead I was grateful to him. It was as if it was his way of saying, 'That was an obvious hurling path you were taking there, boy. I've a different path for you. You'll do more for the game this way.' Were it not for The Accident, I would have won four or five All-Irelands but I'd never have coached Antrim. I'd never have coached Clare. If the powers-that-be in Cork had wanted me to stay on after '85, I'd never have seen the bonfires in Cashel on a wet but glorious November night. Or coached Waterford. In life, you have to deal with whatever comes your way, whatever way it comes, and make the best of it.

A lot like a ball coming back at you in the Alley.

A lot like hurling itself.

People forget that. They compare hurling to sports in which it's easier to get and keep possession and so think that coaching in our game is playing two-man full-forward lines and having your half-forwards behind midfield. Hurling doesn't work like that. If you're expecting your forwards to get the perfect ball every time, you're finished. I remember one league game against Clare when I was able to play everything into my clubmate Eddie O'Brien and Eddie scored five points, but Clare were asleep that day. If you have a set plan, then a good team will soon spot it and cut it out. Now, don't get me wrong – if you're a back or midfielder and have the space and time to look up and pick out a forward, by all means, play it into him. But in championship hurling, you'll only get to do that with one in every four balls. Those other three times, you should play the ball on its merits and trust your team-mates to read the breaks and control that ball. In hurling, scores come from nothing.

Take the 2001 championship. Tipperary's Mark O'Leary scored most of his points through sheer hurling instinct rather than any great plan. Like any good wing forward, he kept on the move and when the ball broke around that half-forward line, he had the anticipation to get onto it and the hurling to control and put it over the bar. Or look at how Seanie O'Leary scored so many goals for us around the square. He never thought, 'I didn't get the ideal ball, I'll wait for it.' He knew it might never come.

The Alley is all about developing that kind of hurling instinct. Anticipating the shots, anticipating the breaks, and then, being able to instantly select and execute the right shot. We play matches in here, similar to handball, except we use hurleys. You literally have to think on your feet in those games. First you must anticipate your opponent's next shot. Then you have to decide instantly what shot you're going to play. Often you'll try to play the ball as far away as possible from him. Or maybe you'll try to kill the point by doubling overhead off your left side. Or maybe you'll play a shot to kill the *next* shot, the kind of forward thinking you need in snooker. Except here, you can't mull over it; you must decide in a split second. Just like in hurling itself.

There's another reason why players should train here more often. It's fun. Hurling is supposed to be fun.

That's why I'm hooked on it.

That's why I took it up all those years ago.

3

THE WAY WE WERE

And it's Christy Ring with the ball!
Mícheál O'Hehir – and Justin McCarthy

A t the start of his best-selling book, *Angela's Ashes*, Frank McCourt gave a damning verdict on growing up in Limerick. 'When I look back on my childhood,' he wrote, 'I wonder how I survived at all. It was, of course, a miserable childhood: the happy childhood is hardly worth your while. Worse than the ordinary miserable childhood is the miserable Irish childhood, and worse yet is the miserable Irish Catholic childhood.' I was blessed. My childhood was Irish, Catholic and joyous.

I almost grew up in Limerick. I was conceived there; well, in the county of Limerick anyway. My father managed a farm in Athlacca, near Kilmallock, for a few years before the family moved in 1945 to Rochestown, close to my mother's home place of Passage West. It was five miles away from Cork city but it might as well have been fifty. Our world was far removed from the city. It was great. We didn't have an alcoholic father or a pious defeated mother moaning by the fire. Most of the clergy I knew were helpful, not pompous. We didn't even mind the rain. When you lived in the country, you embraced the seasons. Each one of them had its own charm. Even if all of them included the rain.

The greatest thing about living in the country was the freedom. There were so many ways to kill time. Like going through the fields with Jip, our wheaten terrier, looking for rabbits. Like fishing in the streams for trout. Like looking for birds' nests. Like hitting blackberries off the briar. Like hurling.

I t shouldn't have been my game. I shouldn't have made it. Not if the odds were anything to go by.

My father was one of the few west Cork men who preferred the small ball to the big one, but his small ball was the kind used for road bowling. My mother never went to see me play; whenever I'd come home with stitches and scars, she'd always say, 'When are you going to give it up?' My sister Una didn't play. Neither did my brother Noel.

I had a hurley in my hand by the time I was fourteen months old. Barry put it there. He was my older brother. I adored him. Maybe it was because he was the extrovert in the family. My father was a typical west Cork man of the land and the time – decent, hard working, resilient, religious, humble. When I became good at the hurling, he'd never say, 'You did me proud there today, boy.' Instead, he'd just go, 'Yeah, ye won. You weren't too bad.' Barry was more expressive, more exuberant. From an early age he told me I was a natural and would some day play for Cork. That's probably why he let me be Ring or Paddy Barry every time we played a game of goal-to-goal on the road and he'd settle for being Mackey. Anything to help me.

I helped him as well. He was nine years older than me so was allowed to go to the big games but he needed money to go. That meant he needed me, or at least I felt he did. When he'd be working for some of the local farmers to finance those match and rail tickets, I'd go out and help him, be it to thin some turnips or bale some hay. Looking back, he didn't need the help; at sixteen he could ride horses, bring in cows and run a milk round all by himself. But he never let on. Every time he came back from an All-Ireland or Munster final he had a red and white hat, match programme and a big flagon of lemonade for me. 'That's for helping me, Justin,' he'd wink. 'I wouldn't have been able to go only for you.'

The best bit though was when he'd describe the games. Going up with my father to Breen's to listen to Mícheál O'Hehir's commentary on their radio was great; hearing Barry's account was even better. It was as if I was at each of those All-Irelands Cork won in '52, '53 and '54. I *knew* Ring. I knew Paddy Barry. I knew Tipp and Pat Stakelum, Seamus Bannon and Jimmy Finn too. In my mind's eye, I could see them all.

We'd try to emulate them. Back then, there was only one or two cars in the area; we thought roads were solely for playing goal-to-goal games. I'd stand on one end of the road, Barry would take up position about forty yards down the other, and we'd have two stones behind each of us for goalposts. The aim was to shoot the old rubber ball past the other fella. The first to three won.

You learned to be an all-round hurler playing goal-to-goal. You had to be able to stop the ball like a Reddin yet have the shot of a Ring. You had to have good anticipation for when that ball came off a stone or the ditch. And you had to be cute. When I scored a goal from twenty-five yards playing for Passage a few weeks before my senior debut for Cork, some people thought it was a fluke because it bounced three feet in front of the goalkeeper. I meant for it to skid off the ground like that. Barry did it enough times to me out on that road in front of our house.

I was seven when I played my first proper game. It was against the rules, really. In our area, you went to the boys' primary school when you were in second class; I was only in first class, down in the convent. But when the boys' school were a player short for the hurling league they were starting up, a few of the older lads around my area told the teachers about me. Those teachers then sent word to the convent. I was reluctant to go up. No one else in the convent had been asked, I only knew a few lads in the boys' school, and I'd be up against fellas who were eleven or twelve.

Sister Carmel had other ideas. She was a forceful woman. She was also from Cloyne, home of Ring. 'Go on,' she told me. 'I've heard you're very good. If you're good enough, you're big enough. You should play.'

I did. It was strange at first but I got used to it. We ended up winning the league. Our prize was a hurley each. After the game, I ran the mile and a half home to show Barry. He was delighted for me. It was one of the best days of my life.

19 March 1955 was one of the saddest. Barry left for America that day. I still remember it well. His smile. His promise that he'd write every week. The hugs. The handshakes. The waves. The tears. The boat pulling out from Cobh. More waves. More tears.

He was true to his word. He did write every week. But as that boat pulled out, I knew part of my life was going away. Back then no one could afford to fly; you might never see a Stateside relative again.

The next time I met Barry I was nineteen. By then, everything had changed.

4

TOUCHED BY A HOLY SPIRIT

A boy comes to me with a spark of interest. I feed the spark and it becomes a flame. I feed the flame and it becomes a fire. I feed the fire and it becomes a roaring blaze.

Legendary boxing coach Cus D'Amato

I never met Cus D'Amato. I never will either, at least not in this world; he took his last breath three months after I took my last Cork training session. That quote of his though has a particular resonance for me. I was once a boy with a spark of interest, provided by Barry. When he went, I needed someone else to feed that spark. Fortunately, I met my D'Amato. My passion for hurling blazes on today.

I was hardly a delinquent as a youngster, unlike D'Amato's most famous protégé, Mike Tyson. I was up to some mischief though when I first came across the provider of the flame. Billy Delaney and myself were playing down in the woods behind the local monastery, when, just as we were coming by the grotto, this huge man with a huge red beard came round the corner.

'What are ye doing?' he bellowed.

'Just chasing, Father,' we muttered. We had heard of this new priest. Father Rock, they called him, or at least we thought they did because that's what his name sounded like. By all accounts, he wasn't a man to suffer fools gladly. The authoritative tone of his voice suggested those reports had been right.

'Who told ye ye could play here?'

'We always play down here, Father,' I said. It was the truth but I feared that it might signal the last words of my nine-year-old life.

And then he took us completely by surprise.

'Do ye play hurling?'

We looked at each other.

'We do, Father. We love hurling.'

And with that, his frown became a smile. Before his arrival, there hadn't been any altar boys in our parish. He wanted to change that. The way he saw it, one of the most effective ways of spreading the gospel was to spread the hurling kind. In Rochestown, one of the privileges of being an altar boy would be to play hurling. And that's what playing hurling under Father Roch proved to be. A privilege.

Roch was a shrewd man. One time, he arranged a game between us altar boys in Rochestown and another group from Holy Trinity, a city-based church also run by the Capuchins. Roch knew they were stronger and more streetwise than us but it didn't seem to bother him. A few days before the game, he told us that we'd be throwing a party for these fellas as they were coming all the way from town. A room in the college was prepared. When the city boys trooped off their bus, Roch was there to welcome them. 'We're holding a party for ye afterwards,' he informed them. 'Follow me; I'll show ye where we're having it.' When the door opened and the city lads saw the tables laid out with lemonade, chocolate, pastries and cakes, their jaws dropped. Hungry looks were directed at their coach, Father Noel, who in turn looked to his colleague. 'But of course, lads, eat away!' decided Roch. 'You don't want to wait till afterwards!' They duly stuffed themselves until about half an hour later, Roch said, 'Lads, I suppose we better go and play that match.' When the ball was thrown in, they could hardly run. We ended up stuffing *them* before having a party of our own. All – as I found out years later – as Roch had planned it.

It took me years to figure out another one of his mind games. As a kid, I couldn't understand why he not only went to the bother of knowing the names of the opposing players but would actually cheer them on. If I was marking a John Murphy and he scored a point off me, Roch would go, 'Good man, John! That's the hurling!' It drove me mad. Which, of course, is why he did it.

Roch had other ways to get the best out of us. Just before we were to play a group of altar boys from Kilkenny, he called us in. 'Lads,' he said, 'today you're playing for Cork.' He then handed each of us a red jersey thanks to an arrangement he had come to with a Father Nessan who was on the Cork juvenile board. Running onto Nowlan Park as an eleven-year-old in that jersey that day was as big a thrill as it was taking to Croke Park ten years later to face the same county in an All-Ireland final. The outcome, thanks to Roch's stroke, was the same.

It's about the only time he ever wanted a Kilkenny team beaten. When I called down to him a few days before that 1966 All-Ireland final asking him to say Mass for me, he did so conditionally. 'Justin,

I'll say Mass that you play well. But I won't say Mass that Cork will win.' Roch loved Kilkenny hurling. Thankfully for me, he also studied it.

It helped that he came from Tullaroan. It may be the second smallest parish in the diocese of Ossory but there's no bigger parish in the hurling world. The local club still leads the roll of honour when it comes to Kilkenny county titles while it has produced seventy-five All-Ireland senior medals. Roch's own cousin, Sean Clohessy, brought one home in 1957. Paddy Phelan, who made the Team of the Millennium and was described by Jack Lynch as the greatest hurler he ever met, won four. Tullaroan was also home to the legendary Lory Meagher.

I didn't know much about Meagher before I met Roch. When Barry and myself would play out on the road, we'd pretend we were either Mackey or Ring; Meagher was a distant figure from the thirties. Occasionally we'd shout that universal hurling line, '"Over the bar," says Lory Meagher', but that was about all Lorenzo Ignatius Meagher meant to me.

Roch changed that. From an early stage, he saw something in me and decided to model my game on Meagher's. For the next five years, Roch must have said 'This is the way Lory would do it, Justin' nearly as often as he said 'Corpus Christi'. Lory – or, as Roch pronounced it, *Low-ree* – was supposedly a stylish, tall, rangy player who was a brilliant striker of the ball both overhead and on the ground. He was also unerring with his frees and sideline cuts and was well able to make space for himself before striking off either side. In short, he could do it all. Roch sensed I should be able to do the same.

He explained though that Meagher had a brilliant work ethic. Making the game look easy took hard work. Meagher would spend hours out in the fields practising, be it just hitting the ball up in the air and catching it or just chipping it over an imaginary bar. When he was a senior with Kilkenny, he'd use a set of dumb-bells that he found stored in a corn loft in the farmyard of his house. I would have to have the same love of the game.

One Saturday Roch got to see first hand that I did. He had told me to be up at the hurling field by ten o'clock that morning with my hurley and sliotar, so I duly obliged. When I got there, he said he wanted me to work on my frees and sideline cuts while he went to plough some of the fields in the sixty-acre farm the monastery owned. When he came back it was three o'clock; he had completely forgotten about me. He never forgot afterwards though that I had still been there, practising away.

Roch made up for not coaching me that day. When I was about twelve, the altar boys were playing this match against Rochestown College. I hardly hit a ball in the first half at centre forward. As I was trooping off the field at half-time, Roch shouted, 'You! Come over here!' Now, when Father Roch said something, you listened; he was a very stern and direct man when the occasion demanded and he obviously felt this was such an occasion. When I ran over to him, he caught me by the shoulder and proceeded to bring me to the centre-forward spot where he put a cross in the ground. 'This is your position! Up to now, you've been playing everywhere and getting nowhere, trying to follow the ball. Stay here! Plenty of balls will drop here. You'll get scores from here. Guaranteed.' I ended up with five goals that day – and absorbing a lesson for life. *Play your position.*

The real test of a coach is what he can teach you on a one-to-one basis. That's what made Roch special. Up in that college field he taught me tricks of the trade which would serve me, and every team I coached, well. Five in particular came in useful.

1. Say the ball is coming down in the air, you're standing on the right side of your marker and you want to keep the ball going forward. If you stay there, you're giving him a free run; he'll either bat the ball down or catch it. So you don't stay there. Just as he thinks you're about to pull right-handed, you cross over to block his path, with your head pointing towards your goal and your backside pointing towards his. Then, in the same motion, you forward pivot on your right foot, bring your left knee up and pull left-handed. Tim Crowley used that tip to great effect for us. I used it a lot myself playing in either midfield or the half-forward line.

2. Back in the fifties and sixties, few players carried a second hurley; they couldn't afford it. Which posed the question: what if they lost that first hurley? Roch said that I ought to try to find out now and again. Instead of striking the ball in the air, I should pull a bit lower to break the other fella's stick. What would I find out? That the odd time, the referee would blow for a free against me. And that almost every time, my marker would be thrown completely out of his stride.

3. Suppose an opponent is coming from one direction, you're coming at him face on from the other and the ball is between the pair of you. If you both pull, the ball could go anywhere. So you don't. Instead, just as he pulls, you stick in the heel of your hurley to hit the bas of his. That way, your hurley is between him and the ball, giving you the room to kick the ball through to pick and clear.

4. Another Kilkenny way of winning the second ball to make space for a clearance. I call it The Sandwich or The Break To Take. Say you're going for a ball, you're on the left, your opponent is on the right and he's slightly ahead of you. Let him pull hard on it; he doesn't know what you're really going to do. So what do you do? Well, you don't just whip on the ball and risk either being beaten to the pull or allowing the ball to ricochet anywhere. Instead, you keep the bas of your hurley at the side of the ball, a few inches to your side. That way, the force of his pull will bring the ball over to your side. It will also bring your hurley more to your left and closer to the ball. As a result, you can keep yourself between him and the ball, by using your backside. All you have to do then is pick and clear.

5. A bit like the third one except this time both of you are shoulder-to-shoulder running for the ball at speed. As he goes to pull on it, you stop and stick in the heel of your hurley to connect with his bas. His momentum brings him forward – and out of the equation. And so you're free to keep him off with your backside before picking and clearing.

Imagine if every player got advice like that.

Roch made it clear that all those skills would be of limited use without a good hurley. One day, he decided to give me one, made by Ramie Dowling from Kilkenny. In a way, it was a present and he pleaded that I take good care of it. I broke it within a week. Over the next few days, I prayed that Roch wouldn't notice I was using another stick. I was afraid how he might react.

The next night at training, he called me over.

'Where's your hurley?'

The game was up.

'I broke it.'

'You broke it?' He sounded hurt. 'Where is it?'

'At home.'

'Well go and get it. That hurley you have there is no good.'

So I went home, reluctantly. What was the point? The hurley was cracked right along its grain. When I came back ten minutes later, I put out the hurley, as if to show him it was obviously a lost cause.

'Give me that hurley!' he scowled before trying to save its short life.

Four years later I was still using the hurley he banded that night.

Roch was more than a hurling man to me. He instilled confidence and discipline into Justin McCarthy the person. As an altar boy,

I'd often have to get up at six in the morning to serve Mass at a quarter to seven. We worked on the farm with him, making the hay or thinning turnips. Yet we could also have a laugh with him. In Seraphic Youth – the name of our religious youth club – there were Christmas parties and trips to the seaside.

He was also a shoulder to lean on, despite his formidable appearance. One summer's night, he called up to our house to say that my father, who had been working in England for a few months, was having a serious operation the next day. We had no phone back then but my father had told Roch's sister, who was based in London, of his predicament; somehow he knew Roch would be the right man to break us the news. And he was. That night Roch also told us he would be having Mass for my father at seven o'clock the next morning. Dad's subsequent treatment for ulcers was successful.

Father Roch left Rochestown to be stationed in a Kilkenny friary when I was fourteen. It wasn't as big a wrench as when Barry went to the States because I was much older, but it was still a sad day. He returned to Cork seven years later. Not only did he say Mass for me before the 1966 senior All-Ireland final but he also fixed my hurleys for the following month's Under-21 final. Six years after that again he said another Mass for me – my wedding Mass.

The woman I married that day, Pat, often says I'm the son Roch never had. She's probably right. After receiving the freedom of Cork for his brilliant social work for troubled kids in the inner-city, Father Roch has been based in the North for the last five years. Before each of our annual trips to him, he's known to get very excited. So do I. And each year, he's still the same Father Roch I met over forty-five years ago. He's now in his seventies but that magnificent beard, roguish look and earthy manner remain. His love for hurling is also intact. We met in August 2001. I slagged him about Kilkenny's All-Ireland semi-final defeat to Galway and he slagged me about taking the Waterford job.

'I'm spreading the gospel,' I smiled. 'Just like you did in Rochestown all those years ago.'

5

RITES OF PASSAGE

Go confidently in the direction of your dreams. Act as though it were impossible to fail.

Dorthea Brandt, *The Book of Zen*

Someone else nearly left Rochestown in '59. Most of the talk in our house revolved around the States, be it about the new coat Una had bought there, the new job Barry had got there or the new car Noel had just bought there. Everything seemed to be happening *there*. So the parents started to think, why shouldn't we all go there?

I could think of loads of reasons. I was an only child in Ireland but I was a happy one; no far away fields could be greener than those of Rochestown. While we had no running water, bright lights or big cars, we had so much else. In Boston, there wouldn't be any Jip to walk, trout to fish or blackberries to pick. Worse, there wouldn't be any hurling.

By now I was hooked on the game. I went to my first Munster final that same summer of '59. Our Under-15 team in Passage was on its way to four city division finals. More than that, I was becoming really good at it.

Maybe it was because I had a hurley in my hand every day. My mother often reminded me what day of the week I was born and that the saying went, 'Saturday's child must work hard for his living.' She had a point. Instilled with the Meagher ethic, I'd often go up to the field in Rochestown College with four or five sliotars and take shots from all kinds of angles and distances, starting off from forty yards out all the way to the opposite 'seventy' as it was known then. I'd spend hours in the handball alley, learning new shots by the day. Even if I was walking through the fields with Jip, I'd bring my hurley, trying to put the ball through that gate forty yards yonder.

America seemed inevitable though. My mother had spent four months over there that summer with the others, and if there were to be more trips across the Atlantic that year, it was going to be myself and Dad making them. Then one night, Father Ferdinand from the monastery called to the house. When my father told him of his dilemma, Ferdinand said he had been in the States for years himself. 'It's a young man's place, Michael. At your age, I think you should stay put.' A few weeks later, my mother was on her way home. That made me glad.

The days of innocence didn't last forever. When I was sixteen, I left school to work as an apprentice boilermaker in Verolme shipyard with 1,500 other men. The Dutch owners and management were real slave drivers, a legacy of their World War II experience. Some of their workings held me in good stead; I'll always remember the sign in our workshop that read, 'If you have five minutes to spare, don't spend it with someone who hasn't.' But for the most part, they were more ruthless than efficient. One day, two local lads went into the hold of a ship after taking their ten-minute tea break. They were unaware that the gas had started to leak so they continued to weld. Seconds later, this huge explosion went off, causing us all to stop working in our tracks. Except the Dutch. While the rest of us took a half-day to honour the deceased, they worked on. As if the war was still on.

Verolme did have one thing going for it. Their hurling team was one of the best in Cork. The inter-firm scene was very serious back then. All the big plants had teams – Dunlops, Irish Steel, Fords, Golden Vale, Youghal Carpets – and all wanted to win. Talk in the workplace was of little else; everyone wanted to help give the team an edge. If I was going into Mick Hemlock to sign for tools for a special job, he'd say, 'Make sure you're there on Saturday, Justin.' If I was working with Johnny O'Connor putting beams into a ship, he'd take it upon himself to do the lion's share. 'We don't want you getting injured,' he'd say. 'We need you right for that game tomorrow.'

I actually couldn't make the team at first; the team had so many players with senior experience. Gradually I became bigger and stronger, and by the end of my first full year with the company I had broken onto the team. When we made it through to the championship final against Irish Refinery, I was picked at right half forward.

I'll never forget that bitterly cold dry January afternoon in Riverstown in 1963, not just because it was the first big game of my life but for how hard my marker was. I had heard of Bernie Aherne. That he was from Ring's home place of Cloyne. That he was a regular with Imokilly and the Cork intermediate team. And most of all, that he played hard. How hard though I had no idea. Bernie was only five foot eight but he was as strong as a bull; like Páidí Ó Sé would be with a hurley. When we were pulling on the ground or in the air, Bernie blew me out of it. After ten minutes I had been on either my ass or my knees five times. It was as if he was saying, 'Don't you know this is a man's game? Sure you're only a boy.'

But I was a confident boy. I knew my skill level and shot were better than anybody else there, and slowly but surely I came into the game. I started to beat Bernie to the pull, and once or twice used Roch's step-over move to effect. Midway through the second half, John Barry of Passage passed a ball out to me on the wing; I soloed inside and finished to the net. By the final whistle, I had scored 1-4 and we had won by four points. After that night, word spread that some young fella from Rochestown had given Bernie Aherne a lot of trouble. For the first time, the name Justin McCarthy had entered the Cork hurling consciousness.

Johnny O'Connor was sure what should happen next. 'You'll make that Cork minor team, Justin. Sure you're better than all them fellas.' I myself wasn't so sure if I was better than all of them. But better than most of them? Yeah, that I felt I was. I practised more than any of them; I didn't drink or smoke; I had even got the better of Bernie Aherne. How many of them could boast that? If luck was on my side, I'd make the team.

It hadn't been the previous year. Five minutes into the trial game in Ballinlough, an opponent came across me and the side of his body collided with the side of my head. I had double vision for the rest of the game but was too proud to tell the selectors. If I could avoid such a freak incident in '63, I was sure I'd make the team.

I didn't; not for the first round against Clare at any rate. I was only a sub. I knew why but decided there was nothing I could do about it; the only thing was to seize the chance if it presented itself. It did. I came on in the second half of that Clare game at wing forward and scored a few points to help us win. When the team was picked for the semi-final against Tipperary, I was on from the start. We were beaten that day in Thurles but I held my own. After that, I knew I could make it – if I had the courage to go against the tide.

When people ask me where I'm from, I say Rochestown, not Passage. There's more than just the two miles that separate the two places even if they make up the one parish. Passage was a heavily industrialised town in the early part of the century; Rochestown was in the country. They were townies; we were country boys. Sure we played with them but we had our own college, our own monastery, our own *identity*. So when some of the lads said in the winter of '61 that we should also have our own club, I agreed.

It was like a lot of GAA clubs, an offshoot of another. When Passage won the intermediate championship in '61, not everyone in the club rejoiced. Some players felt they should have been getting a game and some of them were from Rochestown. When one of the stars of that Passage team also weighed in with the new club, I signed up immediately. I wanted to play a proper game with Martin O'Donoghue. After all, I had spent my whole life playing informally with him.

If Barry and Roch were my two biggest influences, Martin was my third. It was he who showed me how to take my first free when I was only six. Martin was Barry's best friend but when Barry left, he became mine. It didn't seem to matter that I was nine years younger than him; he'd always look out for me. I in turn always looked up to him. We'd play goal-to-goal games together, him playing up the hill, me playing down it. He'd bring me on the crossbar of his bike to all the matches, talk all day about the games, anything to keep my interest in hurling alive. Barry must have told him to keep an eye out for me. Only for Martin, I'd probably have fallen by the wayside.

Martin wasn't the only friend who joined Rochestown. So did Billy Delaney and my neighbour Jimmy Forde. And at first, the new club was great. Playing in the south-east division at adult level that summer in '62 toughened me up. In '63, I was taking frees for the divisional senior team. All seemed well.

It wasn't. When the Cork minor selectors had looked at me, they merely saw a handy player from an unknown junior club. Why go for such a player when you could go with one from the All-Ireland colleges' champions, Farranferris? Why not go with someone from the Big Three of Blackrock, St Finbarr's and Glen Rovers? They were proven; this Justin lad wasn't. No one from an unknown junior club could be.

Passage were monitoring the situation with interest. They knew they could do with me and that I could do with them. I'd often meet one of their best players, Johnny Coughlan, at the pictures in the town and he'd say, 'When are you coming back, boy? Sure you're a senior player!' And after a while, I decided Johnny was right. In the first few days of 1964, I transferred back.

The decision went down very badly in Rochestown. Here they were, a new club on the rise, and their top young player was leaving. The lads told me straight out, 'You're going to lose friends, Justin.' And I did. Before the move, not having a car wasn't that much of a disadvantage. After the move, it was. The lads no longer stopped to give a lift. They didn't even stop to say 'Hi', not even at Mass. Not even Martin.

It hurt badly. But I was ambitious. A few years earlier, I left Rochestown College to go to the vocational school in Passage because I knew taking subjects like metalwork and woodwork was in the best interests of my professional career. Now, by joining a senior club, I was advancing my prospects of playing senior hurling for Cork. I could see where the lads were coming from but I thought they should have tried to see where I was trying to go. Every blank stare, every unanswered salute only furthered my resolve.

It was rewarded. After playing some very good hurling for Passage, I was called up in June to play for the county Under-21 team against Tipperary. It wasn't the most organised set-up. The grade was new to the inter-county calendar and Cork didn't put much effort into it. We had no training sessions and the game was played on a Sunday night in Tipperary town, only three hours after I had played a senior championship game for Passage in the Park. Not surprisingly, we lost. At least though I had fared reasonably well at midfield on the great Mick Roche. It was enough to be selected to play at midfield for the county intermediate team against Kerry three weeks later.

My life changed that night. In more ways than one. When I went down to the crossroad in front of the monastery to be collected by one of the selectors, someone else was waiting there. Martin O'Donoghue had been called as a sub for the same game.

It was awkward at first; we had hardly spoken in nearly a year. Gradually though we started making conversation. When we got to Macroom, I sat down on the embankment to watch the curtain-raiser between the Kerry and Cork junior footballers before Martin gave me some advice I've never forgotten. 'Don't watch the football too closely, Justin. It'll slow down your speed of thought for hurling.'

I heeded his advice. My reactions in that game were spot on. We won by nine points and I scored eight. The next day the *Cork Examiner* wrote: 'If the Cork senior hurling selectors were looking for likely talent then they might well bring Justin McCarthy of Passage on to the selection. Tall, stylish and always appearing completely unhurried, he was in complete command in this type of company.'

What was more, Martin was of the same opinion. Once the game was finished, he ran over to say I had to be on the senior panel for the Munster final after that display.

Macroom was a watershed. Myself and Martin were tight again after it; two years later, he himself left Rochestown to rejoin Passage.

And he was right in what he said that night. Four days after that Kerry game, I *was* called up to the senior panel. Just as Barry had said I would all those years before.

6

LIVING IN THE
SHADOW OF GIANTS

Give us Cork hurling. No one picks the ball except Christy Ring.
Former Cork trainer, Sean Óg Murphy

There's a rule for any team I coach. When I call them to come in, they're to come in fast. The last guy into that huddle does thirty press-ups. Any guy who sniggers repeats the dose. I want them to know that every second in training is precious. You have to be on the move, tuned in, on time.

God knows what I'd have done with Justin McCarthy at his first training session with Cork.

The letter from the county board said that the seniors were training in the Park on the Tuesday night. And they were; the senior footballers, that is. I must have been waiting over quarter of an hour for them to finish up when it dawned on me that none of the hurlers had yet arrived. When I asked one of the footballers, Con Paddy O'Sullivan, if he knew what was happening, he said that he had heard the hurlers were down in the Mardyke. Suddenly it began to make sense. The footballers were playing Kerry the following Sunday so they had first option on the Park. No one had remembered to tell the new fella that the hurlers' training had been switched. All my life I had waited for this moment, all my life I had prided myself on my discipline, and now I was going to be late for my first session.

All kinds of thing flashed through my mind. The saying that first impressions last. That they wouldn't believe me. That my first training session would be my last. But just as my heart was about to sink, I remembered my father was still there. More importantly, so was his motorbike. Seconds later, I was holding onto the back of him and telling him to drop me off at Singer's Corner on Washington Street as fast as he could. I ran the remaining half a mile as fast as I could. When I got there, the hurlers were training away. I was mortified. 'You're a bit late,' said team selector Jim Hurley. His tone was friendly though. When I apologetically explained my predicament, Jim said they had guessed something like that had happened. Then the man beside him stuck out his hand. 'Welcome, Justin,' Jim Barry said. I liked him from the start.

I was never late for another one of his sessions either.

Remember that scene in *Field of Dreams* when the young Burt Lancaster character, Moonlight Graham, walks around Kevin Costner's baseball diamond, in awe of being in the same company as veterans like Shoeless Jackson? That's how I felt in the Mardyke that night; as if I was in Madame Tussaud's and suddenly the wax around me had turned into flesh and blood. Was that really Jimmy Brohan? Was that really Gerry O'Sullivan pucking around with Paddy Fitzgerald? I had seen them from the terraces with my own eyes yet they had seemed to be moving in a different orbit from ours. Now here they were up close. For real. And I couldn't believe that it was.

I also couldn't get over how fast they were training. The speed at which they moved, at which they hit the ball, at which it whizzed past. I realised there and then that everything they had said about senior inter-county hurling was true; it *was* a level above anything I had experienced before.

Denis Murphy noticed I was struggling. In the first three sprints, I was slow off the mark and left trailing behind. Then he came over and told me to watch the whistle in Jim Barry's mouth; that way, I could get out of the blocks quicker. When I did, I was up with the best.

It paid to be cute in Cork training sessions. A year later my clubmate Eddie O'Brien was called up to the panel. Eddie was a cross-country runner with great endurance but he didn't always have to use it with us. The team would often go for a two-mile run starting out on the banks by the Park before going around Blackrock and then coming back into the Park. Eddie would start off like Road Runner and soon be out of sight. We'd do our best to catch up but we never could; every time Eddie would be the first man back by some distance. Jim Barry would say to us, 'Jesus, lads, O'Brien is some runner! None of ye can catch him!' What no one knew was that after his explosive start, Eddie would hide behind the trees along the banks, wait for us to pass, and then come back up while we were slogging around Blackrock.

I don't look back on those sessions through rose-tinted glasses though. They were very limited. Even that first night, when I was in awe of the other players, would have been a basic workout. In my ten years playing senior hurling with Cork, we never had a match amongst ourselves. We never even had a game of backs and forwards. We asked Jim one time why not and he said that we couldn't have lads from the Barrs and the Glen marking each other, that it would only cause club grudges to come to the surface. Jim O'Regan and Willie John Daly also didn't bother with games in training. I think that was a shame. We'd have been better players for pitting our skills against each other. It was one of the first things I changed when I took charge in '75.

An old session wouldn't have been bad as part of a session. We'd have a goalkeeper and a few forwards and backs at either end, while the midfielders would stay around the centre of the field. Every few seconds a ball would be coming for a back to clear and another for a forward to either try to keep moving or take and shoot. Then we'd break up into groups and work on keeping the ball moving across or down the field. For ages. That's all we'd do – keep that ball moving.

We became better players for it. I know that my own wristwork, timing and co-ordination improved from those sessions complementing my work in the Alley, as was evident in how comfortable I became at striking the ball either on the ground or in the air. But we should have been even better players. I found out afterwards that you needed a lot more skills than just keeping the ball moving. Back then, we weren't encouraged to do anything else. We weren't told to solo with the ball (Timmy McCarthy would have been sent home after his second training session) or to hit the ball on the run; we didn't even practise either skill in training.

So many players on those teams never developed. When the ball landed at a back's feet, he'd blow his man out of the way, pull first time and the ball would be up the field. That was it. You don't get that now; if anything, fellas are too prone to picking it. But there's a happy medium – hurling is about a combination of skills – and the sixties wasn't the preferable extreme.

Looking back, our mentors merely trained us; they never coached us. While they were all experienced men who were very good at identifying whether a player 'had it' or not for inter-county hurling, they could never say, 'Well, I'll put it into him.' We had no drills as such. I was never brought aside by any Cork coach like Father Roch would do and be told, 'Justin, this is a skill you should develop more.' All we were told was to play 'Cork hurling', which basically consisted of 'keeping that ball moving'. You weren't allowed to express yourself. If you look at the 1966 All-Ireland final, there's a stage in the second half when I pick up a ball, pretend to go one way, then go the other and put it over the bar from forty yards. That was seldom done. If I had missed it, I'd have heard all about it. When we played Dublin in a league game the following February, I got a ball in midfield, soloed a bit with it, drew a man, spotted John O'Halloran inside and quickly flicked it out to him. John wasn't anticipating a pass, lost it, the ball was cleared and Dublin got a point. Afterwards Jim O'Regan said to me, 'Don't ever do that again. Let that ball in the second you get it.' That I was a good enough player to be receiving the Caltex Player of the Year award the following week didn't matter one iota in his eyes. Neither did the fact that I hadn't taken that bad an option.

If you were to look at it clinically, Cork depended a lot on exceptional individual talent in the thirties, forties and early fifties. When that well of talent dried up, Cork struggled. We just went along with what had been passed on. While our effort and commitment meant we were often competitive, we had a very limited brand of hurling. It's frustrating thinking of how much better we'd have been if someone had come along and said, 'Right lads, there's a time to be direct alright but ye can vary it too. Cross the ball over now and again. Pass the ball out. Don't be afraid to pick it up the odd time. Express yourselves without indulging yourselves.' Ring apart, Cork didn't have anyone who had really studied how the game could be played.

Tipperary did. They had deep thinkers on their sixties team, like Tony Wall, who wrote the first coaching book on hurling. 'We would meet during the week and analyse games and various movements,' Michael Keating himself wrote in *Babs*. 'We came up with ideas and then brought those ideas into Thurles to work on them and develop them. ... Everyone knew where each ball was going. There was a signal for everything. We were ahead of our time.'

They were certainly miles ahead of us. Twelve days after my first training session with Cork, they hammered us in the Munster final in the Limerick Gaelic Grounds. The score at the end was 3-13 to 1-5. We were lucky it was that close. Tipp weren't even going at full tilt.

That day was laced with poignancy. The previous week, Jimmy Brohan had told me that if he didn't make the team, he mightn't even go along as a sub because he had a holiday booked. Brohan had been a wonderful corner back, possibly the best player Cork had in that barren 1954–66 era, but he was getting on. When the team was called out, he was only selected as a sub. Jimmy decided to take that holiday.

He was probably right. If he had shown up, he might have been humiliated like another Cork legend. Paddy Barry had been one of my favourite players as a kid. I was as fond of him in later years too; when I was a selector on the Munster millennium team committee, I insisted that he be on the team as I considered him the second greatest Cork forward ever. The Cork selectors in '64 were not as respectful. With less than ten minutes to go in that Munster final, they took him off. It was scandalous. The man had retired from inter-county hurling a few years beforehand, with his All-Ireland medals. He didn't need to come back. He only did so because the county selectors had begged him to after watching him play in a local championship game against Passage a month before the Tipperary game. While I had impressed that night by scoring 1-4, Paddy had been even better, registering 1-7 for Sarsfields. His reward for answering the call was to be taken off in front of 44,000 people. By then, the game as a contest was over. Ten players could have been called ashore yet the second man they substituted was Barry. At least the crowd acknowledged the injustice. As he made his way to the line, they clapped him off. Tipp folk included.

There was another significant substitution that day. Midway through the second half, I came on at midfield for veteran John Hayes to make my senior debut with Cork. By that stage, we were nine points down. I did quite well, hitting a few balls, but what I remember most is going for a ball which had broken about thirty yards ahead of me. That ball was mine. I was fresh, young and eager; it had to be mine. Then, in a flash, this blur whizzed past me, collected the ball and cleared it down the field. Theo English taught me a valuable lesson that day. As good as I felt my anticipation was from those hours in the Alley and playing goal-to-goal, my speed of thought was still miles behind the best. Echoes of Bernie Aherne came flooding back. 'Don't you know this is a man's game? Sure you're only a boy.'

There was only one way I was going to become the best. I had to play against the best, regularly. The selectors realised this too. I started in our first game back after the Munster final, an Oireachtas tournament game against Kilkenny, and every game after that; it was just a matter of whether they picked me at wing forward or midfield. I felt comfortable playing either position, but I preferred midfield. I still maintain it is the best position on the field to play. You can be by-passed these days more than you would have been in the past because the quality of sliotars, hurleys and puck-outs has improved, but it's still a great place to express yourself. You can become either an attacker or defender, depending on how you see fit. If you're a good striker of the ball with good anticipation, stamina and concentration, it's the place to be. You can dominate matches from there more than anywhere else.

I dominated quite a few games from there the year after that 1964 Munster final. Avondhu knocked us out of the '65 club championship, 6-12 to 3-11, yet the *Cork Examiner* reckoned I had an outstanding game in which I scored 1-3. Shortly after that, a match report of the county Under-21s' win over Waterford read, 'Very much the dominant figure was Justin McCarthy at midfield.' I had scored 1-4. A few weeks later, I moved to there from wing forward against the same county in the Munster senior championship to help us earn a draw. I then started there alongside Teddy O'Mahony for the replay. The pair of us won our battle. That proved to be a big factor in Cork winning that war.

The defeat of Waterford meant another shot at Tipperary in the Munster final. We really fancied our chances of taking them. It wasn't just my game that had improved; so had the whole team's. We had rattled Tipp in our first league game of the season. By half-time I had set up two goals and we were eleven points up. They came back into it – the sun blinded (goalkeeper) Paddy Barry for a goal – but when the ref blew it up, I thought we had at least got a draw. I couldn't tell for sure – the sun was too strong to read the scoreboard – but my marker, Mick Burns, turned round and said, 'I think ye won by a point.' They did. A few months later, Kilkenny also snatched a one-point win over us after we had been ahead for the whole game. It irked that we hadn't won either game but at least we had been in a position to win them. Eddie O'Brien and Charlie McCarthy had added some pace and vitality to our attack. We were competitive again. Tipp wouldn't have it as easy as they had in '64.

A few hours before the match, we were brought upstairs to a bedroom in the Railway Hotel, just across from the Limerick Gaelic Grounds.

Now, there were some bizarre pre-match speeches in my playing days. The night before Munster won a Railway Cup in Croke Park, two of our selectors had enjoyed a bit of a session. There was still no sign of them just before we went out either. The next thing, there was this sound of storming feet down the corridor and a dressing-room door crashed open. 'Sorry about this, lads, but we just want to say a few words,' said Denis Conroy. 'Listen, Munster hurling will never lie down to Leinster. Get out there, do your stuff and give us Munster hurling!' Twenty players just looked at them in complete silence. But then, how else were the Leinster team meant to react?

Believe me though, the Cork team meeting before the 1965 Munster final was every bit as embarrassing.

Between players, mentors and county board officers, there must have been thirty of us in that small room, and so ten of us ended up sitting on the side of the bed. First, we listened to the county board officer Jack Barrett wish us the best. Then our selector from Blackrock, Johnny Quirke, stood up. Johnny had been a great player in the Ring era and made it clear to us what we had to do and what was at stake. Every line he said was said louder than the one before. 'Ye're to go out there and play Cork hurling, lads. Keep that ball moving! And lads, remember, Cork's depending on ye! Our greatest son, Christy Ring, has won eight All-Irelands! John Doyle has won seven! If Tipp win today, he'll surely make that eight! Can we have that, lads? Can ...' And then, just as Johnny was building to a crescendo, the bed collapsed. Players fell over one another; those that didn't, fell around the place laughing. Looking back though, it wasn't one bit funny; it was one big joke. What was meant to happen after that? 'Where were you, Johnny? Oh yeah, about Ring. Go on ...' The moment had been lost. The point had been lost. The *match* had been lost.

Such amateurism was reflected on the field. Tipp murdered us, 4-11 to 0-5. It was put to John Doyle by RTÉ before the game that we would be too lively for them but he replied, 'They can do the running and we'll do the hurling.' And that's what they did. We didn't even run. I broke even with Mick Roche but he still hit his fair share of ball. All his team-mates did more than that. It was, quite simply, a massacre.

That Tipp team were as much a machine as the great Kerry football team of Sheehy, O'Shea and Spillane ever were. They too seemed relentless, invincible, overwhelming. After they hammered us, they went on to beat Wexford by twelve points in the All-Ireland final. It was their fourth All-Ireland title in five years. They also won three leagues in that period.

It was little wonder; they had so many good players. John O'Donoghue was a great goalkeeper. You couldn't get through their full-back line of Doyle, Maher and Carey; if you tried, they'd just put the hurley up to your chest and muscle you away. Wall was a colossus at centre back, while either side of him, Len Gaynor and Mick Burns were solidity personified. English was an exceptional midfield player. Alongside him was Roche, possibly the best all-round player of his generation. Jimmy Doyle was possibly the best forward of his – and one of the top three of any. Babs could be unstoppable on his day.

And then you had Devaney, Nealon, McLoughlin, Ryan. If it wasn't one fella killing you, it was another. They had options all over the place. And yet they were better than the sum of their parts. They could move the ball in any direction because they could all read each other's play. They were strong mentally and physically, individually and collectively. They were like ... Godzilla.

We needed to play a different brand of hurling to beat them. Being told to go out there and play 'Cork hurling' wasn't the way to go about it. We tried to play no-nonsense, direct, hip-to-hip hurling, which was suicide against such a physical side. Getting 'stuck in' against them was just what they wanted us to do, especially their Hell's Kitchen full-back line.

Cork hurling was in a depressing state after that Munster final defeat. It was coming up to twelve years since Cork had last won an All-Ireland, ten since they had even won a Munster title. Ring was gone. Worse, so was the fear of Cork. Now Cork feared Tipp. There were some talented young players coming along like Seanie Barry and the three McCarthys – Gerald, Justin and Charlie – but sure, they were too light and too small. The older players weren't even strong enough for Tipp; what hope had these lads? Hell's Kitchen would shoot them that same look Bernie Aherne gave one of them in a field in Riverstown. 'Don't you know this is a man's game? Sure you're only boys.'

7

WHEN I WAS 21 …

Cork are like the mushrooms. They can come overnight.
Jim 'Tough' Barry

We were sitting down to eat after a challenge game in Nowlan Park when Jim Barry ran in like a schoolboy just after hearing the war was over.

'Lads, ye'll never believe it! Didn't Limerick beat Tipp today!'

He was right. We didn't believe it. We were like those first-class passengers on the *Titanic* who thought it was a joke when they first heard the ship was going to sink. To us, God himself couldn't sink Tipperary.

'I'm telling ye, it was on the radio! Cregan got 3-5!'

When we heard that, we were sure he was only ball-hopping. Nobody lived to get 3-5 off Hell's Kitchen.

But then we began to wonder. Why would he lie? Lads started to leave the table, calls were made; within minutes, the story was confirmed. 'Tough' was right. Eamonn Cregan had scored 3-5. Tipp *were* out of the championship. After that, a huge buzz went around that room in the Kilkenny Imperial Hotel. Fists were clenched, voices became excited; the world had changed. Jim summed it up. 'Lads, they're out of the way now; ye can beat the rest of them. It's up to yourselves.'

We were thinking precisely the same. We could beat the rest. The year up to then had shown that. We had reached the league semi-final and even though Kilkenny had beaten us by twelve points, we had played some very good hurling against them; we just shot too many wides. We had sixteen in all; I shot seven from wing forward. But that didn't bother us. It had been the first time most of us had played in Croke Park. The pitch seemed so long; the posts, so small and so far away. It was better to experience those teething problems in a league semi-final than in an All-Ireland final.

We had also beaten Wexford in Wembley in the annual Whit weekend tournament. That was a milestone in the development of the team. The performance itself was pleasing – I scored five points – but the whole experience was even better. At the time, Wembley was the talk of the world – it would be hosting the World Cup final a month later – and there we were, *there*. It was like a dream. Togging off in those huge dressing rooms; seeing the stewards all around the pitch; playing on the carpet-like surface; walking up those thirty-nine steps to collect our medals; splashing and joking around in the dressing-room mini-pool. The Park had never been like this.

Jim Barry was also doing his bit to bond the team together. He was a lovely man, a real father figure to us young fellas, and a great character. He had been a freedom fighter with the old IRA, sang with the world-famous Carl Rosa Opera Company and was an outstanding boxer and swimmer before he ever trained the Cork team that won the 1926 All-Ireland. Forty years later, he had helped Cork to a further fourteen All-Ireland finals. And yet he had avoided becoming a county board man. When we'd meet up for training during the winter down in the Park, there wouldn't be enough light to do any hurling, so we'd often play soccer as it was the one game you could play on the ground. One night Jim ran onto the field, urging, 'Quick, lads, Con Murphy is coming! Either throw away the ball or start kicking it up in the air!' Seconds later, the secretary of the county board was watching us solo-run like Sean O'Neill. If only he had known moments earlier we had been trying to dribble like Georgie Best ...

Jim had only been a junior hurler. That made the Wembley journey even better crack. After the match, there was a big banquet underneath the stadium for the teams, at which the Irish ambassador stood up and spoke. 'Lay-dees and gentlemen,' he dramatically announced, 'we are blessed to have in our presence today a man who was the greatest hurler of all time. Will you please put your hands together for the great, the famous, the legendary, the one, the only ... Jim Barry!' Jim didn't bat an eyelid; he just stood up and took the applause. The rest of us were in stitches. Peter Doolan and Denis Murphy were going, 'Come here, Jim, you never told us that! How many All-Irelands is it you have again? And there was Ringie, thinking he was the best! God, we're going to have to put him straight!'

The bould Jim just kept on smiling.

'Tough' didn't always catch a ball-hop though. When we were staying in the Lucan Spa Hotel the night before the league semi-final, Gerald McCarthy, Denis Murphy and myself decided to get up to some mischief. A few minutes later, there was a phone call downstairs.

'Hello, would Jim Barry be there?'

'Justin? Gerald? It's Denis. Yeah, he's down here. I'll get him now ... Jim, you're wanted there.'

Moments later, a man came to the phone.

'Hello?'

'Hello, is that Jim Barry?'

'It is, yes.'

'Jim, Paddy Downey here from *The Irish Times*.'

'Paddy! How are you!'

'Fine. Can you talk to us for a few minutes?'

'Oh sure, no problem, Paddy! Work away!'

'Em, this game tomorrow, Jim. You have a young team. What about these McCarthy brothers? Are they any good?'

'Would you believe it, Paddy, they're not related at all. Ah, but they're very good. They've always been skilful but they're hardy now as well. I'll tell you the truth; we're expecting great things from them.'

'And what about Denis Murphy, Jim? One of your more experienced players. He's getting on though, isn't he? A bit past it ...'

'Ah, Paddy, that's harsh. Denis brings a lot to this team. He brings experience, he brings ...'

And on they went, Paddy and Jim, right through the team, until about ten minutes later, Paddy decided to wind up the interview before the man beside him died laughing on a hotel bed.

Moments later, Gerald, Denis and myself were down in the lobby.

'Well, Jim, any news?'

'Actually, there is! You know who I was just on the phone with? Paddy Downey!'

'Yeah? What did he say?'

'He was on about the game. Ah, I only let on so much; I didn't want to give much away. He was asking about ye, actually!'

'Yeah? What did you tell him?'

'Ah, I told him ye're alright. Of course, ye're only blackguards, ye know that!'

Poor Jim had no idea just how right he was.

I don't know if we'd have done anything that year only for those trips to Dublin and London. We could sense on them something was on the verge of happening. With Tipp out of the way, we could beat the rest. We could beat anyone. We were ready for them all.

We were gone. Finished, done, gone. The whole of the Gaelic Grounds knew it too. There may have been only three points in it but an irreversible momentum had gathered. The more the game had gone on, the better Clare had played and the louder their supporters had seemed to sound. Hundreds of Corkmen started making their way to the gates, resigned to the gods having decreed this wasn't to be our day, our year. We were gone after the first round.

They were still leaving in droves when we won a free with little over a minute to go, about thirty-five yards out on the right wing, halfway between the goals and the sideline. Our regular inside free-taker, Patsie Harte, had been taken off. When our next inside free-taker, Seanie Barry, stepped up to the ball, he realised that he had never scored a goal from there before. It was a goal we needed. We were gone.

I wanted to take the free; playing with Passage, a free from that range would be considered a good opportunity for a goal. But playing with Cork, my free-taking duties were confined to long range. This did not qualify.

Then Seanie did something few Cork players have ever done. He went against orders. After looking at the ball, the posts, and then the ball again, he looked over at me. 'Justin, will you have a go for it?'

I hadn't been playing well. In fact, I had thought I wouldn't be able to play at all after waking up with an awful crick in my neck. I couldn't even move it on the way down in the car with Jim Barry. When we got to the dressing room, he gave me a rubdown with wintergreen and oil, and I was able to take my place, but I had been quiet at wing forward. I had fared much better when switched to midfield midway through the second half yet I had hardly been inspired there either. And I needed inspiration if Cork were to stay in the championship.

I knew where to find it. First I prayed to Our Lady. Then I went back in time. When I stepped up to that ball, I was no longer in Limerick; I was back in Rochestown. There I had taken the same shot a thousand times, a hundred times alone the day Roch had forgotten about me. The only difference this time was that there would be five bodies lining the goal. In my mind's eye though, I had seen them in the college field too. And so I went through the same routine I had gone through in Rochestown time and time again.

Seconds later, the wet ball whizzed just above Vincent Loftus's head, hit his hurley and then the back of the net. A minute later, the final whistle sounded; no one had added to either side's tally of 3-8 in the interim. We were still alive. The only thing we were out of was jail. Clare were the ones that were gone.

Two weeks later, we beat them by five goals.

Everyone was gone. Gerald and myself couldn't believe it. Jim O'Regan had told us to be back at the hotel at half-two; that's what time the two of us returned from our little stroll through Killarney and yet now everyone was gone. So were all the cars and gear bags. They had obviously left early; now we were going to be late. It was farcical: 46,000 spectators were going to be early for the Munster semi-final and two of Cork's starting fifteen were going to be late.

We started to panic so we started to run. As we sprinted past the thousands making their way up to Fitzgerald Stadium, a few curious cheers were raised; obviously some people recognised us. The guy at the players' gate didn't. 'Well, where's your gear so?' he quipped. 'Look, get away back now if ye don't have tickets.' We were in an awful state. Neither of us had played in Killarney before and it had taken us ages to even find the players' entrance; now this security man thought we were a pair of comedians, not players. It was five past three. The game would be starting in twenty-five minutes. The teams would be coming out in ten. A new team would be picked ... about now. Jim O'Regan and Jim Barry would have decided to drop us by now. They would have decided to *kill* us by now.

We went from gate to gate but it was the same story; no one from Kerry knew who Justin and Gerald McCarthy were. Con Cottrell did. He was a member of the Cork team that had won four consecutive All-Irelands in the forties and had spotted our predicament. Thankfully, he was more than a former Cork hurler (such status didn't seem to carry much currency with these Kerry officials); he was also a priest. When he told one of the gatemen we were genuine, his word was taken as gospel.

Seconds later, we hit the dressing room to find the rest of the team togged off and the two Jims pissed off. *'Jeezus Christ!'* they roared. 'Where were ye? We're trying to win this game, not shagging lose it! Where the hell's yer gear?'

Five minutes later, we were running out onto the pitch. Ninety minutes after that again, we were being lifted shoulder-high off it. I had broken even with Bernie Hartigan in midfield, Gerald had scored two points and that's how much Limerick had been beaten by.

Others played a bigger role than us that day, mind. Our two other Under-21 players, Seanie Barry and Charlie McCarthy, had scored 2-4 between them, Gerald being the only other scorer. Paddy Barry had made two excellent saves. Our two best players though had been our wing backs. Paddy Fitzgerald was a real tenacious player who took great pride in playing for Cork and was simply everywhere that day. Tony Connolly was also inspired. Although he had only come back onto the team that year after some time in the inter-county wilderness, he had great confidence in his own ability. In the build-up to the game, Jim O'Regan said, 'Connolly, you're on Cregan.'

And Tony replied, 'Sure, that's fine, Jim. No bother there, boy.'

'Oh, you'll be bothered by him alright.'

'Yerra, Jim, I'll take him in my stride.'

Cregan scored one point.

The Cork public could now see we were on for our first All-Ireland since 1954. The team had a nice balance about it. Barry was solid in goal; the full-back line of Peter Doolan, Tom O'Donoghue and Denis Murphy offered him great protection; Denis Riordan at centre back was a no-nonsense player that complemented Connolly and Fitzgerald well; Jerry O'Sullivan and Justin McCarthy were holding their own in midfield; upfront, Seanie Barry's pace and skill on the right wing meant he was impossible to hook; Charlie McCarthy might have been small but he was good for at least one goal a game; his namesake, Gerald, with his wonderful ability to pick and hit without handling, had, in the space of three games, gone from being a sub to a potential legend; centre forward John O'Halloran was a great man to keep the ball moving ...

And yet there was a sense that something was missing if they were going to go the whole way. Or rather *someone* was missing. Ring.

Ring by now was forty-six and hadn't played for Cork in four years, yet there was a strong school of opinion that he was still the best forward in the county. The real Paddy Downey was certainly of that view after watching Ring's display for the Glen in that year's Munster club championship final against Mount Sion. 'He revealed his age only when the spurt to the ball was more than ten yards,' Downey wrote after that game. 'Otherwise he gave us the whole gamut of his enormous skill; the dazzling stickwork, the lightning stroke, the dainty pass – all that artistry that would not have surprised us twenty years ago.'

I had seen up close that he still had it. One night I was playing for Passage when Ring came out the field to take a sideline cut. I stood directly between him and the posts, trying to block him if I could, but the next thing, the ball had been driven though my legs into Patsie Harte who duly put it over the bar. I have no doubt Ring meant it.

There was a lot of speculation whether the players would have resented him taking someone else's place. I know the younger players wouldn't. We didn't see the age, only the legend; sharing the same dressing room as Ring would be the ultimate. He would advise us, show us things we hadn't tried before, while we desperately wanted to show *him* things. I remember another game for Passage up in the Glen which Ring was at in which I chipped a lineball over the bar from forty yards. A few of the Glen lads on the line said that it had been a fluke, so when we won a free about fifty yards out a few minutes later, I didn't bother to lift it; I just chipped it straight over the bar. Then I turned round to the hurlers on the ditch, winked and said, 'That was no fluke.' But when I did, there was no sign of Ring. I wanted him to have seen that.

It wasn't just us young lads that were excited about the prospect of him coming back; so was the whole of Cork. The public felt the attack needed his experience and strength if Cork were to win the All-Ireland. More than that, they wanted to see Ring win a ninth All-Ireland now that John Doyle had eight; to them, no player deserved to be equal with Ring.

The 1966 Munster final match programme shows that Christy Ring was listed as a substitute for Cork. He never showed. Val Dorgan's book, *Christy Ring*, reveals that the selectors voted 3–2 to start another veteran in exile, Johnny Bennett, and that Ring's supposed response was, 'The people of Cork will never see the day when Christy Ring is a substitute on a Cork team to Johnny Bennett.' It was one thing to lose out to a youngster like Con Roche who had been there all along, another to be pipped by a 34-year-old who hadn't trained with the team all year.

The selectors were vindicated. Bennett scored two goals and a point in that Munster final against Waterford. The final result was 4-9 to 2-9. And after that, there was no more talk amongst the team about Ring winning a ninth All-Ireland with Cork. Instead, the motivation turned to Cork winning their first All-Ireland *without* Ring in thirty-five years. The king was dead; long live the king.

They were heady days, those summer days of '66. Being clapped getting off the ferry at work. Signing autographs for the first time. Being interviewed by the national press for the first time. Flirting with the girls in the hotel lobbies after matches. Going out in the evenings with Pat, the girl I had met between the two Clare games. And going down to the Park to be with the team. That was the best bit.

It wasn't the most talented team I've ever played on but it was truly a *team*. It almost helped that we were made up of two different groups – the young fellas and the old fellas – because each one bounced off the other. They'd slag us about that rock 'n roll we were listening to and be telling us not to be staying out all night, while we'd throw back that they were only old men, slipping away for their few quiet pints. We were good for each other. They found our enthusiasm refreshing; we found their experience and maturity reassuring. Not only would they encourage you, but they'd protect you. Even though it was my third year at senior level and I had seen them repeatedly humbled by Tipperary, I still looked up to the likes of Denis Murphy, Doolan, O'Donoghue, Paddy Fitz and Jerry O'Sullivan. A bit of that star-struck newcomer in the Mardyke never left me.

Winning the Munster final meant we were instantly into the All-Ireland final; in those days, Galway played in Munster while there was no Ulster championship either. The day before the All-Ireland, we went up by train, all dressed in our Sunday best. We played cards, had a laugh, told Jim Barry we were fine when he asked us how we were. To us, it was all one big adventure into the unknown. All we knew was that the next day would be the biggest in our lives. That excited us; it didn't unnerve us.

That night, Gerald and myself had our confession heard in a city-centre church; the priests in Rochestown had asked me to leave a match ticket for a Father Angelus, so while we were there, we decided it would be a good way to clear our minds. Not many players these days would think of killing time by talking to God in a church the night before an All-Ireland, but it made sense to us. When I had asked Father Roch the previous day to pray for a Cork win, he had refused. Why not go straight to the top?

The following morning, after Mass and breakfast, we were all brought into a room for a team talk. Standing at the top was Jim O'Regan. We could tell by his face that he was worried.

When we all sat down, Jim went, 'Right, lads, before I start. Denis Riordan. How are you fixed?'

'Sure I'm okay, Jim. I'll be grand when I get out there and warm up.'

'What do you mean you're grand?'

'Look, Jim, don't worry about me.'

Everyone was looking at Riordan at this stage. He was a crucial figure for us; hard, forceful, direct, a real Jim O'Regan player. He had also been playing with Cork since the late fifties without getting within a sniff of an All-Ireland, something that would rankle badly with someone from the Glen. He was desperate to play.

'Denis, come here. Now! Alright. Put your hand up over your head, fast.'

'Jim, I'm telling ya. There's no need. I'll be able to do that when we get out there.'

'Put your hand up over your head! Fast!'

So Riordan tried. And when he did, he could only bring it up so far. His shoulder ligaments were gone.

'You can't do it, Denis! And you're not playing today.'

At that moment, you could hear a pin drop; the hardest man on the team was on the verge of crying. There was no taking him to the side, no putting an arm around him, no telling him the other lads would be going all out to win one for the Gipper. But then, this was Jim O'Regan, this was Ireland, 1966.

I was still sure we would win. Jerry O'Sullivan would be able to do a job at centre back while Mick Waters had hurled beside me in the Munster final. Ever since Limerick had beaten Tipp, we had felt as if we were a team of destiny, that nothing was going to stop us, not even the loss of Riordan. When the Cork captain and myself went up to our hotel room to collect our gear, I said to him, 'Gerald, have one good look around. The McCarthy Cup will be in here tonight.'

The rest of the lads were feeling the same. When Jim Barry and Jim O'Regan had been telling them for the previous month that direct, Cork hurling would prevent Kilkenny from settling, they had fully believed it. We were going to win, it was a certainty, there was nothing to worry about. And so when we got on the bus, led out by a police escort, a song started up, a rebel song. Then someone burst into the number one of the time, 'Yellow Submarine', before Tony Connolly said we should make it a red one. And so we all joined in, belting it out. 'We all live in a red submarine, a red submarine ...' Jim Barry mightn't have been into The Beatles but he liked what he was hearing. 'Keep it going, lads. God, ye're great. Ye'll beat these lads alright.'

We sang all the way to Croke Park. What chance had Kilkenny against a side without fear?

Nothing can prepare you for it. Not Thurles, Killarney, Limerick, the Park; nowhere. When you come out of that tunnel in Croke Park on All-Ireland final day, the roar is so much louder than anything you've heard before. It goes all around you, making the ground seem as if it's moving. You're tested there and then. If you don't have your wits about you, if you hold any shred of doubt about your own ability, you'll get stuck in that moment and won't get out of it. Too many players know just how true that is.

We survived it.

Ninety minutes later, there was an even greater roar. The final whistle had gone. Cue for pandemonium.

There has been a lot of revisionism since Clare won the All-Ireland in '95, that their triumph that day caused scenes not seen in Croke Park since Down won the football in '60. Not true. The outpouring of emotion on 4 September 1966 equalled anything which greeted Down's celebrations. Because for Cork, twelve years without winning an All-Ireland represented an eternity. Back then, the Ban was in force, hurling was the only game in Cork, so when people spoke about sport, it was usually about whether Cork would ever win another All-Ireland without Ring. That whistle didn't signal the ending of a game; it signalled deliverance.

I shook hands with my marker Seamus Cleere and immediately collapsed. Everything seemed to be happening at once. This huge release of tension, this huge release of energy, this sense of incredulity, this awful cramp at the back of my right thigh. The next second, this wave of humanity was heading towards me, led by a familiar face. It was Johnny O'Connor from the dockyard, the same generous soul who had told me all those years ago that I would some day win an All-Ireland. I was now more concerned about whether I'd be able to make it to the steps of the Hogan, but not for the first time, Johnny came to my rescue, giving the thigh the rub it needed. Seconds later, I was being carried off the pitch on the shoulders of thousands.

When I got to the Hogan Stand, Jim Barry was there, tears rolling down onto that trademark bow tie. So too was Charlie, with his jersey half-ripped from his back, smiling that impish smile and beating out the time for that chant. 'Cork, Cork, Cork ...' Looking down, every blade of grass was covered by Cork people. It was incredible, looking at them looking up at you standing between Gerald and de Valera.

And then Gerald lifted the cup, the cue for the loudest roar of all.

A funny thought crossed my mind. 'If only those gatemen in Killarney could see us now.'

The following morning, as our long-lost relative Liam sat in front of us, Gerald and myself lay on our beds, taking in what had happened. Kilkenny, we agreed, had probably underestimated us after the league semi-final. They had certainly been overpowered by our sheer intensity. We hadn't played particularly well – our three goals came from broken play – but they were the type of goals that could only come to a team that had worked hard. The steel O'Regan had instilled into us had rattled Kilkenny. They had never been able to get into their stride. When they finally scored a goal, there was only a minute to go and even then they were still five points behind. Traditional Cork hurling had served us well.

So had Paddy Barry. Paddy was always hyper before a game. Most goalkeepers are the same; ask anyone who has shared a dressing room with Durack, Cunningham or Davy Fitzgerald. In one way, it's because they're arrogant, in another, it's because they're insecure, but most of all, it's because they care. Paddy couldn't just sit in the corner; he always needed to be talking. Before the Kilkenny game, he was going around to the lads. 'Denis, big game now. Paddy Fitz, make sure you mark Eddie Keher tightly. Tom, watch Dillon.'

The lads would offer him the assurance he sought.

'Sure, Keher's way out the field; he won't be near you.'

'Paddy, what are you worried about? I'll take care of Dillon for you alright. Sure, haven't I taken care of you up to now?'

O'Donoghue did end up taking care of Pa Dillon; the Kilkenny full forward was eventually replaced. But Paddy was the one who saved us. Kilkenny couldn't beat him.

There were other heroes, we agreed. Like Doolan, who silenced his critics with a splendid display at right corner back. Like Colm Sheehan, who scored two goals. Like Paddy Fitz, who dominated Keher in the second half. Christ, all fifteen of us had been heroes, we decided. And with that, we decided to catch a few minutes' sleep. The next twenty-four hours would be even more hectic.

They were. First there was the function in the Gresham. I'll never forget how genial the Kilkenny lads were at it; I don't think we'd have been as gracious had we lost. Eddie Keher, Claus Dunne, Paddy Moran, Tom Walsh all came over and talked away with us; Ollie Walsh even had us singing 'The Rose of Mooncoin'. The real star of the show though was our own Johnny Bennett. Johnny was known as the Singing Hurler and even cut records. I wouldn't have known many of them, but there were two songs that we had no problem joining in with him on. 'The Banks' and 'Beautiful City'. We heard them a lot that day. Coming down on the train, in Cork, in our sleep ...

When we were coming into Kent Station, Gerald and myself stuck our heads and Liam McCarthy's out the train window. Mine was closest to the platform and I could see only about ten people on it. I turned round to Gerald and said, 'God, there's hardly anyone here.' Gerald said not to worry, that they were all probably in Patrick Street. I was still a bit disappointed until just as we were walking out the station door, the whole of Cork suddenly appeared in front of us; the gardaí had kept everyone outside. It was an incredible sight, that sea of people. It flowed all the way to Paddy Barry's corner, down

Patrick's Hill, Patrick's Bridge and onto Patrick Street. They reckon there was over fifty thousand there to see us that night. Ireland had never seen a bigger homecoming. We were kings.

There was still a lot of hurling to be played. The Thursday after the All-Ireland, we had the Munster Under-21 final. Seanie Barry, Charlie, Gerald and myself didn't mind one bit. None of us drank or smoked; what better party could there be than to play in front of a packed Park? We destroyed Limerick that night, 5-12 to 2-6. Charlie scored 1-5. Seanie scored 1-1. I had 1-3, totally outplaying Cregan. Afterwards, we showered and brought Liam McCarthy to Passage. Everyone was there – Roch, my old club mentor Dan O'Mahony, Sister Carmel, my parents, my clubmates, my neighbours, Pat. A perfect day.

Three days later, we played Roscommon in the All-Ireland semi-final. Before the start, one of their players came over and said, 'Are you Justin McCarthy?' When I said that I was, he went, 'I saw you playing last Sunday. You were great. Take it easy on me, won't you?' It was a nice moment but I'm afraid we didn't grant his request. By the time they registered their first score Eddie O'Brien alone had run up 4-4. The rest of us had weighed in with another 6-13. It was so embarrassing, we gave them five goals in the last fifteen minutes.

The next day, I went back to work and paid the Dutch for the week I had taken off.

What was it about the Three Macs when we got together? For lads who didn't drink, we had an uncanny habit of getting into trouble. When we had been in London for the Wexford game, we had strolled into one of the city's danger spots before an Irish cab driver spotted three of his naive countrymen and whisked them out of harm's way. Then there had been Killarney when Gerald and myself had put ten years on the two Jims. The night before the second All-Ireland Under-21 final replay though really took the biscuit.

Once more, it had started out as an innocent diversion. The three of us had decided to hang out on O'Connell Street to check out the atmosphere and talent. There was no problem, we assured Jim Barry; we'd be back in the Lucan Spa Hotel well before lights out at eleven. Except, of course, there was a problem. We couldn't get a taxi. At half-ten, we started to thumb for a lift. Eventually, we got picked up but were dropped only halfway. By half-eleven, we were still only as far as Chapelizod. The three big men who had been posing on O'Connell Street were now feeling Lilliputian as car after car passed them by.

At quarter to twelve, one stopped. The front-seat passenger recognised us; Billy Morgan was also in Dublin as the senior footballers were playing on the same bill as us. We gratefully jumped in and then started to think of how we'd get into our rooms without being caught.

When we arrived at the hotel, we peeped in the window. Jim Barry and Donie Keane, one of the selectors, were in the foyer, pacing up and down. A minute or so later, they started to make their way down the corridor. The coast was clear. On the count of three, we breezed into the foyer before sprinting up the stairs, jumping onto our beds and sighing this huge sigh of relief.

A minute later, there was a knock on the door. We didn't let on anything. There was another rap on the door. 'Come on! We know you're there. Account for your movements!'

'We're in bed.'

'Open the door!'

Now Gerald wasn't just the captain of the team; he was the leader of our little gang. Charlie was its baby. So when Gerald turned round to his clubmate and said, 'Charlie, go out there and tell Jim we're in bed', Charlie got up without thinking.

Next thing, the door was open.

'What's wrong, Jim?' Charlie said, rubbing his eyes. 'We were asleep.'

Jim's response was quicker than a bullet from a chamber.

'Well, Jesus, Charlie, boy, that makes you the first fella I've met who wears a collar and tie in bed!'

Gerald and myself looked at each other and started laughing but we soon stopped; Jim and Donie read us the riot act. We tried to explain the taxi situation but they didn't believe us. This was an All-Ireland final. We were meant to be setting an example for the other lads. Seanie Barry, the other senior star, was long in bed; why weren't we? We had let him and the team down. When Jim and Donie finally left, I said what the others were thinking. 'Lads, we'd better play well in this game.'

Looking back, those Wexford–Cork Under-21 finals were a lot like that epic 1991 Meath–Dublin series, the only difference being we had the hurleys and they had the cameras. The more the drama went on, the more intriguing it became. Over 27,000 people watched that third game in Croke Park; only 7,000 had been at the first game in Limerick.

That first drawn game had been a cracker, with both sides scoring 4-9 each. The first replay, in Nowlan Park, was even better. Both camps were desperate to win; the legendary Nicky Rackard stood behind our goal all day, clapping his two hurleys any time the ball came into our goalie, John Mitchell. The *Cork Examiner* was spot on when it claimed, 'Seldom has there been a game with so many playing incidents and talking points.' Seanie Barry's display, though, had to be *the* talking point. He scored 2-8 that day, 1-6 from play. We were trailing by a point, 5-6 to 3-11, in injury time when their wing back, Vinnie Staples, went to collect a ball out by the line. If he cleared it, the game was over, but he missed it, and when he went to gather for a second time, Seanie came sprinting from thirty yards away to flick it away. He then beat Staples to the breaking ball, gathered it out by the sideline, half-turned onto his left and rifled over from fifty yards. It was one of the best five scores I've ever seen.

There were a lot of plaudits handed out around the time of those games. Peter Byrnes of *The Irish Times* described the third and decisive game as one of the best Croke Park had ever seen. And according to Mitchel Cogley of the *Irish Independent*, my display that day was one of the finest individual exhibitions he had ever seen.

I'll admit, I played very, very well that day. Everything just went right from the second the man who became Taoiseach that weekend threw in the ball. Maybe it was because it was Jack Lynch who threw in that ball, maybe it was because I was desperate to make it up to Jim Barry; I don't know. But for some reason I could do no wrong. Every ball I struck seemed to either go over the bar or set up someone else for a score. At one stage in the second half, I pointed a free from midfield but the referee ordered me to retake it because there had been an infringement around the square. I duly put it over again. Wexford even moved Mick Jacob onto me yet he was powerless. It was my day.

It was *our* day. We ended up winning a remarkable game by a remarkable scoreline, 9-9 to 5-9, five of our goals coming in the last ten minutes. Gerald had a fine game beside me at midfield. Charlie scored 2-2. The Three Macs had lived up to their bedroom promise.

It was a Thursday afternoon in December when the father came in with the news.

'Have you seen tonight's *Echo*?'

I muttered that I hadn't; I'd been sleeping since coming home from the nightshift working on a boat. I was wide awake seconds later, though, when the father told me what the paper said.

'You've won the Caltex Award.'

These days, it is known as the Texaco Award. Nothing else about it has changed. It's one of the greatest honours you can receive. Ring had been the only other Corkman to win one.

I'm not sure if I should have been the one to follow him. Paddy Barry, Paddy Fitzgerald and Seanie Barry all must have gone close while Pat Henderson of Kilkenny would also have been in contention. When the *Gaelic Weekly* magazine picked their inaugural All-Star team, I wasn't even included. Mind, I was in good company; Paddy Fitz didn't make it either. Our omission discredited the selection, just as Brian Whelahan's exclusion undermined the 1994 Bank of Ireland scheme. My omission from the All-Stars raised far more eyebrows than my selection as Player of the Year. Mitchel Cogley went so far as to deem me the sportsperson of the year in his column, relegating the Arkle team of Pat Taaffe and Tom Dreaper to second.

Mitchel had been in Croke Park that day against Wexford. That was probably the day that swung the Caltex for me. Other games, of course, helped. Like the five-point exhibition in Wembley. That crucial goal against Clare. My displays in the replay and Munster final. The two points I scored in the last ten minutes of the All-Ireland when I switched with Gerald to wing forward. Even the league semi-final did me no harm; I might have shot seven wides but I also scored four points from play. The Wexford series though was the key. Not only did it capture the imagination of the public, but it was fresh in the memory of the Caltex judges; the last game wasn't played until mid-November. Then a week after that third Wexford match, I put on another exhibition in the league against Clare. That too diluted the memory of Paddy Fitz's colossal display in Killarney.

But you know what I think it really came down to? '66 was before O'Dwyer's bachelors of '75, Loughnane's of '95 or Barry-Murphy's babies of '99. Croke Park had never seen a side of such vitality, youth and boldness. When they awarded me the Caltex, it wasn't so much that I was Cork's best player in '66; it was that I best epitomised the *spirit* of '66.

The day I received the award was a lot like the year I was being honoured for – eventful.

First, there was the scar incident. A few days earlier I had got an awful belt just below the mouth in a league game against Dublin. Stitches had been required so I tried to take them out with a blade in an effort to look prettier. I looked uglier.

Then there was the car incident. I was on the way up with Father Roch, Dan O'Mahony and another Passage clubman, Sean Geary, when Dan's vehicle started to make an awful noise straight in front of the Rock of Cashel. When we got out, Dan shook the car and the wheel fell off; the bearing was gone. It wasn't just the car that was finished; so were we. It was already four o'clock and the function was starting at seven. But just as the rest of us started cursing the heavens, Father Roch started praying to them and blessing the car. A minute later, a car stopped; its driver said he knew who I was and told Sean and myself to jump in. When we arrived in the Gresham, Dan was already there. Parked outside was his car.

The next morning, we again required assistance from Roch and above. The rest of us had made the most of staying in the Gresham and had consumed a big fry-up before it dawned on us that it was a Friday. Catholics weren't meant to eat meat on a Friday. We duly phoned Roch to come over and give us the necessary dispensation. He obliged.

The night itself was a dream. The fanfare going up to receive the award from Jack Lynch. The hotel. The celebrities. There I was, an apprentice boilermaker from Passage, rubbing shoulders with all the greats – Ronnie Delaney, Vincent O'Brien, Rosemary Smith, Billy Morton, Mattie McDonagh, Christy O'Connor Senior, Tony Dunne, Jim McCourt. I still have their autographs to this day.

Sinatra sang, 'When I was 21, it was a very good year.' And so it was for me. But I was also determined to put 1966 in its context. I knew winning the All-Ireland had changed my life, that it had been a tremendous achievement, but I saw it as merely the launching point, not the climax, of my career. One All-Ireland didn't hold much currency in Cork. I didn't want people to be coming up to me years later saying, 'Yeah, you're Justin McCarthy. God, that was some goal you got against Clare in '66.' There were more All-Irelands to be won.

8

A BLAST FROM THE PAST

And then in one game, it could be all over for another year. All the tactical talks, the 'listen hard lads' sessions in freezing dressing rooms, the novenas with the girlfriends, the warnings about keeping the head from the throw-in, staying cool as the roar rocks the stadium in the first ten minutes, will count for nothing as nobody remembers a first-round loser.

Declan Hassett, *The Way We Were*

In life, common sense tells us there are things you do and don't do. Like you don't stub cigarettes out on yourself. Like you look both ways before crossing the road. Like you don't tell Mike Tyson that he's not very pretty. Simple things. Basic things. Obvious things. Common sense.

The same extends to sport. Don't use your new boots for the first time in a game; break them in at home or training. If you pick up a slight injury, don't risk it. Remember that the championship is everything in hurling; challenge games are Mickey Mouse stuff.

And yet us sportsmen continue to ignore those rules. We don't even see them; all we see is the next ball, the next game. It's as if the rules don't apply to us. Especially those of us who are only twenty-one.

I had already upset the city division by deciding to play in Cloghduv that lovely April Sunday evening. It had picked me to play for its team, Seandún, in the county senior football championship that day but I wanted to play with the county hurlers in a tournament game against Clare instead. I quite liked football – it would be my third favourite sport next to hurling and athletics – but it wasn't an art form. Hurling was. Cloghduv would be an opportunity for me to further illustrate that art.

All I illustrated that night was my stupidity. Seconds after the ball was thrown in, I twisted my ankle. Hard ground, new boots, high cogs; it was inevitable. Then I made matters worse. I played on. The sensible thing would have been to come off and make sure I was fit for the first round against Waterford, but then, athletes don't think

like that. In part, it's because we think we're invincible and that we'll
be 'grand'; and yet it's also because we feel we're vulnerable,
replaceable, that if we don't carry on, someone will take our place and
keep it. No one on the sideline thought, 'Take off Justin, just to be
safe. It's a month's time we'll be needing him, not here opening some
pitch.' Four months earlier, I had been told that I had to play in a
challenge game against the county champions, Avondhu, even
though I had been sick all week with the flu and had just been named
Player of the Year. I still had to prove myself. We were disposable,
dispensable, lucky to be playing with Cork at all, particularly those
of us from a small club. And so we'd let on that there was nothing
wrong, that we were 'grand'.

I could do it for only so long. At half-time they had to cut the
boot off, my foot had swollen so much. When I was brought to
hospital, I explained to the doctor that we were starting our defence
of the McCarthy Cup in a month's time and I had to be ready for it.
He looked me straight in the eye and said, 'Mister McCarthy, I'm an
orthopaedic surgeon. Your leg is no different to anybody else's. I'm
not interested when or who you're playing. You have torn ligaments
in your ankle. That's worse than a break. If you want to get your leg
right, you have to go in plaster up to your knee for three weeks.'

He didn't need to say that I had to stay away from hurling for a
good while afterwards. But he didn't actually say it, did he? That was
enough for me. The day after the plaster came off, I went down to see
Cork's last training session before the Waterford game. When I got
talking to the selectors, I convinced them that I could play. They told
me to bring my gear. I just wasn't to be seen with it; they could only
name twenty-one players, I wouldn't be one of them and the county
board would start a war in the dressing room if they knew an extra
body was getting a free ride. And so Dan Coughlan, one of the
selectors, brought the bag in his car. At half-time, it was slipped in
and I togged off. With fifteen minutes to go, I was brought on, all
strapped up. I almost managed to score a goal – a shot of mine came
back off the post – but it was farcical. I could only run in straight
lines; my leg couldn't take going either left or right. When the whistle
went, Waterford had won, 3-10 to 1-8. The All-Ireland champions
had fallen at the first hurdle.

If we were looking for excuses we had plenty. John O'Halloran
suffered an awful belt in the face shortly after half-time; Tom
O'Donoghue was sent off for standing up for Paddy Barry a few
minutes later; I hadn't been fit. If we were to be honest though, that
day in Walsh Park was the first time we came down to earth after

winning the All-Ireland. We never sat down and said, 'Right, we're going all out to retain this All-Ireland. These are the pitfalls. This is how we avoid them.' And so we fell straight into them. We just continued as we were and somewhere along the way, complacency kicked in. Deep down, most of us were happy with our All-Ireland. Which was a sure way to stop us winning the next one.

The following week we went to Wembley and beat Kilkenny. We were anxious to have something to show for the year and prove we weren't a once off. I was so determined I took off work without pay to rest up for the game. I duly played well. Was it worth it? Well, that afternoon I was presented with a medal no one else remembers, two months later Kilkenny were crowned All-Ireland champions, and two years later I was still limping on that leg.

Everything seemed back on track in '68. We blazed through to the semi-finals of the league, playing exhibition stuff at times. We were particularly good in our last game in the round-robin section. 'It was just like old times last Sunday at the Park with Cork playing magnificent hurling and sweeping aside the Clare challenge with a vengeance,' *The Southern Star* reported. 'There was the fluent hurling of the long-striding Justin McCarthy, the superb marksmanship of Seanie Barry and the overall brilliance of the team in general. There's an All-Ireland in that team this year, if only they put their minds to winning it.'

I was of the same view. The team had regained its confidence while Doolan, O'Donoghue, Charlie and myself were buoyant after playing so well in Munster's Railway Cup final success. A month before the start of the championship, we beat the reigning All-Ireland champions, Kilkenny, by six points in a challenge game. Then in our first-round match, we hammered Galway, who played in the Munster championship back in those days. And then we beat Limerick by five points in the semi-final. Even though Tipp had taken us in the league semi-final, we were going to reverse that defeat. I was sure of it.

You know what some Clare players would do a few days before a big match? They'd take off work. You know what Loughnane used to tell them to do the day before a big game? Avoid the sun, don't play golf and take loads of water. You know what Gerald McCarthy, Seanie Barry, Denis Murphy and myself did the day before the 1968 Munster final? We gave a coaching course for Coiste Iomána in the blazing sun in Macroom to a group of young fellas. We didn't drink a bottle of water between us. We didn't think of it. But then, we didn't even drink water at Cork training. Jim Barry used to tell us that water would only give us cramp. If we were thirsty, we were to suck an orange and if we didn't have an orange, we'd just have to brave it out. Sure, we'd be 'grand'.

But of course, we weren't grand. Eight minutes into the game, Jimmy Ryan set up Liam Devanney on the edge of our square and he buried it to the net. Then Babs went on to play the best game of his life. Ten minutes after half-time, he scored a goal of his own to put Tipp eight up. Even then, the 42,000-strong crowd knew it was over. In the end, Tipp won pulling up, 2-13 to 1-7.

It was a crushing defeat. We thought we had got rid of Tipp; now here they were, back with a vengeance, the old order restored. It meant I had yet to beat Tipp in any grade, that it had been eleven years since a senior Cork side had beaten them in any competition, and worse, that '66 was now a tarnished All-Ireland. Over the next year it was regularly thrown at us that we wouldn't have won that All-Ireland if we had had to play Tipp. And that hurt. It hurt because it might well have been true.

There was only one way to win back the honour of '66.

Do what Tipp had done.

Reload.

9

JUSTIN TIME

You know, I got a hunch, fat man. I got a hunch that it's me from here on in. One ball, corner pocket. I mean, that ever happen to you? You know all of a sudden you feel like you just can't miss? 'Cause I dreamed about this game, fat man. I dreamed about this game every night on the road. Five ball. You know, this is my table, man. I own it.

Fast Eddie Felson [Paul Newman], *The Hustler*

A lot of old comrades made way in the winter of 1968. Jim Barry, that gentle, wonderful man, passed away. Doolan, O'Sullivan, Riordan, Fitzgerald, Connolly, Sheehan and Bennett retired or were retired. By Christmas, even one of the young guns from '66 was gone, Seanie Barry's commitments to the Kiltegan Fathers depriving us of a rare talent. A rebuilding job was inevitable. But a transitional period? Not necessarily. We weren't just any county. We were Cork, home of the mushrooms.

The new team sprouted up one Sunday in October. It was an Oireachtas semi-final down in the Park against Wexford, who had just been crowned All-Ireland champions. Not only did we beat them, we dazzled them. Their trainer, Ned Power, was a friend of Billy Delaney's family, and when I called over to their place after the game, Ned was there to tell me that he reckoned the game had been a watershed in Cork hurling. He was right. Only seven of that side had started in the 1968 Munster final. Thirteen of them would start in the 1969 Munster final.

These mushrooms had been nurturing for some time underage, mind. Cork had won two All-Ireland Under-21 titles in the previous three years and contested four of the previous five minor finals. Players from that crop were always going to come through.

Tony Maher took over the right corner back spot vacated by his Barrs clubmate, Doolan. Donal Clifford, sporting the first helmet the inter-county scene had seen, came in at right half back. Roger Tuohy, a small bundle of dynamite from Na Piarsaigh, slotted in at midfield.

Upfront was where the real transformation took place though.

Tomás Ryan, a hard, left-handed player, brought great cut and dash to the right half forward position. On the other wing came Pat Hegarty from Youghal, a good first-time hurler with plenty of cutting and strength. Charlie Cullinane from the Barrs was a very good full forward; cute, direct, strong yet quick. Eddie O'Brien was finally given another chance to establish himself. And then there was one William Walsh.

I've marked a lot of very good players. Eamonn Cregan, Babs, Mick Roche, Frank Cummins, John Connolly, Phil Wilson, Gerald, Charlie, Jimmy Barry-Murphy. Walsh was the best of the lot. I've never seen such a combination of speed, strength and power, but the Youghal man was more than a great athlete; he was a great hurler too. He had a terrific pair of hands, probably the quickest pull in the history of hurling and a remarkable ability to shoot with force at goal while on the move. If he had been from the Glen, the Barrs or the Rockies, he'd have gone down as a legend. Technically, Walsh was the ultimate centre forward.

There was other team surgery involved. The emergence of Tuohy and the progress of Denis Coughlan meant we had an embarrassment of midfield talent but as we weren't so deep in the half-back department, Gerald and myself were redeployed there. Gerald had always been a versatile player while Jim O'Regan, a brilliant centre back in his day, thought I had the necessary maturity and hurling to man his old position.

I didn't mind the move; it was all about giving the side a better balance. It did mean I was more restricted though. I now had a man to stop, a man who would be more forceful than the one I'd be on in midfield. If I cleared twenty balls but he scored three points, he'd have gotten the better of me. I would have to hold my position a great deal more and clear my lines a great deal quicker.

The only time I experienced a spot of bother was against Limerick in February. But then, Cregan wasn't just any player and I was new to the position. I was also able to send a sideline cut from fifty yards to skim the underneath of the crossbar in that same match. That afternoon was a mere blip; the move went like a dream. I found that I was still able to express so much of my game – my anticipation, my ability under the ball and above all, my striking. I'd often take a few steps to make space for myself, pretend I was about to hit the ball to make my man commit, and then put the ball back on my hurley before clearing. Without handling, naturally.

Having two great men alongside me helped too. Clifford, Gerald and myself developed a telepathic relationship that season. If a ball came our way, we attacked it, knowing one of the others would be there to sweep behind.

But then, the whole team was working in symmetry that season. Behind us, young Maher was fitting in well alongside Denis Murphy and Tom O'Donoghue. Tuohy and Coughlan were combining well in midfield, while upfront, Charlie was in his element now that he finally had the hurling and size around him. By March, we had qualified for the league semi-final without dropping a point.

That league semi-final wasn't just any league semi-final. Our opponents in Thurles that day were Tipperary. With five minutes to go, a Jimmy Doyle goal gave them the lead for the first time. Babs then followed it up with a point. But this time we didn't panic. We didn't think, 'Oh, no, here we go again.' The newcomers weren't used to losing to Tipp. A free from Charlie brought us back to within two points. Then, in the last minute, Eddie whipped on a ball on the edge of the square. John O'Donoghue didn't even see it. Cork 2-12, Tipperary 3-8. Seconds later, the final whistle went. You'd have sworn we'd won the All-Ireland.

Three weeks later, we'd won the league. The victims once more were a side that had contested the previous year's All-Ireland final. Wexford couldn't do anything about Walsh that day in Croke Park; he scored two goals. He wasn't the only one to impress though. After our five-point win, the *Cork Examiner* argued that we had established ourselves as the best Cork team since the three-in-a-row side of the early fifties. 'They have the exceptional spirit, speed and stamina of the 1966 side, but have far greater team balance and hurling ability.' I couldn't have agreed more.

The point was reaffirmed in the championship. First, Galway were blown out of the way. Then Clare. And then, in the Munster final, Tipperary again.

Jim O'Regan had us mentally right for that game. We had nothing to get carried away with, he repeatedly told us; we'd beaten Tipp by only a point – in a league match. He also had a special job for Tomás Ryan. The minute the ball was thrown in, Tomás was to take off Mick Roche's trademark hairnet. And that's what Tomás did. He took it off and tore it up right in front of Roche. That set the tone for the rest of the game. By half-time, we were three goals up. At the end, it was 4-6 to 0-9. Walsh had scored three goals, Coughlan and Tuohy had destroyed a rattled Roche, while the backs had been simply brilliant. It was the sweetest win possible. Not only had we claimed back '66, we had claimed the future.

There was a brilliant buzz in the camp in the build-up to the All-Ireland against Kilkenny. The side was brimming with confidence and expectation. It was also fascinating to see the new dynamics of the dressing room taking shape. Gerald, Charlie and myself were no longer the young guns; in fact, Charlie had got married the day before the Munster final. Now we sat back and enjoyed the ball-hopping between Charlie Cullinane, Roger Tuohy, Tomás Ryan and the forever young Eddie O'Brien. Some things didn't change, mind. O'Donoghue and Denis were still the wise old men, while Paddy Barry's intensity was still an easy target for a wind-up. Con Roche would constantly remind him of one puck-out that went astray, even if he let on that it was our corner back that he was talking to. 'Denis, don't forget to watch your back there, boy! You never know who'll decide to hit it!'

I was a happy man that summer of '69. Work was going great; I had left Verolme the previous autumn to work with the Cork Harbour Commissioners. The love life was going great; Pat and myself had now been going out three years. And the hurling was going great; I was on a team that was going to contest a lot of All-Irelands in the coming years.

I was also a far better player than I had been in '66; stronger, more mature, more aware of what I could and couldn't do. In the past, I had a tendency to take long, loping strides which left me open to being knocked off balance if I got hit on the off-stride; now I was taking quicker, shorter steps to keep my feet more on the ground. My striking was also better; in the Railway Cup final, I had scored a free from my own twenty-one. Every time I played, the papers seemed to give me rave reviews.

- The *Cork Examiner*, 10 February, league v. Dublin: 'Either Charlie Cullinane or Justin McCarthy might qualify as Cork's outstanding player. The Passage man is considered a stop-gap centre back but on yesterday's form he might be far more than that.'
- *Irish Press*, 3 March, league v. Clare: 'The inflexible half-back line thrived on the style, speed and invincibility of centre half Justin McCarthy who was such a commanding figure Clare sent four men to mark him.'
- The *Cork Examiner*, 14 April, league semi-final v. Tipperary: 'The Cork half-backs were almost faultless. Justin McCarthy covered with discipline, Con Roche was eluded only occasionally by Jimmy Doyle while Clifford was too good for Flanagan.'
- The *Cork Examiner*, 16 June, Munster semi-final v. Clare: 'Justin

STARTING OUT: In front of my parents' home before heading off to play Tipp in the 1963 Munster minor semi-final. It would be my first start for Cork.

DOCKYARD DAYS: I did a lot of growing up as an apprentice at Verolme but it wasn't all work. There was the hurling and, once a year, sports day.

MEN AGAINST BOYS: Probably the best team I ever saw was the Tipperary team of the sixties. They had everything needed to win and would do anything needed to win. I was introduced to Hell's Kitchen in the 1964 Munster final. (*Irish Examiner*)

GENTLEMAN JIM: Jim 'Tough' Barry was a father-figure to tens of All-Ireland-winning teams, especially to the one of '66. It's a shame Cork haven't named a stand or monument after him.

SMELLS LIKE TEAM SPIRIT: The Three Macs of Gerald, Charlie and myself did nearly everything together in '66, like leading out the parade for the All-Ireland final. (*Irish Examiner*)

DELIVERANCE: Gerald declares the twelve-year famine officially over. (*Irish Examiner*)

HEROES ALL: The '66 team wasn't the most talented I was ever on but it was truly a team. (*Irish Examiner*)

BRINGING IT ALL BACK HOME: The four McCarthys at a reception in Rochestown College. On the far left is the man who made it all happen for me, Father Roch Bennett.

'AND IT'S LYNCH TO MCCARTHY …': I sometimes dreamt of Jack Lynch passing me a ball but I never thought he or anyone else would pass me the Caltex Hurler of the Year Award. On 9 February 1967 though the then Taoiseach did. *(Irish Examiner)*

DECENT, RELIGIOUS, HUMBLE: My parents, Michael and Eily.

JUSTIN TIME: Being a regular with Munster in the sixties was an honour I thrived on. (*Irish Examiner*)

MARTYRS FOR THE CAUSE: Denis Murphy, Seanie Barry, Noel Gallagher, Gerald and myself at a coaching course in Macroom. Looking back, it was madness, being out in the sun; four of us were playing in the 1968 Munster final the following day. We weren't smiling then.

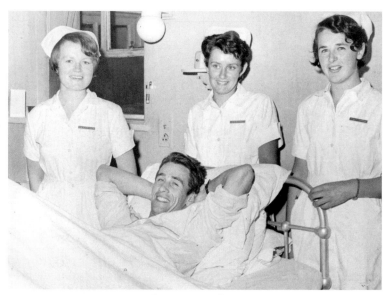

PUTTING ON A BRAVE FACE: There was only one way to survive the Accident: accept what had happened. I often screamed at these nurses, looking for an injection to kill the pain, but we had plenty of laughs as well. (*Evening Echo*)

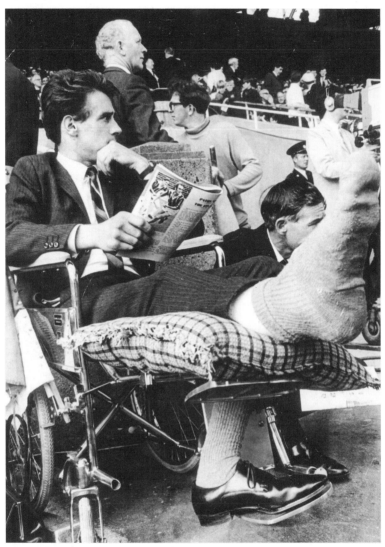

REALITY BITES: Sitting out the 1969 All-Ireland was the worst experience of my career. *(Irish Examiner)*

McCarthy, who played steadily in the first half, was a truly classic centre back afterwards. Whatever else might be said of Clare, they were never tardy in the tackle but the rangy Cork pivot caught and cleared with delightful fluency.'

• *Irish Press*, 28 July, Munster final v. Tipperary: 'In an impregnable defence, Denis Murphy, Tom O'Donoghue, Justin McCarthy and Donal Clifford were superb.'

Their words, not mine.

Even my greatest critic, Roch, sensed I was on the verge of realising his vision of another Meagher.

And then …

10

'THIS PUTS ME OUT OF THE ALL-IRELAND'

Is there another Life? Shall I awake and find all this a dream? There must be; we cannot be created for this kind of suffering.

John Keats

A few weeks after Waterford had knocked Cork out of the 1967 championship, Derry Doody and myself returned to the same county to spend a day in Tramore. It was an enjoyable day, laying out on the beach, going on the rides at the funfair, doing all the regular things you do by the seaside. Then at the end we decided to get our fortunes told for a laugh. I wasn't laughing for long. The woman was amazing. When I showed her my hands, she said that I worked with steel implements for a living. She could also tell that I had two brothers and a sister. She even predicted that I'd marry a tall, dark-haired girl, which was precisely what Pat looked like. It was as if the woman knew me.

Then, just as I was heading out the door, she called me back.

'One more thing. You're thinking of buying a motorbike.'

I was taken aback.

'I am. I've saved £50. I'm going to buy a Honda 50. Any week now actually.'

She shook her head.

'For your own sake, and *for the sake of your bones*, keep away from motorbikes.'

I never bought the bike.

That meant a lot of inconvenience though; I couldn't afford a car. Instead I'd get to work by walking a mile down to the Passage Road and then taking either the ferry (when I was at Verolme) or the bus (when I moved to the Harbour Commissioners). Getting to training was just as difficult. I asked the county board for the hire of a taxi but they claimed Rochestown wasn't far enough away from the Park to merit one. And so I had to rely on the occasional loan of the father's car, on a lift from some understanding neighbour, or, more often than not, on walking, getting the bus to town and then walking some more to the Park.

Things changed at the start of 1969. My clubmate Joe Murphy broke onto the county panel. Joe had a motorbike. By then, the oracle of Tramore had been drowned out by the embarrassment of bumming lifts from neighbours and friends. So when Joe offered to give me a spin to training, I accepted. 'Fine,' said Joe. 'I'll pick you up at ten to seven.'

On Thursday, 28 August 1969, Joe again called to the house at ten to seven. I was just finishing fixing up one of my hurleys, so when I saw him pull up, I grabbed two sticks and my bag and jumped on the back of his bike to head off for one of our last sessions before the All-Ireland.

It had been a splendid summer's day up to then. It was warm, sunny; the kind of day that makes you feel great to be alive. But then, just as we were about only a mile on the road, it suddenly began to rain. I had no helmet and was wearing only a short-sleeved shirt, so we pulled up under a tree until the shower passed. Five minutes later, it had. We got back on our bike and continued on our way to training, not knowing that shower would change my life.

There's a long sweeping bend you take when you enter Douglas from Rochestown. You have to take it carefully because it lasts for about fifty or sixty yards. And that's how Joe took it, carefully. Eventually we negotiated the corner and came back onto a straight part of road when I noticed this car up in front reversing out of a driveway on the opposite side of the road. We kept on going because we were beside the footpath and had the right of way. But just as we were approaching him, the old man for some reason kept on reversing, right across the road …

The next thing, I was lying on the footpath, close to a high wall.

I looked up and there was Joe, roaring, 'Get up, Justin! Get up!'

I looked over to my side and there were our hurleys and gearbags, scattered on the footpath.

Then I looked down. My shinbone was sticking through my pants. There was blood all over my leg.

As true as God, only one thought was on my mind at that moment.

'This puts me out of the All-Ireland.'

Within seconds, there was a huge commotion. Traffic stopped; people gathered around, recognising either the face or the name written across the hurleys lying on the path. Hugh Geary, brother of Sean, came over to tell me he'd tell Pat. Joe – who somehow had managed to stay on the bike – said he'd let them know in the Park. The rest was a daze. People, noise …

The next thing, I was in an ambulance. The pain was now really kicking in but all I could do was talk about missing the game in ten days' time. 'God, after all that training. After being so fit.' The crew told me not to worry about the All-Ireland. Then I realised they were right. Would I even be able to *hurl* again? Would I even be able to *walk*?

Within a few minutes of my arrival at the South Infirmary, Jim O'Regan, Dan O'Mahony and Pat were there too. 'Regan' was brilliant that night. He was one of the hardest men I've ever met and I'm sure his mind must have been racing, thinking about who now was going to play centre back, but his main concern that night was *my* state of mind. 'Take care of him,' he told Pat as he left. And she did. As the clock kept ticking and the blood kept dripping, she was still there.

It didn't take long for my x-ray to be taken. It confirmed that my leg had been broken in three places. My fibula had been smashed. Worse, my shinbone had been broken in two places, just below my knee and just below my ankle, leaving a piece of bone about nine inches long floating in between. The medical team would have to manipulate those bones to put them together again. '*For the sake of your bones.*'

It was eleven o'clock before I was able to go into theatre; you can't be given an anaesthetic within four hours of eating and I had just finished my dinner minutes before Joe had called. When I woke up, I found my leg in plaster up to my hip. The pain was overwhelming. I thought the operation was meant to take it away but it had only made it worse. The pain wasn't just in my leg; it was going right through my heart, through my whole body. I was screeching to the nurses, 'Please, give me something! You have something, give me something. Jesus, please!' But there were only so many injections they could give.

I'll never forget that night. It often haunts me still. I was tired but couldn't sleep because the pain was so severe; I was restless but couldn't move because the leg was in plaster. I was just stuck there, moaning in the dark, looking at the ceiling, living for the next injection, trying to survive.

It's a very lonely experience, being left with just yourself and your thoughts. So many things cross your mind. You replay the accident again and again; the shower, the impact, the fall, the bone sticking out, the bewildered look on the old man's face. Then you think of the future; your life, your career, your hurling. There's only one way to survive – to accept what has happened. You can't fight it, you can't rebel against it; you have to accept that your life has changed. And I did. That night I decided to do only what I could do. Keep as comfortable as possible. Be a good patient. And somehow hang in there for the next injection. When the photographers from the papers called the next morning, I just smiled and gave the thumbs up. It wasn't easy keeping a brave face though. Neil Armstrong and his colleagues were back from landing on the moon and the radio was still playing that famous quote over and over again. There they were, back from walking on the moon, and I couldn't even take one small step here on earth.

The attention helped. The nurses were great crack, there was hardly a day without some paper quoting either me or someone else about how the accident could affect the All-Ireland, while hundreds of strangers were coming up to wish me well. It got to the stage where the hospital had to turn people away. The Friday before the All-Ireland, an RTÉ radio reporter was ushered out of my ward by the head nun. Ten minutes later he slipped back in, drew the screen across the bed and began to interview me. No sooner had he started than the next thing, we could hear the nun coming back into the ward to say the angelus. 'Look,' he said, 'keep on talking. Just whisper instead.' And so we conducted the rest of the interview in whispered tones as she prayed away behind us. When the piece went out, the nun could be heard in the background, oblivious to our defiance. According to the report, she was like the rest of Cork, praying for my recovery ...

Another RTÉ man was very generous to me. Mícheál O'Hehir, who was head of sport at the time, insisted that I go up to see the All-Ireland. He had got on to the county board to make the necessary arrangements and told them not to worry about the cost; his department would pick up the tab. It was a splendid gesture. I now had something to look forward to. My All-Ireland now was to see the All-Ireland.

It wouldn't be the same as going up with the team though. That really hit me when they called up to me the day before the game. Most of them had been up individually – Gerald and Charlie in particular had been great – but seeing them all there together, about to head off to Dublin, was too much. They told me they'd be playing for me. And as they started to stream out of the room, tears started streaming out of my eyes.

The doctors were reluctant to let me go to the match. They feared that the journey and day might be too long. A few days before the game, the doctor had told me to get out of bed for a few minutes to see how I felt. When I did, I wanted to go straight back to bed again, the pain was so severe. But I was desperate to go to Croke Park and argued that I was fit enough from all the training. Eventually, they relented. I could go to the game, as long as I was with a doctor and a nurse at all times.

The morning of the game, I was dressed up in my best suit – the inside of its right leg cut to cover the plaster – before being carried out on a stretcher and rolled into the car. It was some car, an Austin Princess the board had hired from Forde's on Barrack Street. There was a glass partition between the driver and the back-seat passengers, while there was a middle seat that could fold down and allow me put my leg out. The banter on the way up was great too. The nurse was Phyllis Hogan, whose brother I played hurling with at Verolme. The doctor was Billy Christopher, a friendly young intern from Mallow, while the driver was John Drinan, a friend of mine from Douglas who drove taxis. Together, we got on like a house on fire, reading the papers, talking about the match and anything else under the sun. Our first port of call was Lawlor's in Naas where they had arranged for a meal to be brought out to me in the car. The next stop was Croke Park. Just as we were coming towards the ground, we could hear these young Dubliners outside, marvelling at our car. 'Jaysus, it's de Valera!' That gave me a good laugh. I wasn't laughing ten minutes later though. When I got out of the car, I was put in a wheelchair. You feel a very small boy in a wheelchair. Especially when you wonder if you'll end up in one.

I tried to put that thought out of my mind. I had come to watch the game and had been given a great spot to do that, along by the Hogan Stand sideline. But it was tough. When the lads came around the field behind the Artane Boys band, they waved over to me. I in turn smiled and waved the little red and white flag I was holding back at them. Deep down, I was dying that it wasn't a hurley I was holding.

Cork got off to a great start. Charlie had a goal after two minutes, Eddie had another one midway through the first half and coming up to half-time, we were seven points up. Then a rare thing happened. Paddy Barry dropped his stick coming for a high ball, then he dropped the ball itself and then Martin Brennan whipped it to the net. It proved to be a turning-point. Cork scored only another three points after that; Kilkenny scored a lot more. In the end, they won comfortably enough, 2-15 to 2-9.

I don't think the Barry incident was the deciding factor. Kilkenny were bound to rally at some stage, particularly with the team we picked. Privately, I had massive reservations about moving Willie Walsh to centre back. While he had played there the previous year for the Under-21s that had won the All-Ireland, he had since developed into the best centre forward in the country. Why deprive yourself of your best attacking weapon? True, the unavailability of Con Roche through injury didn't help the selectors, but they could have slotted Donal Clifford or Denis Coughlan in at centre back. Instead, they were so concerned about Pat Delaney they decided to move a big man to mark him. It was madness. The biggest threat on the field was our centre forward, not theirs. In the end, the whole balance of our team was upset. Cullinane was moved from full forward to centre forward while a youngster from Blackrock by the name of Ray Cummins came in at full forward for his first championship start. That was a lot of changes just to combat one man. As it turned out, that one man went off injured. When Eddie Keher moved to centre forward, Walsh couldn't stop him. I believe the Kilkenny centre back would have experienced similar difficulty had the right Cork team been picked.

After Keher lifted the cup, he wished me well in his speech. It was a nice thought from a thoughtful man. It was about all that was nice about the rest of the day though. I was completely shattered by the end of it. We didn't get home until midnight. Reality really set in on that trip home. My leg was broken. I might never hurl again. I no longer had an All-Ireland to look forward to. Only the next injection.

Enough was enough. It had been two weeks since the accident and still the pain was intolerable. And so I said to Phyllis, 'Get me the x-ray ye took after the operation. This shouldn't be happening. Something's wrong.' When my request was granted, my suspicion was confirmed. Something *was* wrong. As an apprentice at Verolme, I had learned to read drawings and I could tell from the x-ray that my bone was still out of line. When I pointed it out to the doctor, he admitted it was. A few days later, I was operated on again. They couldn't re-break the leg so instead they tried to manipulate the bone and put a wedge in by the plate to keep it together.

It only made things worse. The pain was even more severe than it had been the first night. It was so bad, I actually tore one of the bed sheets I had been gripping onto trying to bear the agony.

Three weeks later, I was still in pain. I asked for the latest x-ray. From it I could see my leg was still out of line. No one listened. The following day, one of the nurses came in and said, 'Justin, tell your parents to bring in your clothes. You're going home at the weekend.'

I said to her straight out, 'I can't go home! I'd love to go home but I can't. My leg isn't right!'

I kicked up such a fuss that the head nun came in.

'You have a problem with your leg,' she said.

'I do,' I said, 'I'm not happy. My leg isn't right.'

She asked me if I wanted to see an orthopaedic surgeon; up to then I had been dealing with a general surgeon. I said I certainly did.

That night, I was moved to St Finbarr's hospital for an x-ray and then to the Orthopaedic hospital, where I was brought into a private room. When they cut the plaster off, they found the wound where the bone had come out had never been cleaned properly. Had I left it another week, gangrene would have set in. My leg would have had to be amputated.

I knew once I was in the Orthopaedic that it was where I should have been all along. The surgeon, Mister St John O'Connell, was a stern but brilliant man. When he saw the infection, he said he wouldn't be able to operate until the wound was completely clean.

Two weeks later I was brought into O'Connell's theatre. First they re-broke my leg. Then they drilled holes into either side of the bone, from my ankle to my shin. Then they put a steel plate on the bone and tied it on with eight screws that fitted into the holes they had drilled. Then they pulled the skin over and stitched it across.

I could hear them doing it. Sometimes, an anaesthetic isn't enough to knock you out completely if the pain is incredibly severe. The pain was incredibly severe.

I'll never forget the rest of the night either. I honestly thought I was going to die. I was moaning aloud the whole time. 'God, God, God …' Whenever I saw one of the nurses, I'd be screeching at them looking for injections. Eventually, they'd give me one, and I'd be floating for a while but soon the pain would return. Normality wouldn't. The pain would be so bad, I'd hallucinate. 'Where are all those people coming from?' I'd shout out to the nurses, when there was no one there but them and me. That was the toughest night of them all.

It was easier in the morning. The operating nurse was a sister of Dan Kelleher, who used to play with University College Cork, and she said they had done a good job. That meant a lot to me. Then I asked her did she think I'd play again. 'Justin,' she said, 'I have no doubt you will.' It was the best news I had heard in a long time. A few weeks earlier, the doctor in the South Infirmary had said I mightn't. I was afraid to ask O'Connell though, just in case he said I wouldn't. His main concern was that my leg would be right for day-to-day living, not whether I hurled again.

I had some good times in the South Infirmary. Pat would often come up with some extra food because they never had enough for me.

They'd say, 'Well, Mister McCarthy, what will you have? The egg, chicken or tomato?' And I'd say, 'I'll have the egg, chicken *and* tomato.' The crack in the Orthopaedic was even better though. No one was actually sick or dying there; our problems were all bone related. Whenever myself and some of the younger fellas would be let out for some fresh air, we'd fly around on our crutches, having races. One Sunday in November, three of us decided to go down to the Park to see the footballers play a league game. One of the lads had his leg broken in twelve places from a motorbike accident but was able to hold on to it thanks to the brilliance of O'Connell. The other fella was a garda who had his leg broken in four places after ending up on the bonnet of some car that had gone out of control. He had a special device in his Morris Minor that meant he could drive without the use of his legs, so the three of us got in and headed to the match. On the way down, the car started to go to one side. We got out to see what the problem was. It was soon obvious what the problem was. One of the tyres was punctured. That was all we needed; we couldn't even bend down, let alone change a wheel. We must have been there in the drizzling rain for ten minutes before someone eventually took pity on the three cripples stranded on the side of the road and stopped. Just before throw-in, there was a roar from the crowd as three hopped along in single file to their spots along the sideline. That wasn't the most priceless reaction of the day though. A few moments earlier, the stewards on the gate had been rubbing their eyes in amazement, wondering if they really had seen three fellas just hop past on crutches.

That was about my only day out as a patient. The confinement was stifling. From my window, I had a great view of the southside of the city and would often watch on with envy at fellas hunting below in the fields with their dogs. The biggest frustration though was not being able to hurl out in the open. My whole life still revolved around hurling; I'd be reading about the games in the papers every day and be talking about it non-stop with my visitors. I still planned to play again, be it senior with Cork or junior with Passage. I'd often think, 'Well, maybe I'll come back as a corner forward. Or play in goal.' And I'd start throwing and catching oranges off the wall and ceiling, to keep my eye in.

I was still getting plenty of radio requests and cards coming up to Christmas. That helped. So did the television that Con Murphy got me from an arrangement with Fitzgerald's Electrical on the Grand Parade; no one else in the hospital had such a luxury. Con was a regular visitor to me, something which I deeply appreciated. Some of his county board officers were not as considerate. When chairman Jack Barrett asked me how I was doing at a function the following year, I said to him, 'Jack, you're worried how I am alright. Not once did you come up to see me in hospital and I was there long enough.'

And I was there for long enough. I didn't get the plaster off until January. I wasn't let out until the end of February. Six months after the accident.

I went without pay those six months. You had to be working with the Harbour Commissioners for a year to be entitled to full compensation but I had been with them for only nine months. The Cork county board wasn't aware of that. When they dropped me an envelope, there was only a hundred pounds in it, the equivalent of five weeks' wages. Everybody assumed I was going to make a killing in court but that's not how it worked out. I would have had to play the poor soldier there but I was more interested in playing hurling. That cost me big-time. How could they hand out a pile of compensation money to someone who was fit enough to play hurling?

The day I got out, I went tipping the ball around the back garden. It was great to get the feel of a hurley again. I couldn't move a whole lot though. My right leg was now half an inch shorter than my left, as if I had a shoe on one foot and no shoe on the other, while I could feel the plate digging into my instep any time I moved.

By the last week of April, I was fit enough to go back to work. I made another breakthrough around that time too. One of the monastery fields was lovely and soft from the corn being set there so when I came to this slight incline in it, I decided to chance trotting rather than merely walking down it. I was able to do it. That felt great.

Over the next few months, the leg gradually got stronger from daily lifting sandbags I had made. One evening in June, as I was tipping around the back in my tracksuit bottoms, I suddenly decided it was time to play. The juniors had a game against Rochestown up in the college field and I was going to play in it. I didn't bother packing any togs; I just grabbed two hurleys and started to trot through the fields. When I got there, I went to one of the mentors, 'I'll fall in tonight.' And I did, at full forward, where I scored a goal and a few points in those tracksuit bottoms.

That was one of the best nights ever. It didn't matter that I wasn't to play another game for another four months, that I had been desperately slow and hardly able to make space to hit the ball. We had won. More importantly, I now knew I could hurl again, in some shape or form. A new adventure in my playing career had begun.

A few weeks later, so had a different adventure. In a field far, far away from Rochestown.

11

A ROAD LESS TAKEN

Look at every path closely and deliberately. Try it as many times as you think necessary. Then ask yourself, and yourself alone the question … Does this path have a heart? If it does, the path is good. If it doesn't, it is of no use.
Carlos Castenada, *The Teachings of Don Juan*

A hundred yards or so from where I was knocked off Joe Murphy's bike, there stands a distinctive landmark. In Cork, everyone knows it as the Fingerpost. One finger points to Passage; another to Cork city; another to Douglas; another to Carrigaline. The accident that occurred within a puck of a ball of there though pointed me in a completely different direction, a road less taken which has made all the difference. I now often think that that shower of rain was meant to happen. No shower, no accident. No accident, no Antrim.

A week or so before the 1970 Munster final, Father Bertie Troy of St Colman's College, whom I had worked with on courses for Coiste Iomána, told me that Antrim had been on to him. They were only a few weeks away from an All-Ireland intermediate championship quarter-final against Galway and felt that they needed someone to polish the rough edges off them. Father Bertie couldn't make it but he suspected that I could now that I wasn't playing. Two officers of their hurling board would be going to the Munster final in Limerick. Would I meet them underneath the stand at half-time? 'Who knows,' he said, 'it might be a great opportunity for you.'

I had been interested in coaching for some time, which is why Father Bertie had approached me. When that ankle injury in '67 had kept me out of work for three weeks, I spent my afternoons writing notes on hurling and my evenings training Passage. Helping Jerry Keating out with Coiste Iomána had been fun too; I found out not only that I could demonstrate all the skills to the kids but that I could break them down too. It was actually Jerry who suggested that I should become one of the coaching instructors in Gormanston College. Back then, the GAA, in conjunction with the Department of Education, ran week-long coaching courses in hurling and football for teachers over the summer at the County Meath school. Some of the game's top thinkers coached there. Father Tommy Maher of Kilkenny and St Kieran's College was a popular lecturer. So were Ned Power, the former Waterford goalkeeper; Sean Hanley, the Clarecastle and Clare mentor; Des Ferguson, the Dublin dual star; and, of course, Donie Nealon. They were all teachers but Jerry felt that I would hold my own in their company. And so it proved. I also found I thrived in their company in that summer of '69, listening to their views and ideas on the game and bouncing some of my own off them.

The turning-point though had been the accident. As I lay in hospital with my leg in plaster, I often considered the possibility that I might never play again. If that prospect ever became a reality, I decided, there would have to be another way to stay involved in the game; coaching would be it. Many is the hour I killed up in that hospital thinking of how the game should be coached and played.

Antrim was hardly the obvious team or place to try out all those ideas though. It was at the other end of the country. It was also July 1970, around about the time the British army had completely lost the trust of the nationalist community. Only a madman would have considered going into the eye of the storm. But then, I was mad about hurling and I could tell from that meeting in Limerick that Niall Patterson and Frank Smyth were too. This match, they told me, would either make or break Antrim. I would have only a week with the players but that week could make all the difference. They would do anything to have me up. A week's wages to take off work? No problem. Accommodation? No problem. As long as I went up. Even in those few minutes, I could tell that Frank and Niall were good men. So I said yes.

Nineteen days later, the two of them collected me at Connolly Station in Dublin. Then we stopped off to eat at the Airport Hotel. That lunch confirmed what I had thought in Limerick – that these were my kind of people. Niall was a huge man with an even bigger heart, most of which was devoted to hurling. He recalled going to see Antrim play in the 1943 All-Ireland and how Ring was way too good for them, and he joked and reminisced about his own days playing for Antrim. Frank, on the other hand, didn't look like a GAA man. He certainly was though and paid a price for it. For years, he had worked as a civil servant in Stormont, watching less competent colleagues being promoted ahead of him. Antrim GAA though appreciated him. So would I.

The journey up was enjoyable for the most part, listening to

Frank and Niall fill me in on the scene and what they wanted from me. For the *most* part. Crossing the border was no fun. I had never been in the North before. Only when I saw those cars stop and those soldiers bark did I begin to realise what was really happening on this island. Frank and Niall were concerned at that juncture too. Cork was notorious for its republican tendencies; for all the army knew, the guy in the back was the best bomb-maker in the world. When we came to the top of the line, we were ordered to step out of the car. Then the boot of Frank's Volkswagen was opened and my hurleys and bags were thrown out on the road. What were these? Who was I? What was I doing up here? The lads explained that I was up to coach Antrim but the soldiers weren't amused. 'Where are you staying?' they asked. 'With me, on the Glen Road,' interjected Frank. The Glen Road was one of the most active areas in Belfast at the time. We were kept there for another ten minutes. I was getting anxious at this stage because I was sure they were going to confiscate my hurleys. Those were two hurleys Ramie Dowling had made specifically for me, hurleys that would not be easily replaced. I got to keep the hurleys though. When we finally were allowed to move away from the checkpoint, Niall told me not to worry; that they got that all the time and that we would probably get it a few more times along the way. Thankfully we didn't.

I stayed with Frank for the first few nights. Then I was moved fifty miles further up the county, to Eddie McCormack's house in Glenbush, a few miles from where the team trained in Loughgiel. It was a real nationalist heartland. Long before the Troubles started in '69, there had been fierce tension there. Eddie's father told me of the time he took the Union Jack off a pole and wore it as an apron as he fed the pigs on his farm. Shortly afterwards, an RUC officer paid a visit to order him to take it off, saying that such a use of Her Majesty's flag was disrespectful. 'You're right,' said Eddie's dad, taking it off. 'Here, have it.' And with that, he threw it into the pigs, who proceeded to devour it.

I met the players for the first time on the Monday night. Up to then, Niall had been coaching them and you could tell that they all looked to him as a father figure. When he introduced me that night, the whole dressing room listened. 'Lads,' he said, 'you all know me. You know that I've hurled for Antrim, that I love Antrim hurling, that I live for Antrim hurling. But lads, this man here knows a lot more than I do. I want ye to listen to everything he says.'

The first thing I told the players was that we'd be training every night that week and that a lot could be achieved in five training sessions. I also told them that I hadn't taken a week off work and travelled over 300 miles just to lose. I wanted intensity and attentiveness.

We started off with a traditional Cork session, balls moving up and down the field. I was genuinely surprised and impressed by their control and striking. Only problem was, they weren't doing it at a quick enough pace; it was obvious they weren't accustomed to training with so many balls. I called them into a huddle. They would have to speed things up, let the ball go quicker and put more pressure on themselves in training. Then we broke up into groups. Ten minutes of hitting on the ground, then another ten picking and hitting, then another ten working on pulling in the air. All at speed.

The response was excellent. They were mad keen to learn. I trained with them, so they'd often go, 'Show us how you did that there again.' I couldn't show them everything but I'd try to show them something new every night. Like a few skills from the Roch series. Like how to get more weight behind their shots. Like the advantages of being able to strike off both sides. Like some quick pulls on the ground. Like how they should play their position.

There were some communication problems, mind. At times they couldn't make sense of my Cork accent and I had trouble with theirs. The lads from the Glens were particularly hard to understand. They sounded Scottish, as if they were eating their words. Then again, they probably thought I was singing mine.

Then there were our different expressions.

A centre forward to me was a centre three-quarters to them.

I'd instinctively go, 'Hey, pull on that ball there, boy, will ya?'

They'd look at me and go, 'Sorry, what about ya, Justin?'

'Em, just keep the ball moving.'

I was obviously getting something through to them though. As the nights went on, you could see a considerable improvement in their hurling. They were going to the ball quicker, controlling it quicker, getting rid of it quicker. You could also tell that we had the makings of a nice team. Andy McCallan and Aidan Hamill were two small but exceptionally quick forwards from Belfast who could play off each other very well; not only were they both outstanding footballers with Antrim but I reckon they would have made outstanding Cork inter-county hurlers. Brendan McGarry was another brilliant forward whose touch, control and striking would merit a starting place with most Munster teams. Johnny Coyles was solid in goal. Seamus Richmond at midfield was strong and quick to let the ball in. Alongside him was Seanie Burns, a crafty player à la McCallan and Hamill who was also very economical with the ball. Niall Wheeler at right half back would go on to be an All-Star replacement. Probably the best of the lot though was our centre three-quarters, Eddie Donnelly, whose strength, hunger for the ball and ability to score reminded me of Willie Walsh.

I loved it up there. Every day Eddie McCormack had something lined up for me to do in the mornings and afternoons, be it coaching youngsters, doing some sight-seeing, going to the Oul' Lammas Fair in Ballycastle or playing a round of golf in Castlerock. The only downside was that my leg was still giving me fierce trouble. At night it would swell to twice its original size, from my ankle to my knee. Then it would throb. All night.

The game against Galway was set for Ballinasloe on the Sunday. We travelled down on the Saturday. That was an experience. We were held up in Derry for an hour so the Black Preceptory, an offspring of the Orange Order, could march. It was an intimidating but revealing sight for a southerner. It was clear what message the Blackmen were trying to convey – that this was their street, their city, their *London*derry.

We stayed in Hayden's Hotel in Ballinasloe that night. That was the one thing about Antrim – they spared no expense. They were like the Down footballers, years ahead of their southern counterparts when it came to preparation. The standard of their club pitches was excellent; all their gear was set out in advance; the team was put up in good hotels and given steaks before every game.

And yet they didn't have the ideal set-up. Traditionally there was an uneasy relationship between players from Belfast and those from the north of the county. Frank and Niall were very aware of it. They had joined together at board level (Frank was from the city, Niall from Loughgiel); now they wanted the team to do the same on the pitch. It was a point they wanted me to address and I did so in our team meeting in Hayden's. I told them that a house divided cannot stand, that once they put on that jersey they were all playing for the one team, that no one outside Antrim gave a shit where they were from.

A section of the 4,000-strong crowd in Ballinasloe that day was more ignorant of our players' backgrounds than I could ever have predicted. When the lads ran on, they were booed and called 'Orangemen'. It annoyed the lads but it also motivated them. We won. The lads were delighted. Frank was meant to leave me at Limerick for the train back but ended up driving me all the way home. It meant a 300-mile journey back the next day but the way he saw it, the trip down had meant the chance to relive every puck.

The following day as Frank went back to Belfast, I went back to work. My involvement with Antrim though was far from over. Before and after the Galway game, the players and officers had told me that my coaching had helped them hurl with greater speed, economy and confidence. Niall was anxious for me to stay on. Every night for the next three weeks he was on the phone, wanting to know what the team should do at their next training session in preparation for the All-Ireland semi-final.

That semi-final was against Dublin in Croke Park. The night before the game, I met the players in Jury's Hotel and told them the type of hurling I wanted – fast, forceful and direct. I saw very little of it in the first half the following day though. Like a lot of northern teams, the whole occasion had got to them. Instead of making things happen, they were *waiting* for things to happen. Mick Bermingham alone had scored two goals for Dublin. It was a miracle Antrim were only 2-9 to 1-9 behind.

Now, I laughed as much as the next man at the De Mentor sketch by D'Unbelievables. We all know him, the type who rants and raves, mainly because he's incapable of saying anything constructive or technical. There is the odd time though when a bollicking is in order, when you have to display what the Americans call 'righteous anger'. 13 September 1970 was such a time. When the players sat down, looking dejected, I shouted, holding a hurley in my hand, 'Right, lads, up on yer feet!' They all jumped up. And then I tore into them.

'Backs, we're too loose. This isn't a tight pitch like Ballinasloe; this is fucking Croke Park. These aren't club hurlers you're up against; these fellas have played senior with Dublin. How many more goals do you want to give Mick Bermingham? Tighten up! Andy, Aidan – run at them. Make it happen; don't wait for it to happen. That goes for everyone! Make it fucking happen! Take the game to them! Ye're better than them. I want the hurling we've seen in Loughgiel; the hurling we've seen in Ballinasloe. Fast, furious, forceful, direct. Let that ball in fast! Hook, block, chase! That's not what's happening now. You know what's happening now? Right now I'm thinking I've wasted my fucking time going to the far end of the country to coach a bunch of fellas who obviously couldn't give a shit whether they won an All-Ireland or not!!! There's an All-Ireland to be won here! And ye don't seem to want it!!!'

The next thing, there was this crashing noise. In their wisdom, the caterers in Croke Park had put these teacups and saucers on a table in the middle of the room. In my rage, I swept them to the floor with my hurley.

The Antrim County Board was never asked to pay for the damage. It would gladly have done so. The lads went out and scored 1-3 without reply in the first ten minutes of the half. Dublin scored only another two points in the whole game. Bermingham didn't get either of them. Brendan McGarry ended up with 2-2 for us and we ended up winning 3-15 to 2-11. When they returned to the dressing room, the same players who I had ordered to stand up at half-time again rose to their feet. This time they did so on their own accord; this time it was to give me an ovation.

A fortnight later we were all carried off the Croke Park pitch. We had beaten Warwickshire, 4-18 to 3-6, in the final. For the first time in their history, Antrim had won an All-Ireland title. Pandemonium ensued. I couldn't make the celebrations up north – I had work the next day in Cork – but supposedly they had a cavalcade through the Glens of Antrim. For a few days, there were no Troubles. Life was beautiful.

That, of course, was temporary. There was no getting away from the Troubles. I remember the lads being very concerned when there was a big piece on me on the back of the *Irish News*; they thought it might be enough to trigger some unstable loyalist into putting even more steel into me. The team couldn't train in Casement Park in Belfast, while the lads from Belfast lived in constant fear making the ninety-mile round trip to Loughgiel.

One Monday morning our full forward, Paddy McShane, went into the village of Bushmills on the job to collect some rations, sporting a cut above his eye. The guy in there went, 'What happened to you?'

'Ach, I was playing a match yesterday.'

'What kind of a match?'

'Hurling.'

'Get the fuck out of here, you fenian bastard. And don't ever come in here again.'

There were a thousand and one other stories. Like of fellas going to retrieve the ball behind the goal and getting a bullet for their troubles, or the time the army started trying to shoot a fugitive running behind a GAA pitch and one team ducked while the other went on to score a goal. Frank Smyth wanted me to become a full-time coach in the county – the first of its kind in the whole country – but after serious consideration, I declined; it was just too risky. I knew I was right a year or so later when I came up to say a few words to the lads before a league game against Clare. That Sunday night I was in a GAA clubhouse in Belfast with Frank when some fella ran in, shouting, 'Quick, the soldiers are coming.' We were afraid the place was about to be raided, so we all sprinted across the road to this warehouse where we waited in silence for ten minutes. No one came, but as we all held our breath, I remember thinking it was no way to live, living in fear.

The Antrim connection stayed alive over the years. I was asked to talk to the team before the 1974 All-Ireland B final (they lost, to Kerry). There was that incredible day in Ardee. In the early eighties, when the Christy Ring School of Hurling in Gormanston College up in County Meath gave each coach an underage team to develop over three years, I chose Antrim; we duly won the All-Ireland in the third year, the final serving as a curtain-raiser to the Cork county final. I've also arranged games in Cork and held all-day clinics in Gormanston and Rochestown for clubs such as Dunloy and O'Donovan Rossa through the years.

You can do only so much on an ad hoc basis though. You can also be used only so much. In 1988, Jim Nelson, the manager of the Antrim senior team at the time, asked me to become an advisor to the team. I duly said a few words to them before their opening league game against Kilkenny but I wasn't asked to say a word at half- or full-time. A few weeks later Jim again asked me to go to another game, this time against Waterford. That day I had no input at all. So when he asked me to go to a third game, I told him I was no longer interested in wasting my time. It was the same with Dunloy in the mid-nineties. I arranged an all-day clinic for them in Gormanston, something which the players really appreciated, but I sensed when I was asked to help them out before the county final later in the year that the team manager, Seamus Elliott, didn't want me around. Maybe he was afraid that there might have been too many chiefs in the dressing room but he never told me, and if he had gone to the bother, I'd have wished it had been when I was in Cork.

The reality is that they do need outside assistance. A little knowledge is a dangerous thing up there. While fellas are putting in great work and no one can question the commitment and fitness levels of their teams, the old problem is their hurling; their first touch, ability to make space to hit the ball and do things at the required quickness just isn't there. Croke Park is doing little for them. Providing national leagues for the senior county team is not enough. Antrim need serious competition at underage, not adult level; even by minor level it is too late. The GAA has to appreciate – and then compensate for – the fact that Antrim are so isolated. It would bring the game on so much if northern underage teams were given funding to play teams down south.

I'm delighted to see Antrim have decided to help themselves. Appointing Dinny Cahill as county senior manager after their embarrassing defeat to Down in 2001 was a great move. Dinny has a fierce passion for hurling but he also has a deep knowledge of it; his success with the Tipperary minors in 1996 showed that. Dinny can provide that outside assistance they need, from speeding up their hurling to getting players to appreciate the range of shots and options they have. He also brings no baggage. The club scene in Antrim is so intense and parochial that the bigger picture is often missed. I remember a few years ago when the county football manager Brian White invited Martin McHugh to talk to his players. McHugh asked them who was right corner back on the Crossmaglen team that had won the previous year's All-Ireland club final. None of them knew. He then asked them who was right corner back on the Meath team that had won Sam Maguire. They all knew it was Mark O'Reilly. None of them knew his club. McHugh's point was clear; people outside the county only see your county. In Antrim, they've tended to forget that.

You have to admire them though. It's hard to keep hurling alive up there, yet they're doing it. One minute you're in hurling country, the next, the footpaths are painted red, white and blue and there's a Union Jack flying above you. I would consider myself a fanatic about hurling but I've met my equal up there. They have a real sense of the heritage and tradition that is the game, the *art*, of hurling. I've spent nights talking into the wee wee hours with Sambo McNaughton; shown the O'Kanes of Dunloy how I fix and band a hurley; gone to club games in Cushendall, Loughgiel, Ballycastle. I still go up there every year, to visit old hurling friends. Like Dick McKeague of Dunloy and his wife Brigid, who played camogie for Antrim. Like Willie Richmond, a sub on the '70 team. Like Frank Smyth.

I'll keep making that annual trip up north for as long as I live. The truth is, I will always have a soft spot for Antrim and Antrim hurling. They came to me when I was at a crossroads in my life. The path they offered not only had a heart; it gave *me* the heart to try another.

The comeback trail.

12

MOUNTAIN CLIMBING

Nothing is impossible to the faithful and the brave.
McCarthy coat of arms

Shortly after he returned to the Manchester United first team in 1998 after almost a year out through injury, Roy Keane described his lay-off as one of the loneliest experiences of his life. At first, he went to the games at Old Trafford but soon stopped. Everyone was only interested in the team that was *playing*; it was as if he was in the way. 'They say it's a team game, but it didn't feel that way when I was out with my cruciate,' he said. 'At the end of the day, you're on your own.'

I can relate to that. I received plenty of sympathy and support from team-mates and supporters in the lead-up to the 1969 All-Ireland but it was a different story twelve months later. The morning of the 1970 All-Ireland final, Jerry Keating and myself went up to the Skylon Hotel to see the team. I was hardly looking for a fanfare reception but I expected more than the lads and the supporters just nodding, 'Justin, boy.' It was all very distant; there was little warmth, little empathy; it was as if they were wondering, 'What's he doing here?' Just like Keane, I learned things that day. Like that if you're of no use to the team, they don't want you around. Like that people have their own lives to live and will live them regardless of what happens to you. Like that, at the end of the day, you're not that special; you're on your own.

I guess what really stung though was that everyone looked at me as a *former* Cork hurler. It was the same in work. Fellas would go, 'It's a pity about your leg; I mean, it's obvious you'll never play for Cork again.' That summer in '70, Eamon Young told Father Tommy Maher in Gormanston College that he was mad to think that I could play inter-county hurling again. In fact, it seemed Father Maher was the only person who thought I could make it back. That hurt. There are nights even now, at fifty-six years of age, that I dream I'm playing for Cork and then wake up depressed, realising I'm not; at twenty-five, the concept of never again playing for Cork was unbearable. Most lads in my situation would have said, 'Look, I've had a good innings, I have my All-Ireland, pity about the injury but hey, it happens.' I couldn't. That feeling of being a Cork hurler was the ultimate and I didn't want to let it go.

I played a few games for Passage in the autumn. The winter was spent training on my own. I'd go up to the little weights room Father Nessan had built beside the ball alley in Rochestown College. There was no light there but I got over that by bringing a flash lamp; all that mattered was that the room had some weights and a horizontal climbing ladder. I'd also go up at night to a neighbouring farmer's field to do some running. I'd bring Jip and two flash lamps with me, tie one of them around him, put the other on the ground maybe forty yards away and then do thirty sprints between them. One night, I brought no flash lamp. That, quite literally, wasn't a bright idea. The same night I was running around the outside of the field when I suddenly stumbled over this massive body and fell flat on my face. When I looked up, I got the fright of my life. It was a sleeping cow. I jumped straight to my feet. So did the cow. But just as I braced myself for its charge, the cow ran away. Thankfully, it seemed to be even more frightened than me.

By the turn of the year, I was back playing inter-firm hurling as a guest for the city banks. While I could only run on the balls and toes of my foot, it was obvious the leg was getting stronger and that my hurling hadn't left me. After watching the banks play a few times, Dan O'Mahony told his fellow county selectors that I was going well enough for a Cork recall. Before January was out, I was back training with the panel. My first night back was up in Farranferris College. There were no lights there and before the start of the session, Jim O'Regan called me aside. 'Justin, it's fairly dark there. Are you sure you'll be okay?' I said I'd be fine. Farranferris might have had no lights but at least it had no sleeping cows either.

The following week, I was listed as a sub for a league game against Dublin in Croke Park. As it turned out, I ended up starting, at right half back, after Donal Clifford cried off injured. Before the game in the dressing room, John Horgan and Paddy Barry came over to wish me all the best. That meant a lot. We ended up losing by six points but I was never so happy after a defeat. I had played again for Cork; what's more, I had played *well* again for Cork. The following week in his Rambler column for the *Cork Examiner*, Eamon Young wrote how delighted he was to be proved wrong. I was a *current* Cork player. And it was the greatest feeling in the world.

Over the next few months, it seemed as if I had never been away. The week after that Dublin game, I played centre back for Passage against UCC. The *Evening Echo* was impressed. 'I do not know any player in present day hurling who could equal, let alone surpass, the feats of artistry which McCarthy accomplished in this game,' its reporter wrote. 'On one occasion in the second half after an amazing piece of ball control left three UCC players floundering in his wake, he was openly applauded by the College midfield player, Mícheál Murphy.' The following week, I moved to centre forward and scored 2-4 against Cloyne. Then there was a league game for Cork against Limerick in April. Cummins scored three great goals that day but the papers gave me just as much credit. Val Dorgan of the *Cork Examiner* admitted he thought he'd never see me offer such a display in a red jersey again, while John D. Hickey of the *Irish Independent* wrote that I looked 'every inch the hurler' I was 'before the traffic accident'.

And the rave reviews kept coming. Even when a Babs-inspired Tipp beat us by two points in the league semi-final, I was adjudged to have been one of Cork's best performers. When we avenged that defeat three weeks later at Wembley, I put on an exhibition from midfield which included five points, two from sideline cuts. It seemed as if I was on a roll.

The truth, of course, was that I was not the same hurler. I remember another game against Tipp that year. It was back in late March, and although we won, Noel O'Dwyer gave me the run-around in the second half. The pace was just too much; the ground, too hard for my leg. It was the same in the first round of the championship when we played Limerick. I had a very average match that day in Thurles. Unfortunately, so did the whole team, bar Cummins. Limerick won, 2-16 to 2-14. We were out and I was back down to earth.

The autumn of 1971 was a lot like its spring and summer. Most of the time, it seemed as if there was nothing wrong with me; I can distinctly remember outplaying Frank Cummins in a league game in Nowlan Park. But there were other times when it was obvious I was being hampered by the injury; I also recall struggling to keep up with Michael Moroney in a league game against Clare. The leg just wasn't right. I could feel the pound-and-a-half plate and some of the screws hitting my bone. They had come loose from all the running, jarring, stopping and starting. When I went to the doctor, he was straight to the point. The plate and screws would have to come out.

That was hardly what I wanted to hear. For one, it would mean once more going under the knife and revisiting the horrors of yesteryear. Worse, it placed a trip to America in jeopardy. The All-Stars scheme was introduced in 1971, and its sponsors, Carrolls, along with the GAA, had organised a series of games in the States between the All-Stars and the All-Ireland winners, which happened to be Tipperary. As Tipp had a few All-Stars themselves, replacements were needed for the All-Star team, and I was selected to take Mick Roche's place. If either the operation or the ensuing recovery did not go well, I would miss that plane at Easter. I might never even play inter-county hurling again, the way Cork worked.

The operation *did* bring back unpleasant memories. When I woke up after it, the pain was so severe I wondered whether they had taken the plate out at all. I was in hospital for the next three weeks. Over the following few months though, I found I was making a good recovery. At the end of January 1972, I met Jim O'Regan at the Cork county board convention. He was glad to hear the leg was grand. A fortnight later I was picked as a sub for a league game against Limerick.

That wasn't just any league game. After twenty-five minutes, I came on for Denis Coughlan at midfield and started to play really well. A minute into the second half though, I got a bad belt above my eye and had to come off. As I was getting treated on the line, I kept looking out onto the field where it was obvious that the game was going against Cork. I went over to Jim O'Regan.

'Jim, put me back in.'

Jim looked at me as if I was mad. 'Justin, you can't go in, boy. Look at the state of ya.'

I asked again. Jim said no again. With just seven minutes to go, I reluctantly accepted that I had no further part to play that day.

Then Ray Cummins picked up an injury and had to come off. The selectors huddled together and started scratching their heads. They looked at the dugout, then back onto the field, then back at the dugout. Then they looked over at me. The next thing, I was running on the field to play centre forward, my head swathed in bandages. The score at that stage was Limerick 5-8, Cork 4-3. Limerick didn't score again. Cork scored three more goals to win by a point. Even though I had played only twelve minutes in all, the *Irish Press* deemed I was a close second to Mick Malone as Man of the Match. A month later, I was on that plane to San Francisco.

That was a great trip. All the players and their partners were put up by Irish people in San Francisco, and Pat and I got to stay with my sister Una and her husband John. That trip wasn't just a chance to catch up with my sister though; it was a chance to mix with the best players of my generation and a chance to see one of the most fascinating cities in the world. And then there were the games. They weren't exhibition matches; all of us wanted to beat Tipp. The local medical services certainly shared the same view. There were four ambulances outside the Balboa Stadium for the first game. As it turned out, only Tipp pride was wounded; we beat them both times. Coming off the field, Frank Cummins told me that it was as if I had never been in any accident.

All was not well though. I still had no transport of my own to get to training and still the county board were refusing to send a car up for me. So I told them about a fortnight before the league final against Limerick, 'Look, I have no way of getting to training; I'll train on my own.' And I did. I went to the ball alley; I went out to the college field and took hundreds of shots; I went to old Carey's field to do sprints and laps. It was the best week's training I ever had. I felt incredibly fresh without the strain and hassle of getting to the Park after work, while my touch was spot on from all the ballwork. It showed. I hardly gave Sean Foley a puck of the ball. Denis Coughlan and myself ran the show at midfield. When the whistle went, Cork were league champions.

A few months later, we were Munster champions. Waterford were disposed of in the first round, 3-16 to 4-6. Tipp were not so easily overcome; they were ahead by nine points at half-time before we came back to earn a replay, which we won by six. Then Clare were absolutely destroyed, 6-18 to 2-8, in the provincial final, Cummins, Charlie and a young fella called Seanie O'Leary all scoring 2-1 from play.

We were back in another All-Ireland. Another All-Ireland against Kilkenny. Just like in '69. Except this time I'd get to play.

To this day, it ranks as my biggest disappointment in hurling. Okay, so that '72 Cork team was not a *great* team; Walsh and Horgan had somehow been let drift off the scene. But it was a good team. Certainly good enough to beat Kilkenny.

You needed only to look at our full-forward line. It was absolutely lethal. Ray Cummins was in his prime. Cummins's stickwork was actually quite limited; he couldn't, say, clip a ball in the air. But while he wasn't a great *hurler*, he was, to paraphrase Eamon Dunphy, a great *player*. He used his height and reach to maximum effect, had great presence around the square, and his vision and decision making were exceptional. Then in the corners we had Charlie and O'Leary. Even at this early stage, O'Leary was a predator *extraordinaire*. Charlie, meanwhile, was at his peak – and there has never been a better small man than Charlie McCarthy. He had a great turn of speed, a bag full of tricks and the ability to shoot off either side with power and accuracy. What I really liked about him though was that he could move out to a ball coming at speed and whip it across the square first time, be it in the air or on the ground, for someone to finish off. Few corner forwards could do that.

It wasn't just our full-forward line that was on fire that year. So was our centre forward, Mick Malone. He wasn't as skilful or as fast as Walsh but he did as much as anyone could to compensate for Walsh's absence that year; like Willie, he was a forceful, direct player with the ability to cut in for goals. Alongside him were Gerald and Pat Hegarty. In short, we had a brilliant attack.

The point was actually confirmed in the All-Ireland. O'Leary, Charlie, Cummins and Malone scored 5-9 between them. The rest of us chipped in with only two points but still, 5-11 should have been enough to win any All-Ireland. Not the '72 one though. We lost by seven points. We had been eight up midway through the second half. Once more, the fault was not in the stars but in ourselves.

That's what made it so galling.

First, there were the small things. Like the hotel. Now, I know the lads won the '70 All-Ireland having stayed in the Skylon, but I still had, well, reservations about being in a spot so close to Croke Park and beside one of the busiest roads in Dublin. I was used to having a quiet night's sleep from living in the country, so I had hoped that I'd get a room at the back of the hotel. I was given one at the front. My room-mate was Derry Gowen, an officer with the county board. I wasn't happy with that either. I was playing in an All-Ireland the next day; he wasn't. I went to bed at eleven but struggled to get to sleep with the noise. By half-one, I had finally managed to doze off when Derry came through the door. That meant I was awake for another few hours. That morning I didn't feel fresh. I just hoped that I'd be revitalised once I togged off.

That was another thing – what we togged into. Before the game, we were given special tracksuits and socks. Those socks were different to anything we had worn before. They had nylon soles and were very light. During the first half, I noticed that my feet were feeling sore. The ground was very hard and the socks seemed to be moving inside my boots. At half-time, I took the socks off. The skin had come off the soles of both feet. I looked across the dressing room and Con Roche and Ray Cummins were having the same problem. We had to wear those same socks in the second half.

Then there was the biggest thing of all. How we trained for the game.

After the Munster final, the selectors decided we needed something special for the All-Ireland. That 'something special' would be greater fitness; this All-Ireland was going to be eighty minutes long. A new trainer was brought in, a Father Donal Coakley from Glanworth in north Cork who had studied physical education in Strawberry Hill in London. Donal was full of ideas and exercises. His regime was a culture shock to us but we were receptive to it; he seemed to know what he was talking about, and besides, we were flying. A few nights before the final, I was up near the front in the sprints and Jim O'Regan said, 'Justin, I thought I'd never see you in such great shape after that accident.' The same night, I spotted a friend looking on behind the wire. Liam Hinphy was a Kilkenny man teaching in Derry who I knew from the courses in Gormanston College and was down south with a few friends to watch the respective finalists train. When I went over to him, he said he had been disappointed by Kilkenny's session the previous night. 'It was nowhere near as intense as that there,' he said. 'No bullshit, ye're way sharper and fitter than them.'

Liam's words were reassuring. I had been worried that maybe we were overdoing it. The weather had been very warm in the lead-up to that All-Ireland, the ground was very hard, every one of our sessions had been incredibly intense and yet there hadn't been a water bottle in sight. Even a few nights before the game we were doing piggy-back runs and a series of fifty-yard sprints. Was it the right thing to be doing so close to an All-Ireland? I was glad to hear Liam think it was.

A month or two after the All-Ireland, Father Maher, Ned Power, Sean Hanley, Donie Nealon, Des Ferguson and myself were invited up to Croke Park to discuss the possibility of writing a coaching book. Later in the day, I pulled Father Maher aside. 'That All-Ireland in September,' I said. 'We were flying heading into it. Supposedly ye were taking it handy enough. Were ye?'

I will never forget his answer. 'Justin, we knew ye had a new trainer; we knew ye were going like the hammers of hell; it didn't bother us one bit. We knew we'd last the eighty minutes. My philosophy is that you have to keep that bit in reserve for the day itself. Our priority was to keep the lads fresh. Ye left yer fitness in Cork; we kept ours for Croke Park.'

And that was the difference. Up to now, you might have thought I begrudged Kilkenny that '72 All-Ireland. Believe me, my admiration for them couldn't be greater. They totally outsmarted us. The time for us to have had Donal in doing the hard physical training was back in the winter and spring, not a few weeks before the All-Ireland.

Kilkenny, on the other hand, were mindful that hurling is a game of touch and confidence and that you need to be fresh to have both. With twenty minutes to go, we had nothing left in the tank. Kilkenny had plenty. They just ran at us and past us. It was obvious Father Maher had instructed their midfield to keep soloing in. With fifteen minutes to go, Frank Cummins ran through for a goal to level the game. His partner and my marker, Liam O'Brien, had also started to repeatedly blow past me. People put that down to a lack of pace on my behalf but it had more to do with fatigue. It was the same for the rest of the lads. We were killed from the training. How else do you explain a team outscoring us 2-9 without reply in the last twenty minutes of an All-Ireland?

By bringing in Father Donal, our selectors had tried to move with the times. The reality is they were still years behind Kilkenny. Now, I had great time for Jim O'Regan. He had been a very good player, knew the game, gave me some valuable advice when I was centre back and was brilliant to me after the accident. Like every other Cork mentor though, he was no Father Maher. The week before that '72 All-Ireland, I told him I wanted to mark Frank Cummins because I had done well on him in the past. Jim said that I'd be on Liam O'Brien and that Denis Coughlan would be taking up Cummins. When I asked Jim what type of player O'Brien was, his reply summed up generations of Cork coaching.

'Justin, you'll know all about Liam O'Brien by five o'clock on Sunday.'

I took the defeat terribly bad. We had that game in the bag. I had burst my ass to get back to play in an All-Ireland final. And then I had played like that. I didn't go to the function for the two teams that night; I stayed in my room with Pat and a friend called John Motherway, watching TV. The next day, I didn't wait to travel home with the team; I just headed straight back to Cork in the morning with Jerry Keating in his car.

The selectors mightn't have taken that too kindly; the next season I was the only member of the '72 team that didn't feature on the panel. Then again, they might have thought I'd never be the same player with the leg. I don't know. There was little communication in Cork hurling back then. John Horgan and Willie Walsh had been allowed to drift off the scene. There was no one to guide them, advise them, to listen to the factors behind their lack of form or commitment. And in my own case, there was no one to say, 'Justin, what was the story about not coming back with the team? Look, we know you were disappointed but we all were.

We win as a team, we lose as a team and we go home as a team. Listen, we still think you have something to contribute, we want you back, but you need to say a few words to the rest of the lads to clear things up.'

The exile was only temporary. Fourteen months after that All-Ireland, I was called back to the panel for a league game against Kilkenny. I did well; the consensus was that I comprehensively got the better off Pat Henderson at centre forward. And over the next few months, I kept playing well, be it in the half-forward line or midfield. I even had the satisfaction of winning my first Oireachtas medal after we again beat Kilkenny.

But that was as good as it got. I had a poor enough game against Dublin in the '74 league semi-final and was taken off. I put it down as a bad day at the office but the selectors thought it was more than that. When the team for the league final was named, I wasn't on it. The selectors could quite rightly feel justified in their decision – the lads hammered Limerick, 6-15 to 1-2 – but I felt hard done by. With a few minutes to go, they told me to go on but I said, 'Lads, the game is over; leave the team alone.' Tokenism didn't interest me.

A few weeks later in Walsh Park, I was again asked to enter the fray. This time, I obliged. It was no use. Waterford held on to beat us, 4-9 to 3-8. For the second consecutive year, Cork had been beaten in the first round of the championship.

I never played for Cork again.

I would love to have, of course. But they never called. And deep down, I knew in the shower that day in Walsh Park that they probably wouldn't. Whenever I had a mediocre game, they'd put it down to the leg and say I wasn't going to get any better with it.

There's no doubt I was never the same player after the accident. While there were days when there was plenty of give in the ground and I felt fine, there were too many others when the ground was hard and my leg would hurt. I never had the same power in my leg which allowed me to take off like I used to; only 60 per cent of that power came back. But while I wasn't as good as the Justin McCarthy of 1969, I was still good enough for Cork. If the selectors had left me at wing back I think I would have remained one of the mainstays of the team. By then though Cork were in a totally different predicament to the one they faced in '69. They now had a surplus of half backs and a dearth of midfielders, so I was moved up. And while I'd often get by through anticipation and sheer craft, my limited mobility was going to be exposed more often playing such a position. There was always going to come a time when I'd once again be seen as a former Cork hurler. It just happened sooner than I expected.

So did something else.

13

GROWING MUSHROOMS

Ger McKenna gave me a free rein with the team. 'Do it your way,' he said. I told him we had great potential, that perhaps we would win the All-Ireland in three years. It just happened to come straightaway. There'll never be another 1975.

Mick O'Dwyer

It was at the first meeting of the city division board in 1975 that the delegate came straight out with it.

'Lads, we're only wasting our time putting a team in the senior championship.'

Many of his fellow delegates nodded in agreement. Some of them had touted the idea two years previously at a similar meeting and nothing had changed since. What *was* the point in fielding a Seandún selection? Most players were only interested in winning the junior or intermediate championship with their own clubs. Why leave that comfort zone to train as hard as the likes of their city neighbours in the Glen, Barrs and Blackrock? The Big Three were clubs; playing for a club meant playing for the lads, playing for the pride of the parish. Seandún wasn't a parish. Who were you really playing for playing for them? For a division which had never won the county? For your man from Delaneys you tried to split last year? Seandún was only a joke, boy.

Around the same time, another meeting was taking place. Passage was at a crossroads. Eddie O'Brien had gone to America; Martin O'Donoghue was now nearly forty; there were few players coming through. And so it was decided. The club was dropping back to intermediate.

The demotion of Passage was the salvation of Seandún. Our club still had some players well capable of holding their own at senior level, players that would really help Seandún. And so the division decided to field a team in the senior championship after all.

I was approached to coach that team. I accepted. I could see there was the makings of a really good team. From my own club alone there was myself, Bernie Meade, who had played a few league games with Cork, George O'Sullivan, Weeshie Murphy, Kieran Keane and his brother, David (yes, the same David Keane who coached Limerick to those All-Ireland Under-21 titles in recent years). There was Jimmy Nodwell and Jim Atkins from Mayfield, two hardy, tenacious players, and Pat O'Sullivan from Delaneys, a thirty-year-old rangy player who had yet to play for the county but could with the right coaching in him. And then there was a young wing back from Bishopstown called Johnny Crowley. That lad was showing signs of promise.

The challenge would be to get them to play for one another. That hadn't happened in the past. I felt it wasn't an insurmountable obstacle though. The best way to establish a bond and play down our intra-division rivalries was to realise how much we had in common. And so we held team meetings – plenty of them – down in the Victoria Hotel in town and talked about what we were trying to achieve, what we *could* achieve, what we *would* achieve. We had enough talent in the room to beat any one in the county, I told them. If we trained right.

So we trained right. Every player good enough to play senior club hurling was cajoled to go training. 'Come on, we need you, you're a good player; we'll make you an even better one' – many of them had never heard that before. We didn't just train in the division's headquarters either, as good as the pitch in Ballinlough was. We'd go round to different clubs in the division – Mayfield, Brian Dillons, Passage – to let the lads appreciate how big the division, the *cause*, was.

Our approach bore fruit. On 10 May 1975, in the first round of the championship, we beat a highly fancied Sarsfields team that included young guns Tadhg and Bertie Óg Murphy. To most of Cork, our 4-10 to 4-7 victory was a major shock. It wasn't to the Cork senior selectors though. They had seen it coming.

That's why they had approached me the previous week to coach the county team.

Willie John Daly is one of my favourite people. I love meeting him and hearing his stories about Ring and all the games they won together. The man has a great humanity, a great passion, a great knowledge of the game. Unfortunately, it didn't work out for him as trainer to the county team. Cork didn't win a championship game under him in '73 and '74 and then were beaten by Galway in the '75 league quarter-final. After that game, some of the papers claimed the side was physically and mentally unprepared. Willie John thought such criticism was unfair and personal. He was also frustrated that only two or three players were showing up for the sessions before the Galway game. And so he decided that he had had enough. Five weeks before the start of the championship.

A few days after Willie John had secretly called it quits, Jack Barrett and Dan O'Mahony came over to me while I was watching some match in Ballinlough. After a few courteous but bland exchanges, the two selectors came to the point. Willie John had handed in his notice. They were badly stuck. They had nobody to look after the team. They knew what I had done with Antrim, what I did in Gormanston, what I was doing with Seandún. Would I be interested?

I was taken aback. I thought they had come over to ask me to play for them, not *coach* them; I was playing great hurling for Passage at the time, while Willie John's resignation was news to me. I told them I'd need some time to think about it. Dan said he'd call up to my house the next day.

My head was spinning that night. I was playing well enough to make the Cork team, something Jack and Dan said they were fully aware of. Yet I knew that I couldn't be both a trainer and player with Cork. Something would have to give. That was the dilemma. If I didn't take over Cork, who else could? If I did, my inter-county playing career was over; few 31-year-olds had come back after being away from the scene for two years. Then again, what was the point in playing for a team that wasn't properly prepared? That said ... A thousand twists and turns later, I came to a conclusion. Cork needed Justin McCarthy The Coach more than they needed Justin McCarthy The Player. Honestly, that's what swung it.

The following Sunday night, the team played Tipperary in a challenge game in Coachford. I decided to have no involvement on the night because I had yet to train them but before the game Jack Barrett announced to the players that the county board would be sanctioning my appointment on Tuesday. The lads basically shrugged their shoulders. It was hard to blame them; they didn't know whether they were coming or going. Suffice to say, I hadn't inherited the most buoyant team in the world.

The night after our first training session, I told Dan O'Mahony I wanted a meeting with only myself and the players there. 'What about the selectors?' he asked. 'It won't go down well if they're not there.' I felt though that the players needed to know there was now a new regime with a different emphasis. I got my way. It may not have gone down well with the selectors but it certainly did with the players. Training, I told them, would be different, intense but enjoyable. For starters, there would be the novel experience of actually having matches amongst ourselves – twice a week. There'd be loads of ballwork and skills training – at speed; our hurling had to get much, much quicker. I'd be joining in with them, so I'd be able to tell who was slacking off and who was really putting it in. And I'd also be having a good look at all their hurleys and be refining them. Fellas weren't just to have one hurley and rely on a mentor to throw them in a replacement. Each player was to have two or three good hurleys with his name on both sides of them; they were all to be proud of their names and their hurleys.

More than anything, I stressed we needed everyone to put his shoulder to the wheel. We had only thirty days to our first-round game against Waterford. I reminded them that I had taken a big gamble by taking on the job and leaving my playing career behind me but that I was willing to do it for Cork. I didn't want to go back down to Walsh Park and experience '74 again. Every other man would also have to give it his all if we were to avoid a repeat of that day.

The response from the players was fantastic. It didn't seem to matter to them that I was only thirty and had played with most of them, maybe because they soon realised it didn't matter to me. As a rule, I never get close to any team I train. Winning is too important to be compromised by friendships. And it was the same with Cork in '75. Charlie and Gerald were treated the same as anybody else. The days of sharing rooms were gone. In training, the others would hear me going, 'Come on, Gerald, you need to be quicker than that.' 'Charlie, that's well within your range, boy. You should be making that. That's it. Good man.'

One thing I was very conscious of was the need to communicate individually with the players, even if it was just a word of encouragement while giving them back their hurleys. It was a point I stressed in an interview with Pat Courtney of the *Sunday Independent* a week following my appointment. 'I believe players should have their good and bad points explained to them. Over and over again, you see a player given his chance on a team and after a few games he's dropped. Everybody knows why but the player himself. If the player was taken aside and told that he was not, say, putting enough heart into it, that he was picking the ball too much or that he was too slow, he could then work on his weakness knowing what to aim for. Boiled down, you could say that coaching is really advice and communication.'

Now that might seem very basic stuff today. It was even basic stuff in Gormanston and in some counties back in the seventies. But in Cork hurling circles back then, it was revolutionary. I played ten years for the county and I can't recall a mentor telling me to work on a specific skill or weakness. The attitude was, 'Sure, he's lucky to have played with Cork at all. He can find out he's not good enough when he sees the team in Wednesday's paper.'

I was particularly keen to make Willie Walsh feel appreciated. In the past, he had been taken for granted and was left to find his own way up from Youghal to make training. Once I took over, I told him that I thought the world of him and that we'd be arranging a taxi for him to make training. Walsh's response was exemplary.

One player never bought into what I was trying to do. We had thirty-three training sessions that summer and I doubt whether Ray Cummins made ten of them. I don't know what it was about Ray and myself; he was the only member of the '69 panel that didn't come up to see me in hospital either. Maybe he felt he could get away without training because he was living in Kinsale; maybe it was because he felt there was no way he'd be dropped; I don't know. In fairness, he never let us down on the pitch that year but that still didn't excuse what he was doing or – to be more precise – not doing. As far as I was concerned, every player had room for improvement, even Cummins, who, for all his presence and vision, had a limited range of shots. I wasn't a selector so I couldn't drop him but I'd have brought the situation to a head if I had been given more time in the job.

The others though were really appreciating how the sessions were going. They could see their hurling was improving from practising so many shots and skills and playing in match-like situations. John Horgan, Pat Hegarty, Martin Doherty and Willie Walsh came up and told me how different and enjoyable they were finding the sessions.

The introduction of some new players added to the buzz in the camp. My first session as trainer was Jimmy Barry-Murphy's first as a player. I can still see him jumping over that gate in the Farm and coming across with his hurley in hand. When he came over to us, I shook his other hand. 'Jimmy, you're welcome. Enjoy every minute of it.' What a player he turned out to be for Cork.

Jimmy was one of the two fastest hurlers I've come across. The other was his football team-mate and future brother-in-law, Dinny Allen. '75 turned out to be Dinny's only year as a senior inter-county hurler but he was discarded far too soon. He could open up defences with his great flair and vision, and boy, was he fast. We'd pair himself and Jimmy off in the sprints, not just so they'd bring out the best in one another but to save some other poor fella from embarrassment.

Dinny started off with a hurley that two fellas couldn't lift. 'Give me that,' I said one night. 'You can't play with that.'

'It's grand,' said Dinny.

'It's grand alright. It takes you all day to swing it!'

The following night, I gave him back his stick.

'This isn't my hurley!' he said as he swung it in disbelief.

'No? Whose name is that on it so?'

Three weeks later, Dinny tore Waterford to shreds.

The whole team did. Before the game, most commentators had regarded it as a fifty-fifty game, with the papers constantly referring to Walsh Park as a bogey ground for Cork teams. We ended up winning 4-15 to 0-6.

It wasn't just the scoreline that pleased me. It was the way we had played – with speed, passion, authority, directness. From the first minute – in which Charlie scored a goal – to the last, there was no let-up. The lads implemented our game plan to perfection, most notably by using the pace of Barry-Murphy and Allen on the wings. All of a sudden, the side that had been demoralised eleven training sessions ago was now being tipped to win the All-Ireland.

All was not smooth in the camp though. I wasn't happy with where we were training. The Park was unavailable for the year as it was undergoing its metamorphosis from the old Athletic Grounds to Páirc Uí Chaoimh, so the county board had us training down in the Farm out in Curraheen instead. The pitch was poor there. There were no lines or squares marked while there were fields of corn either end of it. We actually had the farcical scenario of our selectors – Jack, Dan, Father Bertie Troy and Paddy Fitz – behind the goals either trying to stop the sliotars going out or retrieving them from the corn. Worst of all, the surface itself was rough and uneven. The only good thing was that the lads had to be sharp to control the ball coming off the bouncy surface but it was hardly the best preparation for Thurles or Croke Park. A few hours after the Waterford game, I asked Frank Murphy – the young Blackrock official who was now the first full-time secretary of the Cork County Board – in the team hotel if there was any possibility of getting a few sessions in the Mardyke. He said he doubted it.

I hadn't been happy with the set-up after training either. The board had us going into this pub in Bishopstown that I felt was too cramped and basic for our requirements. In the lead-up to the Waterford game, Gerald, as team captain, and myself approached the selection committee to ask the board for the use of the Victoria Hotel and to have meals provided after training. I thought it was only fair; the footballers had been getting such perks for a few years as they had tended to be more organised than us; not only did they have an excellent trainer in Donie O'Donovan but they also had some forceful personalities like Billy Morgan. Our selectors had reservations. How would we know what people would want to eat? I said, 'Well, surely someone can ask the players what they want and then ring the hotel and say, "Look, we want ten steaks and twelve ham salads."' After the Waterford game, we finally got our way.

It helped our preparations no end. A meal was a sign to the players that their effort was appreciated, while the Victoria was the perfect venue for team meetings. We had quite a few of them. I would do a lot of the talking but the selectors and players were encouraged to have their say; Paddy Fitz in particular was an outstanding contributor. Then the Saturday night before every game, we'd again run through our game plan, just to have the lads focused right. It was a culture shock to one or two. A few nights before one of those meetings, Jimmy Barry-Murphy, who had a passion for greyhound racing, said, 'Justin, Saturday is a bad night for me. I have the dogs on that night.'

'Jimmy,' I said, 'I know that. But in fairness, the dogs will be there other nights. We won't be if we lose.'

Jimmy was there for the meeting. The following day, we beat Clare 3-14 to 1-9 in the Munster semi-final.

The following month, we beat Limerick by the same scoreline in front of 50,000 in the Munster final, Walsh scoring two goals. Limerick had contested the previous two All-Ireland finals.

Cork were on a roll.

So were another side.

Willie Walsh was getting frustrated. He was pretending not to let on but you could tell. It was coming up to half-time in this particular county championship second-round game and his club Youghal were trailing to Seandún. Outside him, Pat Hegarty was being cancelled out by Bernie Meade. Inside, Seanie O'Leary was being held by our full-back tandem of Denis O'Brien, Jim Atkins and Sean Lucey. And beside him was me. I had yet to give him a puck of a ball.

I had studied Walsh closely while training Cork. You couldn't catch the ball against him because you'd only get your hand blown off, while you couldn't pull against him either because that would only be force against force and he was much stronger. And so I decided on that hot May evening in Midleton to use another trick Roch had taught me all those years ago. As the ball would come down on top of us, I'd go up a little late to bat the ball down, knowing Walsh would be pulling viciously fast. The first time I did it, Frank

Murphy, who was also a top inter-county referee, awarded a free to me, adjudging Walsh to have pulled on my hurley. I duly put the free over the bar. A few minutes later, another puck-out landed on us. Again Frank awarded us a free; again I converted it. That's what was driving Walsh mad. He wasn't out to pull on my hurley.

A few minutes after half-time, a ball came flying in towards us, about two feet off the ground. I tried to block it with my hurley but Walsh pulled so fast and hard that he connected with more than the ball; he also got me right across the knee. It was a wicked belt but I put on a brave face; I didn't want to be the one to break our silence. The next thing, another ball came our way. I beat him to it, soloed up the field and cleared it to one of the lads who duly scored a point. It was Walsh's breaking-point. 'Fuck you anyway, McCarthy!' he said in a tone mixed with disgust and admiration. 'Stay in your shagging position!' A few minutes later, he was moved from his to full forward. That was the moment we had the game won.

Our quarter-final opponents were even more formidable. Youghal had three players at the time starting with Cork; St Finbarr's had five. They were some five too – Gerald, Charlie, Barry-Murphy, Con Roche, Tony Maher. Their team-mates were no slouches either; Charlie Cullinane was still an excellent club player. Together, they were the reigning All-Ireland club champions.

Our morale and confidence was sky-high though. Seandún were also having team meetings that summer. In fact, more thought went into that match against the Barrs than any other I was involved with that year. The game of every player on that Barrs team was dissected. And we came to a conclusion. We had sufficient talent to cope with them. Jim Atkins – a very good, tenacious corner back who would have made it with Cork if he had been given a decent run – could handle Charlie for one game. Weeshie Murphy and Jimmy Nodwell could get the better of Gerald and Con Roche at midfield. Weeshie had played a few Oireachtas games for Cork while Nodwell was a strong, mobile man. I told him in the Victoria the night before the game, 'Jimmy, don't be looking up to these fellas. Throw yourself about. And be direct. You're not playing for Mayfield now; this is senior hurling. If you don't get rid of it quickly, next thing they've got the ball and they're sticking it over the bar. We want quick, snappy hurling. You've shown you can do it in training; now show it to the whole of Cork in the Mardyke.'

Nodwell and Weeshie were outstanding. So were all the lads. Charlie had scored only one point off Atkins going into the last minute. At one stage in the second half we were 3-8 to 1-4 up. The

Barrs got a few late goals but we still ended up deserving winners, 3-10 to 4-5. The All-Ireland champions were out.

People couldn't believe it. The *Cork Examiner* described it as one of the greatest upsets in the history of the county championship. Some of the Barrs crowd had difficulty taking it in. The following Monday at Cork training, Tony Maher came over to me in the car park. 'Well,' he said, 'I hope you're happy now. A group of junior hurlers knocking a senior team out of the championship.'

'Tony,' I said, 'don't forget, Seandún proved that they were good enough to beat the Barrs.'

'Yeah, but ye won't go any further.'

He would have been a brave man to bet on it. At that point, it seemed as if I couldn't lose. The day before that Barrs game, I went for my driving test out in Wilton. When the instructor got into my father's car, he told me to take a right. I did as I was told. Then he told me to take a left. So I did. Then he said, 'Well, what about tomorrow night?'

Now, I had been given three bits of advice before going out there – know your rules of the road, listen closely to what the instructor says and don't say anything to him. I said nothing to him. A few seconds later though, he went, 'I think ye're in with a great chance.' Now, I didn't know if he was having me on, so I just said, 'Ah yeah, sure we'll see', keeping my eyes on the road. Then he said, 'Take a left over here.' By that stage though I had started to think about the game myself and missed the turn. 'Jesus,' I said, 'I forgot about that.' 'Don't worry,' he said, 'take the next.'

Then it came to doing the three-point turn. Everything seemed to be going perfectly, when, at the very last second, I tipped the footpath. When we got back to the driving centre, the instructor started writing furiously beside me. That meant for sure I had failed. Then he tore out a sheet, tapped me on the knee and said, 'Come here, whatever about the driving test, beat those bastards tomorrow; I'm from Bishopstown myself. There, that's your cert. You passed your test.'

And the following night, I passed another. Just like Willie Walsh a few weeks earlier, Jimmy Barry-Murphy was held scoreless by me.

The key to winning the battle with Jimmy was psychological. Early on, a ball broke out near the sideline at the road side of the Mardyke. I was slightly ahead of Jimmy, but just as I was coming to the ball, I deliberately slowed down my stride to cause him to trip over my back leg. Jimmy hit the hard ground and grazed his knee. It meant the concession of a free but it was worth it; the incident irritated Jimmy and completely knocked him out of his stride. He also made the mistake that night of following me wherever I went.

When his goalkeeper, Jim Power, was taking a puck-out, Jimmy stood beside me. My priority was to stop Jimmy getting the ball so I'd anticipate where Power was going to put his puck-out and then move to the opposite side. And every time I did, Jimmy unwittingly followed me, thus taking himself out of the game and allowing either Johnny Crowley or Pat O'Connell to attack the ball.

That was the great thing about playing for Seandún; I had very good players around to cover for me. As much as I enjoyed playing with Passage – and most inter-county players from a small team can identify with this – I had to be almost everywhere playing for them. With Seandún, I was able to focus on merely commanding my own position. As a result I was playing the best club hurling of my life.

After the Barrs game, the papers were speculating that I was going to be recalled to the Cork team. Such speculation didn't change anything though. When the selectors discussed it with me we all agreed it was best if the status quo remained. The team was going well enough without me while I had enough on my plate as it was. I was out almost every night that summer between training Cork, Seandún and Passage (the club were also through to the last four of their competition). Any night I was at home was spent fixing hurleys for players. It was a hectic but an exhilarating time to be Justin McCarthy.

It was also a dangerous one.

It was Dan O'Mahony who warned me. 'Justin, your profile. It's not going down well in some quarters. I'm just letting you know.' I didn't pay much heed to it at the time but looking back, I did become a victim of my own success. It wasn't that I couldn't handle it. Others couldn't.

It was, of course, ridiculous. Cork had lost their trainer only five weeks before the start of the championship; the man who had stepped into the breach was a well-known former player; he was only thirty; he had plenty of thoughts about the game; he was winning; he was still good enough to play at inter-county level; it was only natural that the media thought it was a great story. When Michael Bond masterminded the remarkable transformation of Offaly in the summer of '98, no one begrudged his achievement or the credit he received for it. The man had earned it.

The cult of the manager was nothing new to Irish sport by then though. In 1975 it was. It was even relatively new to British sport. Only in the sixties did people over there really begin to appreciate that it wasn't merely the talent of players that was responsible for success; so was the vision of a leader. There was Busby at Manchester United; Stein at Glasgow Celtic; Shankly at Liverpool. They were soon followed by Revie at Leeds; Clough at Derby. Then in 1974 came Heffo at Dublin. That changed everything. The capital of Ireland was suddenly back lifting Sam Maguires, thanks to one man. The media certainly realised how pivotal Kevin Heffernan had been in the success and started to focus more on the role of the manager. The following season, the phenomenon moved to a different level. The two proudest counties in the GAA world were in crisis and turned to two former young but high-profile players to rescue them. Kerry football looked to Mick O'Dwyer; Cork hurling chose me.

O'Dwyer and myself had a lot in common. He too spoke his mind and believed his county's methods had become outdated. The traditional catch-and-kick style of playing would now be replaced by a more combined game; players would have to be treated properly; the county board would have to be kept at a distance. Most importantly, training would be completely different. 'In my time there was a lot of sprinting and physical work; very little ballwork,' he said in an interview that summer. 'That approach becomes very tedious. I've tried to make training more interesting for the players.'

There was one major difference between O'Dwyer and myself. He had the full support of his county board. I didn't. There was a feeling that I was taking over the whole scene. I was training with the players; running up and down the sideline on match days; having team meetings; being all over the papers. When the Féile na nÓg skills competition was held up in Na Piarsaigh, I was one of the two judges; the other was Christy Ring. And what's more, I was talking about *coaching* Cork. No one *coached* Cork. You *trained* Cork. You got them fit and that was it. The selectors picked the team and the rest was up to the players. Who did I think I was?

I thought my job was to prepare the team as well as possible. Antrim had shared the same philosophy. Seandún also believed no stone should be left unturned. Not Cork though. It was only after the Waterford game that we were given team meals and the use of the Victoria Hotel. It was only after the Munster final that we were finally given the use of the Mardyke. Then came the sliotars controversy.

Even though we had steamrolled the rest of Munster, I thought our hurling would have to improve ahead of our All-Ireland semi-final against Galway. One way to do that was to have good lively hurling sessions. Getting the Mardyke at last would help. So would plenty of good lively balls. When Ger Loughnane used to say his Clare team would go through at least six dozen sliotars a week, most people thought he was only joking. I didn't. New sliotars travel faster and make players sharper than used ones. That's why I told Frank Murphy ten days before the Galway game that I wanted two dozen sliotars for the three sessions we'd be having the following week. Frank said he'd be leaving me six and that the team was costing enough as it was.

I was apprehensive about the Galway game. The mood of our supporters was that we were already in the final, as was reflected in the fact that only 27,000 people bothered to show in Croke Park. Galway though had won the league, beating the big three of Cork, Kilkenny and Tipperary in the knock-out stages. I had been particularly impressed with their display in the final against Tipp. They had been six or seven points down at one stage yet never doubted themselves. Their half-back line of Joe McDonagh, Sean Silke and Iggy Clarke was excellent, while elsewhere they had John and Joe Connolly, Niall McInerney and Frank Burke: all quality players. If you look back at the *Irish Independent* of that week, there's a headline that says, '"I rate Galway a real threat," says Justin McCarthy.' I wasn't talking them up; I genuinely thought they would be very hard to beat.

My fears were justified. After ten minutes, they were 2-2 to no score ahead. A few minutes later, it was 3-2 to 0-1. Their half backs were winning everything while their forwards were running at us in waves along the wings and down the centre. It was only when Jimmy scored a goal midway through the half that we settled down. By half-time, we were trailing by seven points. I was still sure we would win.

We played some really good hurling in the second half. With two minutes to go, we had reduced the gap to a point. Then a ball was played into our goalkeeper, Martin Coleman. Normally Martin would have dealt with it comfortably and driven it up the field, just like he had time and time again in his outstanding Munster final display. This time he fumbled. The ball went out for a 65. John Connolly duly drove it over the bar to make it 4-15 to 2-19. Seconds later, the final whistle went. Our comeback, gallant as it was, had fallen short.

It was a devastating defeat, one of the worst of my career. That team had been shaping up into All-Ireland champions. Even in the Galway game, they had shown in patches how good they were; they just ran out of time.

A week later, I suffered another disappointment. Blackrock beat Seandún by five points in the county semi-final. It had been our first game together in eight weeks. As hard as we tried, we just couldn't regain the momentum we had built up prior to the Barrs game.

It still had been a remarkable season. Both Seandún and Cork had been in a bad way at the start of the season and had ended up having much longer summers than anyone could have anticipated. As a result, I was anticipating been given the chance to continue with Cork.

Over the following few weeks though, speculation was mounting that I mightn't. A week before the commencement of the league, there still hadn't been any official word about who was training or selecting the team, so I contacted Frank Murphy. 'Frank,' I said, 'that league game is next Sunday. Is there any training?' Frank told me that the outgoing selectors would be picking the team and that my services wouldn't be required.

A few weeks later, it was announced that there would be a new selection process in place. The clubs would no longer nominate the county selectors; instead that would be the prerogative of the county champions. Blackrock were county champions. They chose two of their clubmen – Frank Murphy and Jimmy Brohan – along with Christy Ring, Denis Murphy and Denis Hurley. Those five in turn would choose who trained Cork.

On 22 October, I picked up the *Cork Examiner*. The selectors had announced their new management team to the county board. Father Bertie Troy would be team coach for the upcoming year. Kevin Kehilly, the county footballer and physical education teacher, would be team trainer. I was out.

The report went on to say that many delegates expressed their disapproval of how I had been treated. Youghal delegate Noel Morrissey said that he had attended every one of my sessions and had been highly satisfied with my ability as a trainer. Jim Coughlan of St Vincent's argued that I had proven myself as the ideal man for the job. Tony Hegarty of Na Piarsaigh claimed my dismissal would reflect very badly on the GAA in Cork. Michael McCarthy of St Nick's said that I had got a great response from the players and that I should be thanked for the work I had done.

The board responded with a charm offensive. Acting chairman Donal O'Sullivan replied that it went without saying that I had earned the gratitude of the board for my efforts. Frank Murphy agreed, saying that there was no question of myself and the outgoing selectors being blamed for the team's defeat by Galway; it was just a case of the new selectors coming up with what they thought was the best system for Cork and that Father Bertie and Kehilly were the best men for that coach–trainer model.

Neither of their arguments held much water. Donal obviously felt that it went without saying that I should be thanked for my efforts because that's exactly how it was – I never was thanked. The first I heard anything from the board was in the *Examiner* that morning.

Frank's defence was scarcely more credible. Our team hadn't lacked fitness against Galway; sure weren't we the side who had made the comeback? And while I would have welcomed handing over the physical training to Kevin Kehilly, there was no logical reason why I shouldn't have been allowed stay on as coach. If Father Bertie had been the man all along for the job, then why wasn't he the one they looked to to replace Willie John? After all, he was already on the '75 selection committee; I wasn't. The Galway defeat provided them with the perfect excuse to get rid of me; I probably would have been sacked even if we had won the All-Ireland. It had little to do with Cork wanting a qualified PE trainer. In 1990, Gerald was trainer to Canon Michael O'Brien and he was no PE man. In 1996, Cork were beaten by Limerick by sixteen points in the first round of the championship – in Cork – with Kehilly as team trainer, yet the following year, Jimmy Barry-Murphy not only was kept on as team coach but took the physical training as well. Frank just didn't want me around.

I could never say I had Frank on board. There were the rows over the hotel, the Mardyke and the sliotars. There's one incident more than any other though that summed up our relationship that summer. One night down in the Victoria after training, the players were sitting down to eat when we realised there was one meal left over. Across the room was a taxi driver, waiting to bring Walsh, O'Leary and Hegarty to Youghal, so I said to him, 'Look, eat that there. There's no point in letting it go to waste.' But just as he was sitting down to take it, Frank came into the room. When he saw the taxi driver, he pointed out that he was being paid to drive a taxi, not to eat meals. I interjected, saying there had been a meal left over, but Frank was not for turning. As we debated the matter, the taxi driver got up and left. The meal was left untouched.

The sacking was hard to take. If I had been given a decent chance and not delivered the goods, I'd have been the first to say, 'Look, I'm not up to it, get someone else in.' But I had delivered. Cork hadn't won a championship game in three years; with me, they had won a Munster title in three months. Whatever doubt there had been at the start of the summer about whether I was the best coach in Cork was gone by the end of it; the transformation Cork and Seandún had undergone had proved that. What made it even worse was that everyone knew the team had turned the corner and was in a position to win a lot of All-Irelands over the coming years.

I refused to let it get me down though. When my old minor team-mate with Cork, Michael Ellard, called me that same October morning to comment in the *Evening Echo*, I replied, 'I have had bigger upsets than this in my career and have got over them. I guarantee you I will get over this one. I have no intention of quitting the game. There is plenty I can still do for players and teams, not alone in Cork but in other counties too.'

A certain priest from Feakle never forgot those words.

14

CROSSING THE LINE

Even the language of the supporters carried the wail and woe of what was said and unsaid. I hated the question, 'Will ye win?' People knew the answer when they asked you. What they were really saying was, 'We want you to win, we know you can; but you won't.

Clare legend Jimmy Smyth

It was the moment the players decided that something had to be done. Five minutes earlier, all three hundred people in the Gaelic Park social hall had risen to their feet and started to clap their hands and cheer his name. Now, five minutes on, and the ovation was still going strong. It was obvious what the whole hall was thinking. The man had been wronged. Here were the touring Clare team being honoured in New York, and the man who had guided them to a national league final only a few months earlier wasn't there. The response of the exiles only confirmed what the players themselves had thought. When their Stateside trip was over, they would approach the county board. It was time for the GAA world to see some player power.

On Tuesday, 19 October 1976, team goalkeeper Seamus Durack walked into the West County Inn in Ennis and read a statement to the county board. It was with regret, he said, that the players had to attend a board meeting 'to try and rectify the most controversial and unjust decision ever taken at a board meeting with regard to selectors and team management'. They were now demanding the reinstatement of Father Harry Bohan as team manager.

The debate raged for the next two hours. Some county board officers objected to the players' use of the word 'demand', with some suggesting that the very fabric of the board was at stake if 'an outside body' could come in and order a democratically elected institution to change a decision. But that effectively happened. A week later, delegates voted, thirty to nine, for the players to have their way. A few days after that again, Father Bohan and his selectors sat down to discuss how they should prepare the side for the upcoming year.

That meeting changed my life.

The summer of '76 had been as hectic as any other. Passage reached the intermediate county final only to be beaten by a point. Seandún had another glorious run in the senior championship, again reaching the semi-final, before being beaten by Glen Rovers who would go on to win the All-Ireland. In ways, it was a lot like '75. A lot of coaching; a lot of hurling; a lot of fixed hurleys; a lot of excitement; and ultimately, a lot of heartache.

Something that summer though was different; weird; *wrong*. That buzz, that rush that only comes from being involved in the inter-county scene, was missing. While I hadn't been involved in '70 or '73 either, there had been the prospect that Cork would call on me again; in '76, that was a remote possibility. For a 31-year-old brimming with energy and ideas, the prospect of never again experiencing *that buzz* was hard to take.

Then one dirty day that October while I was in the workshop repairing a pipeline, someone said a Father Harry Bohan wanted me on the phone. I knew the name but not the man and had no idea why he was calling me at work. He wasn't long telling me why. Clare were at a crossroads. The nucleus of a good team was there but they had been well beaten in that league final replay and in the first round of the championship. The existing team management had taken them as far as they could. Something else, some*one* else, was needed to give the set-up a new impetus. Would I be their coach?

The last time I had been asked to train an inter-county team, I had to give Dan O'Mahony an answer within twenty-four hours. Father Bohan was left waiting a fortnight. All kinds of voices went through my mind over those two weeks. Some were mine, some were those of the hurler on the ditch, some were even Ralph McTell's …

'*It's a long, long way from Clare to here.*'

Rochestown to Tulla would be ninety-eight miles. It would be the same back. Pat and I were now four years married and Cormac and Ciarán were three and one respectively; that journey to and from Tulla would mean a lot of time away from the three of them. It would also mean taking off work an hour early, spending five hours in a car every time, just me, my thoughts and the road. There seemed to be only one conclusion. 'It just can't be done.'

But then there was another voice …

'*Jesus, it'd be great to be out there.*'

If the 1969 All-Ireland was the toughest game I ever found to watch, the 1976 decider was second. While a part of me was thrilled to see the team I had helped revive go on and win the All-Ireland, another part was dying. As I watched on from the Hogan Stand, I couldn't help feeling that should have been me coaching them. It was the same watching every inter-county game that summer; not being part of that buzz was killing me. Now Clare were offering me the chance to be part of it again.

But then there was another voice ...

'*How can I want Cork to lose?*'

This one shouted loudly for a few days. Ever since I was five, all I had wished for was to play for Cork. Wanting to see them lose was something I had never even contemplated. Until that decisive fortnight. I pictured driving to Thurles on Munster final day in a queue of cars, all of them sporting the red and white – except mine. I imagined walking past old friends and colleagues along the dressing-room corridor as if I didn't know them. And after a few days, I decided I could quite comfortably live with that. If I had to coach Clare against Cork, I had nothing to feel awkward about. I would be 100 per cent for Clare.

I could hear what people would have to say about that though ...

'*Justin's gone to Clare? Sure, he's only doing that to get his back on Cork.*'

You have to appreciate that outside managers were a rare species back in the seventies. Mick Higgins of Cavan and Peter O'Reilly of Dublin had helped the footballers of Longford and Offaly to Leinster titles in the sixties but that was about it. In hurling, it just didn't happen. My stint in Antrim was about the height of it and it was met with great approval in Cork. But then, Antrim were no threat to Cork. Clare were. The only possible motivation to help them would be to get my back on Cork. At least that's what people would think. And after a few days, I decided they could think that way if they wanted. They were wrong. I'd love to still have been coaching Cork but the county board didn't want me and I had long since accepted their will.

I could hear what people would have to say about that too ...

'*Well then he's gone for the money.*'

Wrong again. Going to Clare would cost *me* money.

I went because there was another voice, a voice that drowned out all the others ...

'*This path has a heart.*'

A few months before Dan O'Mahony and Jack Barrett asked me to train Cork, Sean Hanley of the Clare County Board had asked myself and Des Ferguson to give a weekend residential coaching course in the windy coastal town of Liscannor. It was both successful and enjoyable. It wasn't just Clare's foresight that impressed me; so did their passion. At one stage over the weekend, the senior county team's corner back, Johnny McMahon, said, 'Justin, where are we going in Clare at all?' And then he joked, 'You might come up to us sometime.' And I remember leaving Liscannor that Sunday night thinking, 'God, it is a pity they can't make the breakthrough.' Now, less than two years later, Father Harry Bohan was asking me to help them make that breakthrough.

There was also a tone in his voice that reminded me of Frank Smyth and big Niall Patterson that day in Limerick. There was sincerity there and a desperation there that said they were badly stuck. I could not stand idly by. I wasn't going to be one of those lads who would boast that they could never coach against Cork while coaching no one. People like that couldn't see the bigger picture, that what I was doing wasn't anti-Cork hurling but pro-hurling itself. Hurling needed me in Clare.

There was just one problem ...

'How the hell do I get up there?'

By the end of 1976, I still had no car. I just couldn't afford one. And contrary to what the begrudgers would later claim, neither could the Clare County Board. Then one evening over that critical fortnight, I got talking to my next-door neighbour, Pat Behan, and told her I might be going up to coach Clare. 'Only problem is,' I said, 'I don't have a car.'

'That's not a problem,' she instantly replied. 'Leave it with me.'

The following day, she came back with quotes from two car-hire firms in Cork. Tom Moloney's would hire out a car for £15 a day as long as I would have it back to them the following morning. 'There you are,' she said. 'No more excuses.' And after that, there were none. Father Bohan got the news he wanted to hear.

People don't think of Clare as a traditional hurling county but it is. Michael Cusack, the founder of the GAA, was a Clareman. Two hundred years before Christy Ring was conceived, Clare produced a legend of its own by the name of Thomas O'Gorman from Kilmurray-McMahon. At six foot six, O'Gorman stood out as a hurler in his own county but it was when he emigrated to Paris to escape the Penal Laws that he really came into his own. Over there he organised hurling games, which catered for the thousands of Irish and aroused the curiosity of the native Parisians, including one King Louis XV who was enthralled by reports of this giant of a man. When Louis went to see O'Gorman he was not disappointed and duly arranged a commission for him in the Irish Brigade. O'Gorman went on a roll after that. He earned the title of Chevalier, married a wealthy French woman and became a successful figure in the French wine business. To avoid *his* head going on a roll though, he had to return home to Ireland; the heads of Louis's grandson and others weren't so fortunate when the French Revolution broke out.

O'Gorman was only the first in a litany of great players produced by the county. There was Doctor Tommy Daly, Jimmy Smyth, Liam Danagher, Matt Nugent, Tull Considine. Dan McInerney was another player who walked onto the Munster team. When I was six or so, Dan was an engineer involved in the construction of the dam for the Inniscarra power station, and in the afternoons he and a few friends would go down to the field in Rochestown to practise. I'd go down to see them and bring my old broken hurley along with me. When the ball would go behind the goal, I'd race to puck it back to them. Dan I remember was the best of them. He had this trick I loved. When he was pucking about and the ball broke in front of him, he wouldn't bother going down to lift it; he'd just sandwich the ball between the inside of his foot and hurley to raise it to his hand. Even then, I knew Clare were a proud hurling county.

Thing is, while Clare had a proud tradition of hurling they didn't have a tradition of *winning*. There was the All-Ireland in 1914, the Munster title in 1932 and the league in 1946; that was it. After that was a series of false dawns. In 1955, a young Liam Danagher cried in his bed when his Limerick-born parents teasingly asked him a few hours after that year's Munster final, 'Where's your great Clare team now?' And over the years, a lot of other kids and grown men and women were reduced to tears. Every big-match defeat was etched into the collective psyche of the county; just like republican folklore is loaded with a litany of failed rebellions. There was the '55 Munster final. And the one in '72. And the one in '74. And those Under-21 finals in '72, '74 and '76. The '76 league final replay was only the latest in a string of crushed dreams. I inherited a group of players reared on defeats.

I was fortunate to inherit other things though. The management structure was excellent. Father Harry was – and is – quite possibly the most amazing, most decent man alive. Everything he did, he did with an open heart, be it setting up the rural development company to attract people back to live in rural Ireland or making sure everyone was able to get to training on a wet winter's night. He was a brilliant speaker and had a great way with the players, constantly reminding them of where they were from and what they represented. He was also a firm believer in delegation. The way he saw it, Colum Flynn was there to do the physical training, I was there to do the hurling and he was there to co-ordinate the whole thing.

I had also been handed a good bunch of players. Most of them had been on those Under-21 teams that had reached all those Munster finals, regularly beating Cork and Tipp on the way. They were also an intelligent bunch. Ger Loughnane, Colm Honan, Sean Hehir and Sean Stack were all school teachers and all students of hurling. They were also the most forceful and lively Clare team I had seen. Within a few weeks of taking over, I could sense that there was something there and that they could sense it themselves.

There was a lot of scope for improvement though. The first thing I did was look at their hurleys. Most of them were from the same source, which meant most of them weren't conducive to good hurling. They had good ash but the balance and shape of them were all wrong. See, it's okay to have a thick heel if the bas is big but the bas of these sticks weren't, which meant they were unbalanced. In fact, each bas was far too small for the ball to be controlled and struck properly, while most of them had very thick handles with no real grip or feeling. Most of the hurleys were an inch too long. The first hurley I took away with me was Pat O'Connor's. When I gave it back to him, he was like Dinny Allen eighteen months earlier. After that, there were hundreds of nights spent out in the shed, fixing, reshaping, balancing and banding the hurleys of Clare players.

The other thing I noticed was that their hurling would have to speed up significantly. Commitment and forcefulness wouldn't be enough come the summer when the ball would be flying off that hard ground. See, playing in the league is like driving a car in the country. You're going along at your own pace, thinking everything's fine, feeling in total control. Then you hit Championship City and suddenly you're thinking, 'Jesus, there's traffic everywhere.' You have to be that bit cuter and sharper to be able to do things quickly and instinctively, be it switching lanes without crashing, or killing that breaking ball and whipping it down the field. But that instinct can be developed. What does not initially come naturally can come to feel like second nature – through practice and experience.

Quickness was emphasised in every hurling session. At least ten sliotars were used every night. A ball was coming their way every time which meant they had to think and hurl faster. In the past, too many of them couldn't hit the ball on the turn or on the move; they would slow down and hit from a standing position. I stressed to them they wouldn't win Munster and All-Ireland titles like that. Johnny McMahon at corner back could no longer just go to a ball in training nice and handy, pick it up in his own time and look up to see who was up the field. I'd be on to him right away saying, 'Johnny, you do that in a Munster final, boy, and there'll be four fellas on top of you. You must go to every ball here in training as if there's a man alongside you and you must then clear it as if he's trying to hook or block you.' I didn't want him waiting behind his man; he was to go and attack that ball, trusting that he'd have the hurling to control it.

I'd then take the forwards down to one goal and go behind the endline while they'd go behind the sideline. Colm Honan might be first in line and I'd puck a ball out to the right wing. Colm would have to run onto it and put it straight over the bar without slowing down. Just as he was shooting, I'd then hit out another, maybe out to the left, so Colm would have to be on the move again. Every player would have to take six shots in rapid succession. Everything had to be quicker. They had to read that ball quicker, go to it quicker, control it quicker and strike it quicker.

The full back, Jim Power, was a case in point. Jim was a big man who took these big strides going to the ball and took this big swing *if* he got it. We wanted him to take shorter, quicker steps going to the ball and then develop a quicker striking action *once* he got it. He didn't have to drive the ball eighty yards down the field; he merely needed to get it out of the danger zone fast and trust the hurling of his team-mates to win the breaking ball.

Then there was that famed half-back line of Loughnane, Stack and Hehir. People would say, 'Well, they're three very good players; there's nothing you can show them.' But there was. If a ball broke behind them, they weren't getting back quick enough to offer cover for the full-back line. Loughnane needed to develop a more wristy shot to get greater distance into his clearances and would have to practise hitting on the turn. Stack was a stylish player who loved to solo out with the ball but was leaving himself open to being hooked or blocked down. Hehir also tended to be too deliberate on the ball. I wanted them and Gus Lohan releasing the ball quicker and longer.

The thing was, most of them had come from colleges hurling where they were encouraged to play to set patterns. That was fine at that grade but at senior inter-county level they just wouldn't have the time to look up to pick out a man. Even if they occasionally did, the opposition would soon close down that avenue of attack. I wanted our backs and midfield to let that ball in early. And our forwards were going to have to develop the hurling to be able to take it whatever way it came in, low or high. I also wanted them to take a chance and take responsibility by trying to take their point from fifty yards out on the wing. Playing the odd cross-field ball was fine but doing it time and time again was a cop-out, a cop-out which playing to certain patterns provided. Twenty years later in *Against the Wind: Memories of Clare Hurling*, several players would tell the author the most valuable thing I taught them was to play every ball on its merits rather than be dictated by set patterns.

Seamus Durack would have to be more precise with where he was hitting the ball; he was under no threat of being hooked or blocked taking puck-outs. I didn't want him to just puck out the ball as far as he could; he had to look down the field, see who was in front of his man, or maybe spot a space between the midfielders and half forwards and land it there. I didn't want him pucking out high balls towards Johnny Callinan's wing; Johnny was poor in the air. He was to send them out in front or to the side because Johnny's touch and pace meant he was a great man to win it on the floor.

Everything I said they took on board. If there was a man short in training, I'd drop in and play on any one of them. One night I might be on Loughnane and say, 'Hey, Ger, I got that ball too easy there, boy. You're the one playing in Thurles next Sunday, not me.' The next night I might be on Johnny McMahon and I'd be going, 'Johnny, attack that ball. Don't wait for me to get it. Get out in front and get it yourself.' And they took it in the spirit it was intended. They knew I wasn't there to show them up but to bring their *game* up. I read that when Mick O'Dwyer was first in charge of the Kildare footballers, they used to drum their fingers, waiting for him to make another reference to the great Kerry teams he coached. That never happened when I was with Clare. I only mentioned Cork or a Cork player when we were preparing for a game against them. I wanted Clare to believe they were better than Cork, to take chances and express themselves.

And that's what they started to do in the space of a few months. Jackie O'Gorman was a brilliant, experienced corner back who had a tendency to take a lot out of the ball when he was hitting it; now he was getting to it and getting rid of it quicker. Ditto Loughnane and Hehir. Upfront, Noel Casey, Pat O'Connor and Jimmy McNamara were getting more chances from receiving faster, more direct ball, while they were keeping the ball and hurley closer when soloing. Throughout the field, fellas had become more comfortable at hitting the ball with the hurley caught short. By April 1977, we had qualified for the league final for the second consecutive year.

Problem was, Kilkenny were again the opposition. The previous year, the same team had won the replay by five goals.

CROSSING THE LINE 111

More baggage for a county reared on defeats.

You can't always be honest with your players to get the best out of them. That league final in '77 was a classic example. Our left corner back was Johnny McMahon. Johnny was a nice tidy player who had won an All-Star the previous year but he didn't win it for his performance in that year's league final replay. Kilkenny's Mick Brennan destroyed him that day, scoring a brace of goals off him. I felt that if we put Johnny on Brennan again, he'd more than likely be taken asunder again; not only would he not have the confidence for Brennan, but at five foot seven, he wouldn't have the strength and force for him either. The week before the match, I told Father Harry at training in Newmarket-on-Fergus that we should move Jackie O'Gorman to the left corner and switch Johnny to the right. Now, I wasn't a selector and Father Harry was initially wary about changing the shape of the team but he eventually said he trusted my judgment, so I called the two players over.

'Lads,' I said, 'there's a few plans for next Sunday that nobody knows about, only ye. Jackie, you're going left full back; Johnny, you're going right.'

Johnny instantly went, 'I'm going on Eddie Keher?'

'Yeah, you are.'

'God, I don't know.'

'Well, Johnny, it's like this now. I think you're one of the best corner backs in the business. We need a lively player on Keher, to play outside him. Keher is made for you.'

Then I turned to Jackie. 'And Mick Brennan is made for you. He's durable, tough, strong, but you'll be able for him.'

Jackie wasn't initially enthusiastic. 'Feck it, I hate switching,' he said. O'Gorman though was one of the most unselfish players I've ever coached and quickly added, 'I'll gladly do it if it'll help the team.'

'Grand,' I said, before looking back at Johnny. He was still looking at me.

'God, Justin, how do I play Eddie Keher?'

And so the three of us went to the far end of the field.

I started off with Jackie. First we went through what Brennan would do when he got the ball in his hand. He'd look to come at Jackie and hit him hard; Jackie would have to steel himself to withstand that contact. He'd also have to expect Brennan to then look to pop out and get his shot in for a point. Brennan was a rare breed of player who could hit the ball with both his hands and his hurley fully extended; it was remarkable how he could get the power and accuracy to score with such a stroke. Jackie would have to alter his normal blocking technique considerably. Every other player he had faced would be hitting the ball closer to their body; to block down Brennan, Jackie would have to extend his reach significantly. And so we went through it, me being Brennan with that fully extended swing of his, and Jackie being Jackie. Within minutes, I wasn't getting my point anymore; Jackie was standing up to me and blocking 'my' trademark shot.

Then I went over to Johnny. The big thing I tried to impress on him was that Keher liked to wait for his chance and get a first touch on the ball but what he didn't like was someone ruffling him out of it and getting to the ball ahead of him. Johnny would have to be aggressive coming to that ball and make sure Keher didn't get it. 'There's no reason why you shouldn't, Johnny. Don't look at him as Eddie Keher. Look at him as a player that you're faster and livelier than, a player who you will beat to the ball.' Then we got Jackie and a few of the other lads to hit some balls into us, with me being Keher and Johnny being Johnny. And pretty soon, Johnny was knocking me out of the way and getting out in front to win and control every ball.

We worked on it again the next night in training. And the next. Heading towards Thurles on Sunday, I knew Jackie O'Gorman and Johnny McMahon wouldn't be the losing of the game for us.

Kilkenny had more than Brennan and Keher on their team though. They had Noel Skehan, Fan Larkin, Pat and Ger Henderson, Brian Cody, Frank Cummins, Joe Hennessy, Liam O'Brien, Pat Delaney – every one of them a past or future All-Star. As a unit they had contested five of the past six All-Ireland finals. I told our lads that Kilkenny were only names. I asked them how could Kilkenny beat them. If it was a matter of fitness, we'd win after the work they had done under Colum. If it was going to come down to hurling, we'd win again after all the hurling sessions we were after. 'But what, lads, if it's a matter of determination … ?'

I got exactly the response I was looking for. Before the game I stressed the need for a good, aggressive start. If either a back or a midfielder won a ball, he was to let it in early; if a forward won it, he was to carry it and make something happen, be it creating an opening for a goal or winning a close-in free. And that's what happened. Jackie O'Gorman took a free about ninety yards out from the Kilkenny goal; Pat O'Connor won it, carried it and took a shot that came back to Jimmy McNamara, who duly buried it to the net. The game was less than a minute old.

Ten minutes later, Tom Crowe chased down Skehan after the

Kilkenny goalkeeper collected the ball on his fourteen-yard line. What followed was quite remarkable. It was one thing for Tom to block down Skehan; another to somehow flick the ball into the net while on his knees. After that, there was no question who had the greater determination either.

Kilkenny did keep plugging away to try to deny us. Even Cork tried to keep us down. One of their selectors, Christy Ring, was sitting behind the goal and at one stage called Paddy Grace over to offer the Kilkenny coach some advice. It was of little use. At the end, the scoreboard read 2-8 to 0-9 in favour of Clare. Thurles erupted. Father Harry described it as the best day of his life, a delighted President of Ireland, Paddy Hillery, came into the dressing room to congratulate his native countymen, while every neutral at Semple Stadium couldn't get over the outburst of emotion which that final whistle triggered.

And it was a terrific victory. Kilkenny boasted the best attack in the country; it was inconceivable that they wouldn't score even one goal. Keher scored only one point from play off Johnny McMahon. Mick Brennan scored three yet everyone agreed Jackie O'Gorman was the game's outstanding player. The rest of the defence were excellent, while Colm Honan and Michael Moroney got the better of Cummins and O'Brien in midfield. That night, there was a parade through Ennis and bonfires all over the county. I went straight home to Cork. There would be other celebrations for this team.

It wasn't as if the rest of the Clare set-up got carried away with the league win. Far from it. The following Wednesday they were back training. I was against that. I felt we shouldn't have resumed training for another week, which would still have left us with over a month to prepare for the first-round game against Tipperary. In Cork, we'd always take ten days off if we had a good run in the league; you couldn't just roll over from league to championship and expect to keep fresh. It was particularly important in the case of this Clare team. They couldn't refuse training. Mick Moroney was a farmer and one night he said, 'Justin, I've been baling hay all day and I'm wrecked. All I see are bales in front of me.' So I said to him, 'Alright, Mick, take it easy tonight. Do your hurling and then go home.' But once the hurling session was over, Mick stayed on for the physical training, saying he didn't want 'to let the lads down'. They were all like that. Colum was great to get them pumped up and fit but I was worried whether he'd have them fresh. John 'Goggles' Doyle, the famous captain of the 1932 team which reached the All-Ireland final, did a lot of the groundwork on the pitch in Tulla and would often say to me as he opened the gate at training, 'For God's sake, will you tell them to ease down on that running; they'll be killed from it.' And that was my fear, especially if we took no break between league and championship.

Colum though felt there could be no let-up and Father Harry sided with him. That disappointed me. While I was glad to see they weren't satisfied with a league title, the players could become stale and be found to have gone to the well too often. Father Harry and Colum's decision was governed by good intentions but also by an element of insecurity and inexperience.

We had to go to the well in that first-round game against Tipp. Just before half-time, we were eleven points to two down. Our backs were standing off their men, our forwards were waiting for the right ball to come in, our midfield were non-existent from general play, while every one of them seemed intent on picking the ball off the ground every time. We got a goal just before the break but it didn't stop me giving the lads an even bigger bollicking than I gave Antrim in Croke Park seven years earlier. I told them that they were half an hour from being forgotten about. They responded to scrape out a draw.

A week later, the same two teams once more came face to face. So did two other old acquaintances.

Frank Murphy and myself were bound to clash that day. Frank was a strict – and very good – referee, while I was one of the first mentors who liked to run around – and sometimes onto – the pitch. In the old days, team selectors and managers had simply been too old to do so but I was only thirty-two. The players liked me moving around, urging them on; Jackie O'Gorman, the O'Connors and Johnny Callinan in particular would often ask me before a game to give them a shout later on. This particular day in Limerick though Frank felt I was getting too involved. At one stage in the first half, the ball went out for a sideline ball to Clare next to where I was standing. It was a wet day which meant the sliotar was heavy so I sneaked in a dry one to Michael Moroney. Frank though spotted me taking it out of my pocket and putting the old one in.

'Take that ball out of your pocket!' he said in that stern, schoolmaster-like voice of his.

'I have no ball in my pocket,' I said.

'You do! I saw you putting it in there!'

So with that, I produced a ball that was in my pocket and the game continued with it.

What Frank didn't know was that I had two dry balls in my pocket in the first place. And that the ball he got wasn't the one he had wanted.

We just about won, 0-13 to 1-7. It was a good thing our backs were brilliant the same day.

It was a similar story against Limerick a fortnight later. Again we lacked that fluency which we had towards the end of the league but again we grinded out a result, 0-14 to 1-9. For the lads, it didn't matter if we won ugly. They lived and worked with Limerick people every day of the week; obtaining bragging rights for a whole year was the sweetest feeling in the world.

Our next opponents would create even more banter in the workplace, especially in my own.

Our Munster final opponents were Cork.

15

KICKING ON HEAVEN'S DOOR

The fact that Justin McCarthy trained Clare was a big factor in Cork. We all had tremendous respect for him but when a fellow county man is training another county, it's bound to galvanise the team. It added a cutting edge to the whole thing.

Jimmy Barry-Murphy

A month or so after I had accepted Father Harry's offer to coach Clare, Cork came to Tulla for the last league game before the winter break. Doctor Daly Park was like a fortress back then; opposing teams seemed almost intimidated by it. Hundreds of spectators would be allowed inside the wire, while outside, the crowd would stretch all the way back to this windswept hill overlooking the field. It all led to a special atmosphere, an atmosphere in which Clare almost always thrived. And that was what happened on that drizzly, dreary December day. Cork were up for it but they were to find that while it was one thing to win All-Irelands in Croke Park, it was another winning in the heart of east Clare.

If that day felt surreal for a team just after winning an All-Ireland, it was particularly strange for me. Less than eighteen months earlier, the same two sides had met in the Munster championship and I had been coach to Cork; now I was going around to the Clare players in the puck-around while Cork warmed up at the other end. The weirdest moment though was the drive home. I was just coming into Sean Hehir's home village of Kilkishen when I was overtaken by this car. Its occupants didn't recognise me in my hired car but I could instantly tell that it was a taxi for the Cork team, John Horgan's blond hair in the back a dead giveaway. And a thought struck me as I watched his head pull away into the distance. In an ideal world, John and myself, being two neighbours and friends, would have been heading back to Cork in the same car. But we weren't. We were in different cars because we were now in different camps. I had crossed the line.

That day though hardly prepared me for 10 July 1977. Nothing could have. John's taxi and my hired car were about the only Cork-registered vehicles which had headed to and from Tulla that winter's day; the whole county seemed to be going to Thurles for the Munster final. That trip to Tipp was the toughest journey of all. Every other car leaving that morning was shouting for Cork. Just because I was hoping for a Clare win didn't mean I could float over the convoy to Semple Stadium. There was no avoiding all that red and white; no getting away from those supporters looking into my window wondering whether it was really me and then shouting, 'Hey Justin! Up Cork!' As I say, the toughest journey of all.

The ordeal didn't end upon arriving in Thurles. When I went up to meet the team in the Anner Hotel, Cork were there too. We walked past each other as if we were total strangers. Then after the team meeting, the Clare party made our way to the ground in a convoy of cars behind a police escort paving a route through the masses. As that siren sounded out, I looked out the window and spotted familiar faces from home, all making their way to the ground, all wishing for something I had always wished for myself. And that too was surreal, looking out at them and thinking, 'Today, lads, I'm not on your side.' And yet I was always fully aware why I was in Thurles. At no stage did I think I was in the wrong dressing room or that if we lost, at least it would be to Cork. I wanted Clare to win every bit as much as Father Harry did.

The same man empathised with my predicament. Before the game in the dressing room, he told the players, 'Hey, lads, we have to remember Justin as well today. He doesn't want to be the only Corkman going back disappointed.' The corollary of that though was being used next door. I later found out that more than one selector made the point that there was no way another Corkman was going to stand between them and another Munster title. As Jimmy Barry-Murphy would later say, the McCarthy Factor galvanised Cork.

So did some comments published on the morning of the match. A few days beforehand, one of the Sunday reporters had asked Martin Doherty and myself to assess both teams. Martin pointed out that while I had obviously helped raise Clare's game, they looked like a team that were on the verge of burn-out and would struggle against a full-forward line of O'Leary, Cummins and Charlie. I, meanwhile, said that the Cork defence would hardly be as tight as the ones we had faced in our three previous matches. Both were honest assessments but only one was used as the headline. Unfortunately it wasn't 'Doherty claims Clare are past it'. Instead it screamed, 'Cork defence the weakest link', while the subheading read, '"Will be easier for Clare to score today" – Justin McCarthy.' In hindsight, it would have been better off unsaid.

It's what I thought though. The biggest challenge I had with Clare was to convince them they should not be afraid of Cork. Clare had an inherent fear of Cork teams, particularly ones that had just won an All-Ireland. I told our lads though that we were the form team, that Cork were living on the past and that all the pressure was on them as they had two championships to lose. I also went through every Cork player and how they could be exploited. Martin Coleman was a good shot-stopper but lacked physical presence. Brian Murphy was a sticky marker but couldn't clear the ball forty yards and would struggle if Pat O'Connor stayed on the move. Noel Casey would be too strong for Martin Doherty. John Horgan was brilliant to anticipate, pick and clear ball that dropped over his head but he lacked pace; he wouldn't like to be taken on by Enda O'Connor. The midfield of Tim Crowley and Tom Cashman were both weak off their left side. The Cork attack was dangerous but could be contained by the aggression, force and skill of our backs. They also had their limitations just like anyone else; Charlie had a preference for pulling off his right; Jimmy Barry-Murphy always side-stepped to his left any time he won a ball. I wanted our lads to realise that there was no reason to look up to Cork as if they were gods. They were beatable, especially by a team as good as us.

That was even more evident fifteen minutes into the game. When Tim Crowley blasted a penalty to the net after only seventy-five seconds, the lads didn't panic. Instead they took the game over. Casey won a ball over on the wing, powered past Doherty and passed to Enda O'Connor who slapped the ball past Coleman. Then Casey slipped past Doherty again and finished well himself. Midway through the first half, we were 2-4 to 1-1 ahead. This didn't look like a team that was afraid of Cork.

While Casey was proving too strong for Doherty though, there was another mis-match at the other end. Three months earlier, just before we played Offaly in the league semi-final, Cork had asked the Clare County Board for a challenge game in the Mardyke. I had been against it. We had enough competitive games coming up; what was the point in helping Cork shape up for the championship and letting them get a better look at us? The game though went ahead and Cork did take a lot from it, namely to play Jimmy Barry-Murphy on Gus Lohan. Now, I want to make it clear that Gus was a tremendous servant for both Galway and Clare. He also had a very good league final; we didn't miss the injured Sean Hehir that day at all. The

Mardyke though showed that Gus was simply too slow for Jimmy. And the point was further underlined in Thurles after the selectors decided to stay loyal to Gus. It was a noble gesture, and in fairness, it would have been hard to drop Gus after his display in the league final, but he could only play a central defensive position – and only then on a slower player than Jimmy. Soon after Casey's goal, Jimmy set up Cummins for one and then blew past Gus to score another himself. After twenty minutes, Cork had gone a point ahead.

Clare didn't bow. There was still only a point in it a minute before half-time. Then came an incident which remains one of hurling's greatest 'If only' debates. Ray Cummins and Jim Power had been exchanging verbals and nudges all day. Just before the break, Cummins fell to the ground. Noel Dalton gave Power the line. Dalton had let a lot go up to then; Power had a split head as he walked off and Father Harry maintained afterwards that the same full back had twice been struck by two different Cork players. As for the incident itself, it appears there was a clash of heads.

That call more than influenced the outcome. It defined it. It was always going to be hard to beat such a good Cork team with fifteen men, virtually impossible with fourteen. And that's how it proved. The heart and workrate we showed in the second half would have been rewarded against a less confident, less focused team, but Cork to their credit did not wilt. Seven minutes after the break, Cork were as many points ahead as Jimmy broke through for his second goal. That ended the game as a contest. We battled on and actually outscored Cork in the remaining part of the match but when Dalton signalled for the ball, the scoreboard read 4-15 to 4-10 to Cork.

Cork claim they would have won even if Power had stayed on; that by then they had taken control of the game and had faced the wind. I don't go along with that. Cork hadn't irreversibly taken control of the game; they had merely enjoyed a period of dominance, just like we had enjoyed one in the first quarter of the game and were capable of having another in the third. I'm not saying we'd have won only for the incident. I just think it's impossible to say Cork would definitely have won regardless.

Losing to Cork hurt as badly as losing to anyone else. In fairness, Martin Doherty and John Horgan felt for me; as I walked off the field they came over to say, 'Hard luck, Justin, no fault.' It was a nice touch but it didn't make the journey home any easier. As I drove home with those red and white flags waving out the car windows in front of me, other images raced through my mind. Cummins dropping to the ground; Power walking; Jimmy blowing past Gus; the awful finality that was the final whistle. I knew though that the players and supporters of Clare were every bit as dejected as I was. I hadn't wanted Clare to win for Justin; I had wanted them to win so that I could see the gleam in Ger Loughnane's eyes, the tears in Father Harry's and so that those Clare supporters on the way home from Thurles would know just once what it was like to feel what every other passenger in this mass movement was now feeling.

And so that's why I said what I said in the dressing room after the game. They'd be back the next year. And I'd be back with them.

In March 1996, by which time he had become the biggest figure in the game, Ger Loughnane accepted an invite to speak at the Ballincollig Gaelic Week debate with Mick O'Dwyer, Niall Cahalane, Jason Sherlock and myself. A few days before the big night though I got a call from Brian Callinan, the Ballincollig club chairman. Loughnane had told him he couldn't make it. He was coach to the Munster team at the time and any night he wasn't training them he was training Clare. On top of all that, he had to help his wife move her business to new premises in Ennis. Brian told me that there were a lot of businessmen and gardaí from Clare living in Ballincollig and Loughnane was the one they had all wanted to see. So I called him.

'Ger, I hear you're out for that talk.'

'I am. It'd be great if I could make it but there's Clare, Munster, Mary's new business ... I can't be everywhere.'

'Jesus, Ger, you'll be an awful loss. Everyone is expecting you to be there.'

'I know but I just can't fit it in. I mean, going down all the way to Cork right now ...'

'Ger, I know it would take a big effort to come down to Cork. You'll remember I know all about that trip; I made it many, many times. And Ger, I'll tell you, there were nights when I cursed going down to Clare but I still went. Now, I'm not involved with this club but I know they're good people and I'm asking you personally: if there's any way you can extend yourself, please do.'

Loughnane's tone changed. 'What time is it on?'

'Eight o'clock.'

There was a moment's pause.

'I'll be there.'

It lashed out of the heavens that March night, the kind of night AA would urge you to stay off the road unless you absolutely had to travel. At quarter to eight, Ger Loughnane walked into that clubhouse in Ballincollig. He was still there five hours later, talking and laughing away with O'Dwyer, Jayo, Cahalane, various club members and myself. And he still had to drive back. It would have been three in the morning by the time he got back to Shannon. Not easy that. I know.

For four years I travelled the same route and beyond.

First, I'd have to leave work early. We weren't supposed to finish until half-four but I'd clock out before that, losing half-an-hour's wages every time. Then I'd walk the mile to Moloney's on Patrick's Quay and collect the car before popping back across the river to the house to collect a few sandwiches, my gear and the batch of hurleys I'd have fixed the night before. And then at quarter to five I'd hop back into the car, steeling myself for the journey ahead.

The old Mallow road was notorious. It had 360 bends, which was some going for a route that was twenty-two miles long. If there was a truck in front of you, you couldn't pass it out; you'd have to wait until you hit Mallow. It wasn't plain sailing after that either; there were those bends outside Buttevant, the roadworks in Limerick and the cattle crossing the roads of rural Clare. In all, it would take two hours if we were training in Newmarket-on-Fergus, two and a half hours if we were in Tulla. The journey back wasn't easy either. There was no such thing as meals after training in those days, so I'd pull over outside either Bunratty or Patrickswell to eat my sandwiches and drink my flask of milk. By the time I'd be coming into Cork, it would be quarter to one.

There were times when I questioned my sanity. Once when we were training in Newmarket, I was just coming into the village and going down the hill near Halpin's garage when I hit black ice. Before I knew it, my car was skidding right across the road and someone else's was heading towards mine. It could easily have been the end. Luckily I was able to u-turn and point the car towards Limerick and the other driver was able to react quickly enough to round past me.

Another day it was snowing as I set out from Passage. By the time I hit Mallow the whole countryside was white, so I pulled over to phone Dessie Crowe, the county board secretary. Now, I wanted Dessie to say it was desperate there too, that I could turn around, that I should be back with Pat and the kids. But he didn't. 'God, it's a fine day here,' he replied. My heart sank. I had to go on. And as it turned out, Dessie was right. By the time I hit Limerick, there wasn't a sign of snow. We trained away.

I also recall one particularly awful Saturday afternoon. I dropped Pat and the kids off at her parents in Buttevant like I would any Saturday we had training, and then headed towards Tulla through the driving rain. When I got there, the pitch was waterlogged, so we had to try to find a pitch somewhere else. And as we headed to Cyril Lyons's home place of Ruan, I asked myself, 'What in God's name are you doing here?'

I got my answer in Ruan. We had a terrific session and every player was there. When I hopped back into the car, I was on a high. And it was the same every time I left Clare those four years. The journey back to Cork was always manageable because my mind was racing, thinking about the session we had and the games ahead. Really, that Clare side were special.

The hurling world saw that for themselves on 1 May 1978. Our second consecutive league final victory over Kilkenny in Thurles was even more impressive than the first. This time we won 3-10 to 1-10, all our scores coming from play. Jim O'Sullivan of the *Cork Examiner* noted the improvement. 'Last year,' he wrote, 'victory was gained principally through the determination of the team as a whole, allied to a great start and superb second-half defensive covering. This time it came about largely as a result of a mature, confident and skilful performance from a side that on the day did not have a single weak link. It was, in essence, the kind of display that one would have expected from champions.'

And so it was. Clare were close to being the complete team at that stage. The full-back line was now more controlled, the half backs were more adept at sweeping in and covering for one another, while all six were able to make space for themselves and clear on the turn and run. The midfield and forwards were now livelier and better on the ball and able to take their points on the run. What pleased me most though was the authority and confidence they were all hurling with. When they trailed to Kilkenny by four points at half-time in that league final, they knew they'd still win. No previous Clare team had felt that way against Kilkenny.

There were more bonfires and open-top buses after that win but the team themselves remained rooted to the ground. When Sean Stack collected the cup, he barely made reference to it; instead the thrust of his speech referred to the upcoming championship, 'our real objective'. A month later we took a step closer towards achieving that objective. The team were again in rampant form in the Munster semi-final against Limerick. With fifteen minutes to go, we were 3-12 to 0-8 up. Limerick did rattle in three consecutive goals to make a game of it but again our lads kept their cool. With a few minutes to go, a Brendan Gilligan goal gave us a seven-point lead. We kept it. It meant we were back in another Munster final.

MOULD BREAKERS: Going up to coach Antrim in 1970 gave me a new lease of life. That mission also transformed these men: that All-Ireland intermediate title we won was the first national hurling title Antrim had captured.

BACK IN THE BIG TIME: Everyone but Father Tommy Maher thought I'd never hurl again for Cork after the Accident. By 1972 though I was on the first-ever All-Star trip with Father Maher's most famous protégé, Eddie Keher.

DEFINING MOMENT: Losing the 1972 All-Ireland final was the most crushing defeat of my career. The manner of our collapse would define my coaching philosophy. *(Irish Press)*

SQUEEZED OUT: Most of this 1975 Munster championship team that I coached would go on to win three All-Irelands. Dinny Allen, Willie Walsh and myself though were discarded. My face in particular didn't fit with the county board. *(Irish Examiner)*

OPPOSITE END: Behind Seamus Durack's goal in the 1977 National League final. It would be one of the greatest days in Clare's history, but a lot of Cork people felt I had no business being there or coaching Clare. (*Irish Examiner*)

MEN APART: The Clare team that won the 1978 National League was probably the best side never to win an All-Ireland. It was an honour to coach them. *(Clare Champion)*

THE DIFFERENCE: People have overlooked the main reason why the Clare team of the nineties won All-Irelands and the team of the seventies didn't. One side didn't have to come up against Charlie McCarthy and the line of legends behind him. We did. *(Irish Examiner)*

FRANKLY SPEAKING: Frank Murphy, secretary of the Cork County Board. (*Irish Examiner*)

A HELPING HAND FROM THE PADRE: Fr Michael O'Brien might not have been joint coach with me in 1984 but he did play his part as a selector. So did our trainer, the onlooking Noel Collins. (*Irish Examiner*)

GIVE HIM AN INCH AND A YARD OF GRASS: I had to fight hard for Seanie O'Leary's inclusion in '82 and '84 but each time that faith was repaid. He scored four goals in the '82 Munster final and a goal in each Championship game in Centenary year. (*Sportsfile*)

SOLDIERS OF DESTINY: They could have gone down as the team which lost three All-Irelands in a row. Now they're remembered as the team which won probably the most prestigious All-Ireland ever. (*Irish Examiner*)

THAT WINNING FEELING: The Cork dug-out in the closing moments of the Centenary All-Ireland. (*Irish Examiner*)

THE HARDEST-WORKING MAN IN HURLING: Ger Cunningham was the only player I've coached that maximised his full potential. He practised in the Alley and the field more than any player I know. (*Inpho*)

THE PRODIGIOUS SON: Tony O'Sullivan had been written off after the 1982 All-Ireland. I never lost faith in his ability though. Neither did he. This was about the only time Aidan Fogarty won a ball off him in the Centenary All-Ireland. *(Inpho)*

BACK TO BASICS: The day after I coached my last championship game with Cork, I was competing in the Poc Fada competition in the Cooley Mountains.

Another Munster final against Cork.

To this day, I've never experienced an atmosphere like it. It could be argued neither has hurling itself.

On that Sunday in July, 54,000 people crammed into Semple Stadium. Another 4,000 were left out when the gates were locked half an hour before the match. John Horgan would later admit he doubted at one stage whether he would even make the game, he was so far back in traffic. It was that hectic.

I had no doubts of making the game. I had no doubts about its outcome either. I wasn't the only one. When TG4 did a documentary about the career of Ger Loughnane, Ger admitted that he was certain we would win. As I had told the lads, Cork were living off their past glories; we were now *the* team. That feeling was widespread throughout the county. Those supporters who used to skeptically ask Jimmy Smyth 'Will ye win?' were vibrant about this team's chances. Goggles Doyle, who had seen more Clare teams than nearly anyone else, articulated the mood of a people when he told the *Examiner* a few days before the game, 'Last year, the lads *felt* they could win it. This year they *believe* they are going to win it.' While such optimism was welcomed, it also created an unprecedented air of expectancy. That added to the unprecedented sense of tension.

It showed in the first half. Cork were engulfed by the atmosphere; in that first thirty-five minutes they appeared rattled for the first time since their emergence three years earlier. We were doing scarcely better. Good first-touch players were scrambling to pick up the ball, while forwards were shooting poorly under pressure. It was ten minutes before the first score came and another eleven before there was a score from play. By half-time, the two best teams in the country had generated eight points between them.

What was even more incredible was that none had come from the Cork attack. Instead, four of their five scores had come from long-range frees from John Horgan, who had managed to get a police escort to ensure he made the game. With their side only two points behind having played against the wind, the Clare supporters rose to their feet as the players came off the field. Clare's moment, they sensed, had come.

There has been a lot of pub talk about what was said in the respective dressing rooms over that next fifteen minutes. Some people will have you believe that we were singing, sure we had the game won. What happened next door, meanwhile, is also the subject of some conjecture. In Ollie Byrnes's book *Against the Wind*, John

Horgan says Christy Ring didn't say a word. Jimmy Barry-Murphy told Ollie that he did and duly galvanised Cork. I myself have heard that Ring went, 'When I was playing against Clare, I could beat them on my own. There are fifteen of ye!' How true that is, I don't know. What I am sure of is what happened in our quarters. Anyone who believes a dressing room with characters like myself, Father Harry, Loughnane, Hehir and Callinan would start up a premature celebratory song is beyond saving. We spoke to the players like we normally would, telling them the game was there for the taking in the next fifteen minutes.

I was confident we would. That Clare side was a superb second-half team. Often it would take them a while to get into their stride but at some stage they'd take off. This day they didn't. The second half was as scrappy and tense as the first. We were struggling in midfield. Before the game, I told our pairing that I wanted Johnny Callinan to go on Tom Cashman and Mick Moroney to take up Tim Crowley. When the game started, Cork changed Cashman over to Moroney. Our lads switched again but then so did Cork. Johnny ran over to me and I told him to switch again but within seconds, Cork had swapped over again. And basically, our lads gave in first. It was to prove costly. Although Johnny had done well on Tim Crowley in the first half, Cashman was too lively and crafty for Mick and would go on to be the most dominant midfielder for the second Munster final in a row. If Callinan had been on him, it most likely would have been a different story.

It wasn't just our midfield play that was out of synch. While our backs were over one of the greatest attacks ever, the Cork defence were containing our forwards. There was little fluency to our hurling. The routine Clare second-half express wasn't running. And midway through the second half, Cork sensed it. Within a few minutes, they rattled off a few quick points. The Cork crowd, starved of scores, greeted those points as if they were goals. An air of inevitability began to hover over Thurles. You could almost sense our players hearing those roars from the Cork crowd, roars that were saying, 'It's not going to be your day again, lads.'

The lads did keep in there. With three minutes to go, we were only three points behind. In the closing seconds, Loughnane launched one last delivery aimed at dropping in around the square. The wind caught it and dragged it over the bar. A few moments later, Loughnane was on his knees, fisting the ground in anger. The final whistle had gone. Cork had scraped through, 0-13 to 0-11.

That whistle was like a dagger to the heart. I couldn't believe it when it was all over. I felt as if the game had never started. We needed a goal – even a Cork one – to kick-start the whole thing but it never took off. And that suited Cork more than us. We didn't frighten them in those first ten to fifteen minutes after half-time and their confidence rose from that. For all the strides we had made in the previous two years, Cork could draw on the knowledge that they had previously won in front of fifty-thousand-plus. We couldn't.

No one could speak in our dressing room afterwards. No one could look up; hardly anyone could *move*. I've never been in a more sombre dressing room. I don't think Christy Ring was either. When he walked through the door, he seemed unnerved by the desolation all around him. When he saw one of our lads sitting down on the bench, personifying dejection itself, Ring went over to him and said, 'Fair play, hard luck, you had a great game.' The same player, who was wearing a tracksuit, honestly muttered, 'I didn't play at all.' Then Ring came over to me. 'Justin, hard luck. Ye were very close. It could have gone either way.' Then he shook my hand the way you would at a funeral with a relative of the deceased. And then he was gone.

As it turned out, so was that Clare team. It never recovered from the trauma of that defeat. The following year we were beaten by a point in both the league semi-final by Tipp and the Munster semi-final by Limerick. Father Harry stepped down after that, which meant I was both manager and coach for the 1980 campaign, but again we fell short to Limerick in the first round. That left me facing a harsh, cold reality. I had brought the team as far as I could.

I said my farewell to the team on 29 June 1980, the same day they said hello to the new Cusack Park in Ennis. It was a big day for everybody; the pitch had been closed for redevelopment for nearly four years and GAA director general Seán Ó Síocháin was there to reopen it. Before the match, I told the lads it would be my last game and that I wanted to go out on a high with a win. And they did win, by eight points, which was no small achievement; our opponents, Galway, would be All-Ireland champions two months later. When the lads came back into the dressing room, I asked them to sit down. I had always said to them, 'Lads, I'm only passing through. I'm just here to give you some advice that will help inspire you to greater things but one day I'll be gone.' Now that day had come. I pointed to the walls of the new spacious dressing room. I said it was a pity that we hadn't the use of it before but that I was sure that they would have great days in Cusack Park in the years ahead. I thanked them for the effort, commitment and respect they had given me for four years, and said that I had great respect for them and the people of Clare. 'Lads, I have no regrets whatsoever coming to Clare. I feel privileged that I did. Thanks again for everything.'

And as the lads clapped and I sat down fighting back the tears, one of the players came across the floor, bare-chested. 'Justin,' he said, 'there's my jersey. Have it.'

There are many men who have won more All-Irelands than me but few of them have been paid a tribute as high as that. By giving me that jersey, that player was saying that he would literally give me the shirt off his back, that he had given me all he had to give.

That wasn't just any jersey or any player either.

That jersey was number five. That player was Ger Loughnane.

16

LEGACY, LOUGHNANE AND LIBERATION

Many people are due many thanks so today could become a reality. I'm thinking first and foremost of Clare teams down the years. Some of those Clare teams were better than this one but they were not as fortunate. We now accept the Liam McCarthy Cup on behalf of all those teams.

Anthony Daly, 3 September 1995

Hardly anyone knows this; not even, I dare say, Loughnane himself.

Shortly after he was fired as Clare Under-21 coach following his side's shock defeat in the 1992 Munster final, a close associate of the new selection committee called Trixie Twomey phoned me to say that they felt I was the man to get the best out of the team. Now, a part of me was tempted to take the job. While it had been twelve years since I had coached the senior county team, my love affair with Clare had continued. I had given numerous coaching courses up there over the years, some run by the county board, some on the request of different clubs. I also knew this Under-21 team had a lot of promise; Jamesie O'Connor was still eligible to play and the word was that it was an even more promising group than the class of '92. I declined the offer. Loughnane had been one of my players. He would have prepared that Under-21 team well; they just happened to lose by a goal to a gifted Waterford team. I felt he had been treated scandalously. The job should still have been his. To take it would be to betray him, to dance on his grave.

There were a lot of interesting developments in Clare hurling over the following three years. Within weeks of saying no to Trixie, I accepted the offer to coach the county's minor team. Again it was based on loyalty; one of its selectors was my close friend Noel

O'Driscoll, who had been a selector with the senior team when I had been there. As it turned out, we won nothing in those two years; a talented Tipp team beat us in a replay in '93 while the following year Cork took us on their way to the All-Ireland final. Still, I thoroughly enjoyed being involved with those minors. They were a great bunch of lads and we prepared them well; we just didn't get the breaks. But then, little was going right for Clare at the time. The 1993 Under-21 set-up ended up being a farce (Seanie McMahon couldn't even make the team), but worst of all was the senior team's loss to Tipperary in that year's Munster final. It was painful to watch; Tipp were even more superior than the 3-27 to 2-12 scoreline suggests. After that, many were convinced that the county would never win anything.

The following February, Johnny Callinan, on behalf of the county juvenile board, asked me to give a talk at the Queen's Hotel in Ennis to over two hundred hurling people. At it, I told them Clare could still make the breakthrough if they cleaned and speeded up their hurling. A new psyche would also have to be harnessed, one that was more ambitious and less prepared to accept defeat so easily. I also urged everyone in the room to keep the faith. The county, I said, should have the goal of winning an All-Ireland by the year 2000 and every club should give everything they had to ensure that vision became a reality.

They didn't have to wait six years for it to come true, of course.

One man had a vision of his own.

I've heard even Clare people bad mouth Ger Loughnane. I've heard them say that he was too dictatorial, too confrontational, that he and his side were too arrogant. But Loughnane and his side needed to be all those things. Let's be clear on one thing. Only for Loughnane, they'd all still be sitting on the fence, looking at the Clare team of the nineties as a team that should have done something but didn't. A revolution is what Clare needed. Loughnane was smart enough to identify that.

Loughnane had a few things going for him. He was not a prisoner to comparisons. No one could say to him, 'Ah sure, the team of '66 never did that' because the Clare team of that or any other year hadn't won a Munster or All-Ireland title. Loughnane wouldn't have lasted more than a summer in Cork (I didn't, in '75). There's no way the Cork County Board would have given him the scope he would have sought, like when he stopped Ollie Baker, Eamonn Taaffe, Fergal Hegarty and Frank Lohan playing in the 1995 Munster Under-21 final. When any county board official was let near his team, they knew their place. They weren't the show; he and his team were. Loughnane appreciated that if his team were to think like winners, they couldn't be distracted by negative thoughts and hangers-on. That's a big reason why the gates of Cusack Park were closed.

The Clare set-up under Loughnane was the closest thing to professionalism that the GAA world had seen. Unlike me, he had the advantage of being based on the ground, so he had greater flexibility to call all the shots. If his team trained on a Friday night, he had the option of saying, 'Right, lads, we're going again tomorrow morning.' Only Mick O'Dwyer had enjoyed such scope before.

That enabled his team to change how the game was played. Loughnane rightly recognised that Clare had reverted to being laborious and ponderous on the ball, but he didn't just recite what I had preached to him as a player; he ensured their hurling was quicker than anything the sport had seen before. That was because they had the physical fitness to play it, a fitness level which only Loughnane had envisaged. That meant his team could burst through challenges and still keep possession of the ball, such was their energy and confidence; if someone did that pre-1995, you'd say to him, 'Hey, hit the ball faster; don't be killing yourself.' And yet it worked both ways; they needed a good skill level to play at that speed. A lot of people, especially in Cork and Tipp, failed to give Loughnane credit for that.

He also gave his team the leeway to express themselves. The Lohans were allowed to come across their goalmouth and clear the ball; before, you'd get dropped for taking a risk like that. But Loughnane was right to give them that freedom. Clare needed to be arrogant. I often said to the team I coached, 'Lads, ye're too nice, too honest; be more arrogant.' Loughnane recognised that. Although that 1970s team had a lot of strong characters (remember, it was they who insisted Father Bohan be reinstated as manager), they were of a different Ireland. Loughnane was right when he said recently that the young Clare person of 1995 would have been more confident and assertive than his equivalent in 1977, that the contrast between both Clare teams was a microcosm of Irish society itself. Anthony Daly ruffled feathers when he declared in 1997 that Clare were no longer the whipping boys of Munster but he was right. For too long Clare had been whipping boys. Whenever Cork were stuck for a challenge game, they'd go, 'Ah, sure, we'll ring up Clare' and Clare would willingly oblige. They were available to help everyone else while winning nothing themselves. Under Loughnane, they looked up to no one. And rightly so. They had to defend the patch they had fought so hard to attain. That Clare team were no more arrogant than Cork or Tipp had been for years; it's just that some people in the hurling world found the new order hard to accept and would have preferred if Clare, as Daly put it, had fecked off back across the Shannon after that cute little All-Ireland they won in '95.

I was in Croke Park that wondrous day. I jumped out of my seat when Eamonn Taaffe, one of the minors I had coached a few year earlier, scored that goal and I jumped out of it again when the final whistle went. I had waited nearly twenty years for that day. Clare is a special place. No other county has such a grá for our culture and arts, and yet that own county's identity had been suppressed for so long. That day they were finally able to stick out their chests and say to the nation, 'We are Clare.' It was an emotional time. After the game, everyone connected with Clare must have walked around the stands, looking for someone else to share the moment with. I was no different and within minutes, I had met up with Johnny Callinan, Seamus Durack, Enda O'Connor and Dan McInerney. I had my camera and took some photographs to record the moment. And it was a poignant moment. For I couldn't help thinking, 'Jesus, those guys were so close to a day like this.' And I could tell that they were thinking exactly the same. As thrilled as they were, a part of them was dying, going, 'Look what we missed out on.'

Which raises the question: why did they miss out on it? What didn't their Clare team have that Loughnane's team had?

I don't think any victorious captain has given a better speech in Croke Park than the one Anthony Daly gave that day in 1995. It was emotional, respectful, gracious, dignified, a speech which captured the pulse of a moment and a people. There was one part of it I disagreed with though. As moved as I was when he acknowledged the Clare teams of yesteryear, I think he flattered them somewhat. The only Clare teams that were better than the one of 1995 were those which won Munster in 1997 and 1998. The side I coached would have given them a mighty match, but the one Loughnane coached was livelier, fitter and meaner.

That was because of the set-up they had. No such set-up was possible in the 1970s. My friend Colum Flynn, who was a physio to Loughnane's team, made an interesting comparison between the two eras in Ollie Byrnes's book *Against the Wind*. 'Things weren't as professional as they were in 1995,' he said. 'We didn't have the resources or the financial back-up, even the basic amenities. We had the nucleus of a fantastic side but we didn't have the full backing of the county board. Maybe it was bureaucracy.' Now, some of what

Colum says is right. We didn't have the same resources or financial back-up as Loughnane's team had. But how could we? There was no sponsorship back then. That Clare team was as well prepared as any hurling side had been prior to Babs taking over Tipp in '87. I was generally considered to be one of the top coaches in the game, Colum was an excellent trainer, and Father Harry did everything to facilitate the players and us. I remember getting that Clare team free adidas gear and boots from my friends and neighbours, the O'Connells, who ran the adidas franchise in Ireland; few teams had gear that good back then. The Clare County Board were also far-sighted; remember, they had the courage and humility to allow Father Harry to approach an outside coach at a time when that simply wasn't done. Both teams were simply children of different eras.

Mike McNamara seems to have forgotten that. In his insightful book, *To Hell and Back: The Inside Story of Clare Hurling*, Mike writes, 'As far as I was concerned, they [the double-winning league team] were only a bum outfit that should have won championships but didn't. That Clare team looked at success, stared it in the face and couldn't grasp it. That annoyed me. For me, they either hadn't the gumption or were a bunch of idiots.'

Now, Mike Mac can think he can throw that theory out unchallenged in Clare because he has his two (well-deserved) All-Irelands and three Munsters while the likes of Callinan, Stack, Durack and Honan don't. Well, I've won two All-Irelands and seven Munsters and I can tell Mike Mac that those men weren't a bunch of idiots or part of a bum outfit; they were an exceptional group of intelligent men and talented, honest hurlers. I've coached Gerald McCarthy, Charlie McCarthy, Jimmy Barry-Murphy, Ray Cummins, Tom Cashman, John Fenton (I could go on and on) and to me, they didn't have any more gumption or intelligence than the Clare team which Mike Mac ridiculed.

But then, Mike Mac isn't the only recent Clare mentor to indulge in some questionable revisionism. I was amused by Ger Loughnane's analysis of my time with Clare in his book, *Raising The Banner*, for the simple reason that some of his claims were laughable. Ger said that while he himself had great time for me, 'a lot' of the other players didn't 'take to' me. That's just absurd. Some teams are slower to take to you than others but that Clare team took to me. To this day if you were to ask Durack, O'Gorman, McMahon, Power, Stack, Moroney, Callinan, Honan, the O'Connors, Casey, indeed, the whole team, how they saw and see Justin McCarthy, I'm certain they'll tell you how much they respected me and the advice, the individual coaching, the encouragement, the fixed hurleys and the hundreds of hours on that road from Rochestown to Tulla that I gave to them.

It wasn't the only criticism that Ger had of me. He contends that Justin McCarthy was 'a good coach for his time'. He says that while I had a great knowledge of hurling, I 'lacked the ability to get inside players' heads'. He says that 'the backroom mix wasn't right' and that Colum and myself had 'many conflicts'. He says that after the 1977 Munster final, Clare made the mistake of feeling sorry for themselves about the Jim Power incident instead of addressing the real problem which was that the pace of our game was 'short'. None of those arguments hold any water.

First, the notion that I was a good coach 'for my time'. When Sean Stack lifted that national league trophy in 1978, I was only thirty-two yet it was the fourth major inter-county trophy that a team of mine had won – and I hadn't had a Justin McCarthy or a Ger Loughnane or a Len Gaynor to learn from. And when exactly was my time? Four years after finishing with Clare, I coached a team to win an All-Ireland final by ten points, which was some going considering even the great Ger Loughnane didn't win one by more than two. In the nineties I coached Cashel to their first county title and then Ballincollig to probably the most keenly contested county championship in the country – the Cork intermediate championship. I know the game has moved on since 1985 but I've moved on with it. I'm an even better coach now at Waterford, having learned from my own experiences and indeed the Loughnane Revolution. Ger is the one living in the past if he thinks the rest of us are.

I wouldn't have won anything with all those teams if I lacked the ability to get inside players' heads. I certainly wouldn't have won two national leagues with Clare. Remember, Kilkenny had hammered us the year before Father Harry took me on board. We wouldn't have beaten that same star-studded Kilkenny team twice if I lacked the ability to get the players 'out of the old ways of thinking'. You have to remember that the league was taken more seriously back then and that it was very important that Clare won something if they were to make a breakthrough. Ger himself admitted in that TG4 documentary that he was certain we would win the 1978 Munster final. He wouldn't have felt that way if I had been unable to get through to him and the others.

I also find his assertion that the mix between the backroom personnel 'wasn't right' equally implausible. Colum and myself worked together for four years and in all that time we had only one dispute, in the lead-up to the 1977 championship. And at no stage did we transmit our difference of opinion to the players. Ger claims, 'Harry should have said, "Colum, you do that. Justin, you do that."' But that's exactly what Father Harry did. He made a call, sided with Colum on that one and I went along with it. When the Cork County Board were putting the squeeze on me in 1985, Colum wrote me a letter of support saying how respected I was by clubs he knew in Cork and how grateful Clare should still have been for all I did for them. To this day, we're still friends. Yet you'd swear from Ger's book that Colum and myself hated the sight of each other.

Ger is also out of order trying to get people to believe that Clare spent the whole of 1978 sulking about the Jim Power incident. We dusted ourselves off and went about improving Clare's hurling, from the speed of our game to the range of shots and options each player could have. It was actually in '78 that Sean Stack half-joked with me, 'You know something, you're a fucking hard man to please. What do you want us to be? Perfect?' I said, 'Exactly.' It's been like that with every team I've coached; even after winning the Centenary All-Ireland I explained in a much-publicised interview how every one of my Cork players had room for improvement. That Clare team was even better in '78 than it was in '77, just as Loughnane's Clare team was even better in '98 than it was '97. We both just didn't play well enough in our last game of the season to conclusively prove the point.

I still have huge respect for Ger Loughnane. What he did with Clare was one of the greatest coaching jobs in the history of hurling, which means he has to go down as one of the greatest coaches in the history of the game. And I still value dearly that jersey he gave me. Because back then Ger could afford to have coaching heroes; back then he had no agenda. I'm honestly not bothered that Ger gave me faint praise in his book. I hardly expected him to tell the newly converted masses that there was another Clare coach who once said that the county needed to quicken up its hurling. I'm also in good company. I've noticed that in order to boost up Ger Loughnane The Coach, Ger has played down Ger Loughnane The Player. If Ger was as average a player as he is now asking us to believe he was, then that old Clare team of ours had no business even thinking of winning Munster or All-Ireland titles. I must have been an incredible coach 'for my time' and had an incredible ability to get into players' heads for that Clare team to even think of beating Kilkenny and Cork if one of our top players was that ordinary. When I was asked by *Legends of the Ash* author Brendan Fullam to pick an all-star team from my time in the game, I could have opted for so many other outstanding wing backs: Tom Cashman, Dermot McCurtain, Con Roche, Joe Hennessy, Sean

Stack, Paddy Fitzgerald … But I told Brendan, 'I have picked a panel to win. This team can't be beaten.' That's why I went for Seamus Cleere and one Ger Loughnane. No matter what they – and Ger himself – say, he was some player, just like he was some coach.

Want to know what was the big difference between the Clare team Ger played with and the one he coached?

It wasn't that he and Mike Mac were over one and Father Harry and I were over the other.

It wasn't intelligence.

It wasn't gumption.

It wasn't that we trained in Tulla and they trained in Cusack Park, as much as I'd have preferred if our big-match preparations were in a stadium-like setting.

It wasn't even Jamesie, as much as I'd love if we had him.

I'll tell you in one word what it was.

Cork.

Go back to Mike Mac's book. When recalling Clare's first-round game in 1995, he writes, 'We were worried about Cork, in particular their corner forwards Kevin Murray and Kieran Morrison.' Now, I've given those two players some praise in my *Examiner* column through the years, but they were – and are – hardly Charlie McCarthy, Seanie O'Leary and Mick Malone, the corner forwards the old Clare team had to face.

Look who else was on those old Cork teams. John Horgan. Martin Doherty. Dermot McCurtain. Tom Cashman. Denis Coughlan. Johnny Crowley. Gerald McCarthy. Jimmy Barry-Murphy. Ray Cummins. Players that would walk onto any team of any era.

Contrast that with the Cork team that had Mike Mac so worried in '95. Only Ger Cunningham, Jim Cashman and Brian Corcoran would have made the Cork team which just about beat the 'bunch of idiots'. John O'Driscoll, Pat Kenneally, Peter Smith, Darren O'Donoghue and Mark Mullins wouldn't; none of them played more than two championship games for Cork again. And yet Clare beat them by only a point, thanks to a last-minute Ollie Baker goal. Only for that one moment, we probably would never have heard of Mike McNamara. Ger compares the old Clare team to a horse and says that it had no one to drive it over the first fence. I would argue that we jumped every fence but the last. That last fence was some obstacle, an obstacle his side never had to face – a great Cork team. Ger would later do a magnificent job of getting his team to jump over every fence but look at what their first fence was – a five-eighths Cork team. It is to Ger and Mike Mac's credit that their side did not have the fear of Cork that the old team did but you must remember that, as Ger himself has pointed out, the Irish person of '95 was more likely to question his place in the world than the Irish person of '75. More importantly, his team had less reason to fear Cork. Would they have jumped over the three-in-a-row Cork team? Maybe in '97 but not in '95. And there would never have been a '97 if they hadn't made the breakthrough in '95.

So in that regard, Anthony Daly was right. The Clare team of '95 *was* more fortunate than others. They came at a time when Cork were weak and the side Babs had built was on its last legs. By pointing that out, I'm not taking anything away from their achievement. I'm just putting things in perspective for those like Mike Mac and Ger who have taken away from ours.

Because that 1977–78 team did achieve a lot. In that gracious victory speech, Daly also referred to the county which his team had just beaten. Offaly, he said, were an inspiration over the years, a county which Clare looked at and said 'Why can't we achieve that?' What Daly wouldn't have known was that Offaly used to model themselves on Clare. At the end of 1977, Clare put on one of the best exhibitions of hurling I've ever seen, destroying Offaly in a league game in Birr. When I went into the hotel after the game, Damien Martin and a few of the Offaly players came over and asked if I had a few minutes to spare. Offaly, they said, were going nowhere. What were Clare doing that they weren't? What could they do to be up there challenging with the Kilkennys and Corks like us? We stayed talking for two hours, during which I told them to consider getting an outside coach. Three years later, Dermot Healy guided them to an All-Ireland title. Over the next fifteen years as Offaly kept winning and Clare kept losing, I often thought about that day in Birr. Our greatest legacy though was something which Ger himself has occasionally acknowledged – we gave school kids like Liam Doyle and Anthony Daly heroes. It's just a shame we couldn't have given them some half-days.

I believe that if that Clare team hadn't encountered one of the greatest Cork teams ever, they'd have won it all. Clare were over Kilkenny those two years and I'm certain they would have taken Wexford too. It was commonly acknowledged at the time that Clare were the second-best team in the country. Ger was voted Hurler of the Year in 1977 and Seamus Durack ensured it stayed in Feakle by winning it in '78. Our status was also reflected in our All-Star representation. In '77, Clare won four; All-Ireland finalists Wexford only took two. In '78, we won three, the same as All-Ireland finalists Kilkenny. Not bad for a team that never saw Croke Park.

It cut me up that they didn't. Thurles, Limerick and Cork are all great hurling amphitheatres but Croke Park is the GAA's Carnegie Hall. I'd love to have seen Jackie O'Gorman on that stage; he was as good a corner back as I've come across. Durack had everything you would want in a goalkeeper: brilliant wristwork, footwork, reflexes, commitment and attitude. Johnny McMahon and Jim Power deserved a better reward for how hard they worked on improving their game. Mick Moroney mightn't have been the fastest or most stylish of players but boy, could he clip a lineball over the bar. Colm Honan had terrific balance and a nice sidestep and was good to take a long-range point. Johnny Callinan was an exceptionally intelligent, lively and courageous player. Jimmy McNamara, who had been an All-Star replacement with me in '72, made them dance many times on that hill in Tulla by sweeping that ball off his left and over the bar. Noel Casey and Pat and Enda O'Connor would also have thrived in Croke Park; they weren't lacking gumption or intelligence either.

And then there was the half-back line. Stack with his inspiring runs out of defence. Hehir with his single-mindedness and durability. And of course, Loughnane. They should be remembered as a unit but if you were to ask me who was the best of them, I'd have to say it was Ger. He wasn't as fast as Stack or as rangy as Hehir but he was tidier and livelier than either of them. It hurt me that Croke Park never got to see him opening up his shoulders and letting that ball go up the wing.

What separated Cork from them? Very little. Who knows what would have happened if Power hadn't been put off in '77 or if Casey had elected to kick that ball in '78 rather than try to pick it up? Ultimately though Cork just had that extra bit of know-how in the closing minutes of that '78 game. But that was an exceptional Cork team. I now think it is time the side who put them to the pin of their collars were also acknowledged as exceptional. I'd go so far as to say they were the best side never to win an All-Ireland.

Such a claim, of course, is debatable. Other things are not. It cannot be disputed, for instance, that I had a wonderful time in Clare. I have so many pleasant memories of my time there. Goggles Doyle and his smile opening the gate for me in Tulla. Collecting Clareman Paddy McMahon in Charleville and going to the games in Tulla. The farmers on the quiet roads of Clare nodding 'Hi Justin' while driving their cattle into the fields. Dan McInerney in the hotel before a match, advising and wishing the players the best. A jubilant Mícheál O'Hehir, whose father trained the 1914 All-Ireland-winning Clare team, in our dressing room after the league final wins in '77 and '78. And above all, those hurling sessions with the players and those magical match days in Tulla.

Before I went to Clare, Jerry Keating's sister-in-law, Eva Bride, who had worked in the county, gave me two bits of advice. The first was never to bring up politics there; the second, that once they warmed to you, they'd take you in as one of their own. And so it was. They never got to know my politics and I never got to know theirs, while they soon accepted me as one of their own. There was even a time in '77 that I considered playing for them but just like with Cork in '75, I concluded that I couldn't play *and* coach. To this day, I have a lot of close friends in Clare. I always will.

One will always stand out. Father Harry Bohan continues to aspire and inspire. After spending twenty years building two and a half thousand houses in rural Ireland for returning emigrants, he has now set up a company to build a £20 million research and retreat centre to see how Ireland can become a more rounded, caring, holistic – I suppose, utopian – society. As I say, a remarkable man and one I feel privileged to know. I also consider myself fortunate that he phoned me on that winter's day in 1976. Back then, I was at a loose end. My own county didn't want to have anything to do with me; my days involved in the inter-county scene seemed over.

There was just one problem. By finishing up with Clare four years later, my inter-county days seemed over again. No way would Cork want me to cross back over the line. It was back to the quiet fields.

But then, I had never left them.

17

A Sort of Homecoming

Never demean the time you spent in the trenches
Pat Reilly, *The Winner Within*

We were walking down the grassy bank when there it was, below on the plateau we used for a pitch. And judging by the way it was strutting around, that massive black bull wasn't going to be moved.

Jerry O'Sullivan wasn't in the mood to make way for anyone either. For over ten years he had been playing adult hurling for Ballygarvan and had never won anything until committee member Edmund Forrest had approached an outside coach who he was friendly with. After that coach agreed to help out, Ballygarvan went straight on to win the 1974 Cork South East Division junior B championship. That coach wasn't involved the following year because of his commitments with Cork but now he was back in 1977 and the club had a chance of winning the junior A championship for the first time in its history. So when that outside coach beside him went, 'Jesus, look at that bull!', Jerry just replied, 'Justin, let me handle that bull.' And with that, he ran down the slope with his hurley.

Two of the lads followed. It didn't take them long to hunt the bull into the next field. No sooner though were they walking back towards us than the bull turned and charged, sending the lads flying for cover.

Now, at that moment, I wasn't thinking, 'Feck it, anyway, we're not going to get training tonight.' I was thinking that some of our best players might get seriously injured or even killed. But Jerry and the lads were hell-bent on training that night. After getting their breath and nerve back, they decided to tackle the bull again. Shortly afterwards, the bull was back in the other field, its backside warm from a few slaps of Jerry O'Sullivan's hurley. And this time, the lads remembered to close the gate.

That farmer's field in Ballygarvan was a long way from Thurles where I had been involved with Clare on Munster final day a few months earlier. While that was the only time we came across a bull in there, we'd often have to chase cows out of it. The surface itself was littered with hollows, we had only makeshift goalposts, no dressing rooms, while sliotars would rebound off the electricity wires running over the middle of the field.

Rarely have I had so much fun coaching a team.

If ever a team played for the pride of the parish, it was this one. The village itself was only fifty yards long, made up of a shop, a church and two pubs, so we didn't exactly have a big pick. And yet, every night, we'd have twenty-three players out in that farmer's field. Anything I'd say, they'd believe. Anything I'd ask from them, they'd do. They wanted to show that Liam McCarthy wasn't the only GAA man to come from Ballygarvan.

That autumn, we qualified for the divisional final. Four thousand people were in Ballinhassig that day. Our opponents were Tracton, the division's most successful club, and overwhelming favourites. We felt our spirit and honesty though would compensate for any talent deficit, while we had our best players positioned where they could be most effective. Jerry O'Sullivan, a great man to deliver long and quick clearances, was at centre back. Another influential player was Billy Dillon, who had played with Blackrock but was now living in the area. That day we decided Billy would start at full forward for the first ten minutes to try and get us a quick goal before moving out to centre forward where we would need him most.

Billy set up an early goal to give us a huge lift. Tracton though didn't lie down and gave as good as they got. It was a ferocious contest with little fancy hurling but plenty of hip-to-hip clashes. You need to realise, a South East final is as intense as an All-Ireland final. That's because, to the people of a rural area like that, it is their All-Ireland final. The Carrigdhoun division consists of ten or so clubs outside the senior grade, all of them within close proximity of each other. The rivalry is extreme. If you go into Tracton, all they'll talk about is hurling. The same in Ballinhassig. And the same in Ballygarvan. And that's why, when we won by two points, the whole community went absolutely crazy. That night, the whole village was lit up with bonfires, while the road was covered with people drinking and dancing. I saw grown men and women cry that night. At long last, their Liam McCarthy had come back to the home of Liam McCarthy.

I was well familiar with the South East division by then. When I had played with Rochestown for those few years in the early sixties, we competed in the South East. My love affair with the division was then rekindled in 1972. Carl Daly, the chairman of Ballymartle, felt his club had slipped back and wondered could I come up and polish up their hurling in the weeks leading up to the championship. I liked the sound of the challenge so I said yes. I had no car but Carl would call to my house twice a week and give me the spin out to Ballymartle.

Ballymartle was a lot like Ballygarvan only it had more of a winning tradition. They used a silage harvester to cut the grass of their pitch, which was slanted. They had no dressing rooms either. We'd have to tog off at the side of the ditch and often when we'd finish training, our clothes would be wet from the dew. But it didn't matter. They were lovely people and their commitment and enthusiasm were inspiring. The team had quite a few sets of brothers, such as the Sheehans, Hurleys, the Dalys and the Webbs. Georgie Webb was a very good player, in the Jerry O'Sullivan mould. A bull wouldn't have got in his way either.

Neither did Tracton, Ballymartle's old rivals. That 1972 South East junior A final in Ballinhassig was one of the wettest days I can remember; I had no raingear and got soaked to the skin. We won in another close and intense affair. Afterwards I went back to Carl Daly's house for tea, and then, down to Allen's pub in neighbouring Riverstick. The place was going mad. It was some sight. And some feeling.

By 1981, I was still preaching the gospel in the South East. It was my first year having finished with Clare but it was my third involved with Shamrocks, a club from Shanbally, outside Ringaskiddy. Pat O'Neill had worked with me as a boilermaker in the Harbour Commissioners and was actively involved with Shamrocks so I decided to help them out. They didn't have that same raw spirit as Ballygarvan had, but then, there was no need for them to drive bulls and cows off their pitch. They were very well organised. Administrators and mentors like Pat O'Neill, Joe O'Driscoll and Neilly O'Mahony would be in their element at inter-county level. It was a pleasure to work with them.

Success hadn't come as quickly with Shamrocks as it had with Ballygarvan and Ballymartle though. In 1979, Tracton turned the tables on me, beating us in the final after three epic games. I have mixed feelings about those games. I was delighted for Ballygarvan, who had hosted the three games in their lovely, new, bull-free Liam McCarthy Park. It was also a lot of fun at the time being involved in those games. They were the talk of Cork. Father Michael O'Brien was training Tracton that year, while the excitement and tension created by the two drawn games meant more than 6,000 people descended on Ballygarvan for the third game. A few months later, the South East board honoured both teams with a function in the Grand Hotel in Crosshaven. A song was even written about those games. The bottom line though was that we had lost the last one by a point.

In 1980, we were determined to go one step further. We did too, beating my old friends, Ballymartle, in the final by a point after trailing by seven at half-time. The turning-point was when we switched our wing forward to centre back. That player was Joe Murphy, the same player who had given me a spin on his motorbike that fateful night eleven years earlier.

A year later, another former Cork and Passage player decided to play with Shamrocks.

It happened by chance. Joe O'Driscoll and Pat O'Neill had called over to my house a week before the final to talk about the team's preparations, when something hit me. 'Do you know lads, I could actually play for ye on Sunday.'

They laughed.

I said, 'I could. I missed last year with Passage. It's been more than a year since I played.'

'Yeah,' Pat smiled, 'but you're not transferred.'

'I could transfer.'

Pat stopped smiling. 'Would you?'

'I would.'

And I did. That Tuesday night, my transfer was sanctioned without any objections. I had played eighteen years for Passage without winning any form of a championship medal; now I was one game from winning one with Shamrocks. No one in Shamrocks was going to claim I was robbing some poor fella's spot either; I had given three years to the club and brought them to a South East final every time. I just felt like playing.

People thought it was only a ploy to distract Carrigaline. 'He'll never play on Sunday,' they said. But that Sunday, there I was, marching with the rest of the lads behind the Carrigaline Pipe Band. I played centre forward on a young fella called Tony O'Donovan. Tony's father was Dáithí O'Donovan, a well-known local figure who had been on the Carrighdhoun team which had reached the 1945 county final. During the first half, a ball came down over by the popular side. The sun was in my eyes but I managed to flick the ball overhead with one hand. I also managed to catch Tony in the eye though and he was badly cut. It had been a complete accident but Dáithí, understandably, was upset. As the game was delayed, he roared out, 'McCarthy, I always knew you were a dirty player!' Tony had to go off. I was sad to see that but I just had to get on with it. And I did. I ended up scoring 1-5 and we won by five. The shock transfer had paid off.

There was another surprising development that summer.

On the first day of July, I was in work when one of the lads said, 'I see you're a selector.'

'A selector? With who? Shamrocks?'

'No, with Cork. It's in the paper, sure.'

I got the paper, went to the sports pages and there it was. The previous night there had been a meeting of the Cork County Board at which the senior county selectors had been chosen and I was one of them.

It had been an extremely lively meeting, going by the report. Cork's shock defeat to Clare in the Munster semi-final the previous month had caused the system of appointing selectors to come under review. Since 1975, the county champions had appointed all five senior selectors, a system which the Big Three of Blackrock, the Glen and the Barrs wanted retained. They were outvoted on the night though. Instead, the new system would see delegates electing four of the selectors, with the other being a nomination from the county champions.

It was also decided that delegates should elect those four selectors there and then. Four of the outgoing selectors were put forward for re-election but only Frank Murphy and the team coach, Gerald McCarthy, got back in. Johnny Clifford and Paddy Fitzgerald had paid the price for the Clare defeat and had been replaced by Denis Hurley and a nomination from the men of the quiet fields, one Justin McCarthy.

It certainly hadn't been a nomination which the conservative forces within the board had desired. Denis Conroy had urged delegates not to vote for anyone who had 'defected' from Cork, a clear reference to my association with Clare. Other delegates though saw through that argument and I was flattered that they recognised the contribution I could make.

That contribution would be limited. When the selectors met at our first meeting, Frank Murphy cut straight to the chase. 'Gentlemen, the coach's job. I propose we leave it the same as last year. I see no reason why we should change it.' I found his argument ironic. Gerald was being kept on in '81 after winning only the league while I had been kicked out in '75 after winning a Munster championship. But I said nothing. I had no problem with Gerald being in charge. He was a good coach, a friend and deserved a second chance.

Gerald was glad to have me on board but I knew some officers and even players would be initially cool to me. I had deserted Cork's cause in the past; how loyal was I to it now? The rivalry between Cork and Clare had been intense in those years. Even to this day when I'm talking to old team-mates like Gerald and Charlie and Denis Coughlan, we'll talk about everything except the time I was involved with Clare. Those were tense days. In the 1977 Munster final, I ran onto the pitch to give a Clare player some water when there was a break in play. Beside him was Dermot McCurtain, who asked for some for himself. But as soon as he said it, I was gone. So, for a player like him, who hadn't worked with me in '75, I would hardly have been someone he either respected or liked; I would have been the fecker who hadn't given him water in a Munster final. Even a lot of the players who knew me would have assumed I was getting money in Clare, completely unaware that I lost money coaching there.

One of our first games that season was a tournament game against Limerick. We were to meet in Cook Street and when I arrived, Denis Conroy and a few other officials were already there. I said, 'Good evening, gentlemen.' They muttered, 'Evening.' That was the sum of our conversation. From being so highly respected in Clare, I was back in my place in Cork. It was going to take time before being accepted back into the fold.

Gerald helped. Before we played Clare in a league game in Cusack Park, he came over and said, 'Will you talk to the team? You know Clare.' I was surprised but I appreciated it and went on to give a very good speech about the Clare mentality and what Cork could expect to be up against. In hindsight, it was an important moment. While the players privately would have respected me, some would have been suspicious of me. That speech in Ennis would have left them under no illusions which side I was firmly on. It helped break the ice. So did the fact I fixed a lot of their hurleys.

Gerald would have seen me as an asset. We would discuss the team and how different players were going and he'd want my view when we'd be looking at the opposition. But when it came to actually coaching the team and taking the sessions, I gave him a free run; I'd take shots with Ger Cunningham and that would be it. It was a strange role for me because it was the first time I had been involved with a team without being either a player or a coach, but Gerald was the coach. As a coach myself, I knew the last thing he needed was interference.

Going into that 1982 championship, Cork had won the previous two league titles but done nothing in the championship. It was a massive year for everyone, especially Gerald. The selection committee was divided on some key positions and players. I liked John Fenton but Frank didn't. It was the same when it came to Seanie O'Leary. Frank made a strong case though for another member of the three-in-a-row team, Martin Doherty. I wasn't so sure. I had good time for Martin – he would often come up to the Alley – but he was now based in California. I didn't think he'd be able to do himself justice, missing training and only flying in for games. The other selectors though sided with Frank. Martin played in the first round against Tipperary in the Park.

He played well in that game. We won it convincingly, 1-19 to 2-8. Jimmy scored 1-3 at full forward but the man everyone was talking about afterwards was Tony O'Sullivan. Tony was barely overage for minor but already he had tremendous skill, footwork, accuracy and confidence. He scored seven points as well in our next game. Clare were wiped out, 3-19 to 2-6, with Kevin Hennessy also impressing, scoring 2-1. A bit of me was sad to see Clare humiliated like that but then another part of me was saying, 'Well, they beat us last year.' Just like in those Munster finals of '77 and '78, there was no disputing where my loyalties lay. Home was now where the heart was.

Frank felt the team could be going even better. A few weeks before the Munster final against Waterford, he pushed for Ray Cummins to be recalled. I wasn't in favour of it. Ray had been a tremendous player but he was now thirty-four and hadn't played for Cork in over a year. Again though Frank got his way, and again, in fairness, his judgment was justified on the day. Most people had anticipated a close game but from the moment Cummins got an early goal, it was one-way traffic; it was so embarrassing that at one stage in the second half Cummins chose to hand-pass for a point when it would have been easier to take his goal. O'Leary showed no such mercy, scoring four goals, while Tony and Pat Horgan weighed in with nineteen points between them. It ended up 5-31 to 3-6. After that, everyone assumed we'd win the All-Ireland.

That was one of the reasons we lost it.

There were other reasons though. In the weeks leading up to that final against Kilkenny, I found history was repeating itself. Just like in '72, we were doing far too much strenuous physical work. I had a lot of time for Noel Collins as a trainer but I felt Gerald was giving him too much scope in those weeks. The way you judge a hurler in the last week of training is by looking at his appetite and sharpness. In training that week, too many of our players weren't sharp or fresh. When Jimmy felt there was something wrong with the hurleys I gave him, my worst fears were confirmed. That night I said to Gerald, 'I'm hoping I'm wrong but some of the lads aren't as fresh as I'd like them to be.' Gerald said, 'Well, there's little we can do about it now.' And he was right. There was little we could do except ease off, ask the players to rest and make sure our match-day preparations were spot on.

They weren't. They were disastrous.

After Mass, we went back to the Grand Hotel in Malahide for our team meeting. Before Gerald spoke, Derry Gowen, the chairman of the county board, was asked to say a few words. Derry said more than a few words. He went through every player on the team, telling them what to do and what was at stake. It was madness. That was Gerald's job, not his. What made it worse was the room had no windows and was extremely stuffy. By the time Derry was at the half-forward line, he had been talking for fifteen minutes. You could see the players were bored and getting restless and that the tension was rising. I remember thinking, 'Christ, will he ever end? Gerald has to talk yet. This team is going to be talked out.'

When we got to Croke Park, it was Frank's turn to say a few words. In fairness, he kept it short; he looked tired that day, drained from the hassle of organising tickets. Gerald again offered some words. Then, just as we were heading out, the chairman of the Munster Council, Donal O'Sullivan, was brought in to say a few words, being a Corkman. I couldn't believe it. I said to myself, 'This team is totally confused.' They went out onto that field and their minds weren't straight.

It showed. Kilkenny physically tore into them in the opening twenty minutes and Cork didn't respond. Coming up to half-time, there was only four points in it but Cork were visibly struggling. We were accustomed to things flowing for us that year but they weren't flowing in that game. Just before half-time, the Kilkenny full forward, Christy Heffernan, scored two goals. The second half was a formality. Cork lost every significant duel. Heffernan cleaned out Martin. Cummins hardly pucked a ball off Brian Cody. Tony wasn't allowed breathe by Paddy Prendergast, while Jimmy didn't get clear all day. No one was able to raise either his game or the team, the sign of a side that was talked and burned out. A team as talented and as well prepared as Kilkenny were always going to take advantage of that. It ended up 3-18 to 1-13, a scoreline that said it all.

It was a harsh defeat to absorb. I was disappointed for the players but especially disappointed for Gerald because I knew that result meant he was gone. I was also hurting myself because we hadn't performed and I also suspected I'd be gone with Gerald. That night though I was talking to Jimmy and Frank in the bar and I said, 'Lads, we should plan now for '84. Coming back and trying to win it next year would be sweet but Centenary Year is the one everyone will want to win.' The way I saw it, it might take two years for Cork to catch up with Kilkenny. The lads nodded but said little. They were understandably still trying to take in what had just happened to us that day.

A lot of what I envisaged that night came to pass. The following month, Gerald was thrown out. So was I. A new selection committee was brought in, with Johnny Clifford, the former Cork and Glen Rovers player, as the team coach. And despite his efforts, Cork found they were still somewhat short of Kilkenny, losing the 1983 All-Ireland final by two points.

I could never have foreseen what happened after that though.

18

McCarthyism

A politician will double cross that bridge when he comes to it.

Oscar Levant

Christy Cooney's phone call came out of the blue. So did his question: 'Justin, are you interested in going forward as a selector tonight?' I hadn't even known the county board was voting its selection committee for the 1984 season that October night, let alone contemplated putting my name in the hat.

My initial answer was no. I had been in twice before and promptly kicked out each time. Other candidates had known weeks in advance that the vote was imminent; I had been given two hours' notice. As attracted as I was to the notion of being involved with Cork in the biggest year in the GAA's history, the prospect of humiliation was greater. I didn't want to make a fool of myself by being rejected again.

Christy was persistent. He appreciated that I had been burned in the past but argued that the delegates from the country clubs would also appreciate that and would feel I deserved another chance. 'No, Justin, I think you should go forward. Remember, it's an open vote. I'll make sure you're nominated.'

I'm still not sure where Christy was coming from. This was long before he was the chairman of the Munster Council or the Cork County Board; back then, he was merely a delegate from Youghal. Maybe other people had suggested to him that I would be a good man to have in for the Centenary Year; maybe it was because he knew I had great time for his clubmate Seanie O'Leary; I don't know. What I do know is that he was persuasive. I eventually caved in. Florrie McCarthy, a delegate from my own club, Passage, would second the nomination.

Late that night, the phone rang again. It was Florrie. I was in, third past the post. Father Michael O'Brien, Denis Hurley and Tom Monaghan had also been voted in, joining Joe Desmond, the representative from county champions Midleton.

It had been a serious race with some serious casualties. Gerald,

Frank and Johnny Clifford were the three men who missed out. In ways, it was remarkable. They were from the Big Three, Frank was the most powerful man in Cork GAA, while Gerald and Johnny had each led Cork to All-Ireland finals the previous two years.

In other ways though, it wasn't. Cork hadn't won an All-Ireland since 1978 and Frank had been on most of the selectorial committees in the interim. Gerald and Johnny had both failed to land the big one. Father O'Brien, meanwhile, was seen as an up-and-coming coach, while Denis and Tom were likeable figures in county board circles, a scene they both knew well.

Who would actually coach the team then became the talk of Cork. The *Evening Echo* ran a story with the headline: 'Cork have the coaches but who will be doing the steering?' Would it be Father O'Brien? Would it be me? Would it be Johnny Clifford without selectorial powers? The piece even speculated it could be a joint effort. As far as I was concerned though, there was only one man for the job. After my experience in '82, I wasn't happy to be just a selector. That year I contributed somewhat but could never really get my teeth into the team. If I had my way, it would be different for '84.

A few hours before the five of us were to meet to pick a coach, Father O'Brien called me at work. 'Look,' he said, 'we should have a chat about this meeting. We'll meet on the way down.' So we did, in a cul de sac on the Boggy Road, a few hundred yards from Páirc Uí Chaoimh.

When I got into his car, he asked me if I was going forward as coach. 'I am,' I said. 'Are you?'

He paused for a moment, and then said, 'I don't think so. I'll vote for you. The others mightn't but I will.'

I've sometimes wondered what motivated him to take that stance. He had developed quite a reputation, winning five Harty Cups and three All-Irelands with Farranferris and several Fitzgibbon Cups with University College Cork, and had been a selector with several All-Ireland-winning minor teams; perhaps he felt he wasn't ready to coach an inter-county senior team and that his time would come down the line, as it did in 1990. Whatever, we headed down to the Park in separate cars, needing one more vote to get our way.

When the five of us met, the coach's job wasn't long coming up. Joe Desmond, as chairman of the selection committee, proposed Johnny Clifford. He said he had worked with Johnny the previous season and had been impressed and did not see the point in changing the coach. Although Johnny was due to undergo heart surgery, Joe had been informed he would have made a full recovery come spring.

By then, he could coach; in the short-term, he could advise. The nomination was seconded by Denis Hurley. He too had been a selector in '83 and liked Johnny.

After Denis had his speak, I countered. 'Look, we have coaches in the room. I don't think it should go outside the five people here.' Then Father O'Brien proposed me. That meant it all came down to Tom Monaghan. Whoever he gave the nod to would coach Cork in Centenary Year.

I knew Tom from playing with him on the Cork intermediate team in '64. I was also aware that he had good time for Johnny Clifford. I had some for Johnny myself. He too had sustained an injury – in the eye – early in his career and had heroically come back to play for Cork, while I also knew only too well that it was harsh to dismiss a man who had been in the job for only one championship campaign. But I was also aware that I might never get another chance to train Cork. Johnny would later say that he had got the shortest trial in history but he was wrong about that. I had, in '75. Johnny hadn't wept for me then and I wasn't going to weep for him now. I had no reason to apologise to anyone for trying to seize this chance.

I was also sure that I was a better coach than Johnny. He once said, 'I have no great theories on hurling but I do believe the best way to get anything from anybody is to become their friend.' I had a thousand theories on hurling and becoming friends with the players wasn't one of them. Whether Johnny was popular with the players was irrelevant; this was about who would get the most out of those players. While he was a good coach, I was certain that I was better at instructing players, devising drills and game plans, and conducting training sessions. If Cork were to win the All-Ireland, they would have to win with the players already at their disposal becoming even better.

I didn't say that to Tom and the others in so many words. What I did argue was that Cork would need a new plan of campaign after failing in the previous two All-Ireland finals. There would also have to be more emphasis on hurling. Although I wanted Noel Collins to stay on as team trainer, I wasn't going to give him as much scope as he enjoyed under Johnny and Gerald. I could also bring the players into the Alley, do up their hurleys and advise them more fully than I could as a mere selector. I also made reference to my previous coaching successes. It was important to highlight that my methods had worked with many teams.

I let the others bring up the matter of Johnny's health. But when Joe argued that he would be fine come March, I said that March would be too late, that we needed to be well into our hurling programme by then and that it would have to be our coach conducting it.

Joe and Denis kept making a strong case for Johnny. 'The man deserves another chance,' they said more than once. Tom was asked a few times if he had made up his mind but he in turn would ask to hear more. After about half an hour though, he finally came to a decision. 'Lads, I'm going for Justin. I respect Johnny, he did a good job last year and he's unlucky to lose out. But Justin knows the scene. He knows what has to be done.'

Joe and Denis immediately congratulated me. As far as they were concerned, a collective decision had been taken. I let them know that I valued that response and that I knew I'd have their full co-operation even though they hadn't voted for me. Then, after the handshakes, we made our way out into the dark. At last, I was back.

Or so I thought.

A few weeks later, a very interesting article appeared in the *Evening Echo*.

'Father Michael O'Brien and Justin McCarthy have been appointed joint coaches to the Cork senior hurling team, while Noel Collins will continue in his role as team trainer,' wrote Michael Ellard. 'These appointments were sanctioned at last night's meeting of the Cork County Board.'

Now, technically that article was accurate. Ellard only reported what had been said at the meeting. But it was wrong in another sense. Father O'Brien was never joint coach to that team. I devised and conducted every training session and team talk in the following two years, as it was the brief given to me at that first selectorial meeting in the Park. At no stage was the idea of joint coaches discussed that night. The only thing was when I was accepting the congratulations of the other four selectors, I had also thrown in, 'And thanks to you, Father, for nominating me. Sure, you can always give me a hand out.' So when I read Ellard's report, I smiled. The county board had found the loophole they wanted.

It wasn't the only passage of the article that amused me. Frank Murphy was quoted as describing Father O'Brien and myself as 'experienced men' whom the board 'had every confidence in'. He had also paid a flow of tributes to Johnny Clifford, 'a great motivator' with a 'marvellous hurling brain'. 'We hope that his loss to us will only be temporary,' said Frank. The *Echo* reader may understandably have assumed Frank meant that Johnny would take the job again in a few years' time. Frank though had wanted Johnny back much earlier than that.

The previous week, he hadn't such confidence in Father O'Brien and myself.

When Joe Desmond rang to say the General Purposes Committee wanted to meet us, I asked why. He said he didn't know. I speculated that maybe they wanted to talk to every Cork selection committee about how to approach Centenary Year. To me, it wouldn't have been a bad idea. It was a huge year and Cork would have been feeling confident of challenging for honours in every grade in both codes. 'You're probably right,' said Joe. And looking back, I probably was. They certainly made it clear how they wanted us to approach it.

I had never been at a county board meeting before, let alone a calling of the GPC. I did know certain things about it though. I knew that it was chaired by the county board vice-chairman, which in this case was Denis Conroy, and that all other members of the county board executive sat on it. It also consisted of a handful of delegates voted by the county board. Its brief was to finalise and ratify various county board matters, such as the appointment of referees and venues.

When we entered the room, we were asked to sit down by Conroy. And so we did, the five of us. Straight across the table were Conroy and Frank Murphy. Behind them, there were a few other rows; in all, there must have been about twelve of them there. Then Conroy stood up and said, 'Gentlemen, I'll be brief and to the point. We understand you've picked a coach for the Cork team for '84. What we're saying here, and I, as chairman of this committee on behalf of the county board, am asking you to do is reverse that decision and pick Johnny Clifford. We feel he's the man for the job and that he'll bring back the All-Ireland to Cork in Centenary Year.'

He went on. He had 'the best medical advice' that Johnny would be 'fit as a fiddle' come March, which was when he would really be needed. We could change our decision without losing face, he argued. It all would be a formality if we agreed.

I was flabbergasted. When the selectors had decided on who the coach should be, that was meant to be the end of it. Only then did I truly realise that they would never forgive me for coaching Clare. In ways, I was naive to think otherwise. This, after all, was the same Denis Conroy who had insinuated that I should never be let near a Cork team again because of my association with Clare. Everyone that night knew who he was referring to and everyone at this GPC meeting knew he was referring to the same man again. By pleading for Johnny's reinstatement, it wasn't so much a case of 'Let's get back our man' as 'Let's get rid of your man.' If the five of us had agreed Father O'Brien should be team coach, I don't think we would have been facing the GPC that night.

After Conroy had spoken, Joe Desmond, as chairman of the selection committee, got to his feet. 'Mister Chairman, I'm sorry but we've already made a decision. We're not going back on it. We feel it was made in the right order.' I was impressed by that interjection. Remember, Joe Desmond had nominated Johnny Clifford to be Cork coach only a few days earlier; now he was standing by Justin McCarthy.

Frank Murphy acted as if Joe had never spoken. Once Joe sat down, Frank stood up to give an even more passionate speech about Johnny Clifford. Some of the phrases that Ellard would later quote were first aired that night. Johnny was a great motivator and a great servant to Cork hurling. He had innovative ideas and methods. He was building a team. His health wasn't great but he'd be in tip-top shape come the spring. In short, he was the man to lead Cork in Centenary Year.

When Frank eventually finished, Joe Desmond again stated that we had made a final decision. Conroy then again reiterated that we could always change our mind. 'Will you at least go back and think about it?' he said.

'There's no going back, Joe,' I said within earshot of everyone. 'There'll be serious repercussions if this is reversed.'

I meant I would go public. It would have caused a furore. Cork County Board delegates had democratically voted its selectors. Those selectors in turn had democratically elected a coach. Now the GPC were undemocratically trying to squeeze that committee, ambush it, split it.

Thankfully, Joe Desmond was a democrat. Like the rest of us, he had been caught off guard but once something had been agreed, he was going to stand by it. 'Mister Chairman, we respect what you're saying about Johnny Clifford. I worked with the man last year. But we're not going back on our decision.'

And yet they still went on. It came to the stage where I had to say to our chairman, 'Joe, we're only wasting our time. Let's go.' And as we were walking out, we were again asked, 'Will you think about it?'

On our way downstairs, I called the four other selectors together. As hard as it was to absorb the absurdity of what had just happened, one reality had certainly registered. 'Lads,' I said, 'our days are already numbered. There's only one way we'll survive and that's to win that fucking All-Ireland.'

If Limerick, Tipperary and Offaly didn't know what force propelled the opposition that blew them over that year, they know now.

It was a team driven by a man driven by the memory of that night.

19

PICKING UP THE PIECES

Well, there you are. I did my best and they took me off. That's my fucking lot with Cork.

Seanie O'Leary, February 1984

Losing an All-Ireland final is like losing a bride at the altar. You feel passionate about something, you put your heart and soul into getting everything right for that one day, and then, at the final moment, it's taken away from you. It is not any game or girlfriend; a piece of you dies. Just as you can never forget winning one, you never forget losing one either.

We were inheriting a team that had experienced that ordeal twice in twelve months. Many of the players felt they would never win another All-Ireland. Some might have feared the side did not have the talent for it; others, that they did not have the heart to risk going through such pain again.

Jimmy Barry-Murphy would have been one. Twice he had been outstanding in the earlier stages of the championship, twice he had been captain yet twice he had flopped in the final.

John Fenton was also at low ebb, despite winning an All-Star. He played some outstanding hurling in '83, particularly during Midleton's march to the county title, but had suffered the humiliation of being taken off in the All-Ireland final. As he approached the sideline that day, Fenton threw his helmet to the ground. It was little wonder. He had been first called up to the senior panel in 1975. Nearly nine years later and he still hadn't established himself as a Cork regular. That was an incredible predicament for a 28-year-old. Brian Corcoran, the next great player east Cork produced, *retired* at twenty-eight.

Seanie O'Leary, meanwhile, was only a sub in '83. At thirty-one, he felt his course was run.

The rest of the panel were scarcely in better emotional shape. The way I saw it though, they were still Cork hurlers, a breed different to all others. It was our job to reinstil that old Cork cockiness into them.

The first thing we had to do was to make it clear what we were about. Within a week of that General Purposes Committee meeting, we called a meeting for the Cork Regional Technical College, at which twenty-eight players were to attend. I reminded them that the fate of Cork hurling for the following twelve months was in that room. Five or six players weren't going to fall from the sky. If Cork were to win anything, they would all have to become better players. I also said I was asking players who had won All-Irelands and were household names to improve their training and discipline. There was only one way they could get over their All-Ireland blues – to win the Centenary Year title. The players agreed. 'Well then, this is a historic night,' I said. 'Tonight was the night the Cork hurlers decided that they were going to win the 1984 All-Ireland.'

A new plan of campaign would mean a change of scenery. Páirc Uí Chaoimh is a fine place to be when the days are long but during the winter it can be grey, cold and tedious. I mentioned to Noel Collins that we needed to get out of there for some winter sessions and asked whether we could get the track, gym and hall out in the RTC where he worked. The county board were initially reluctant about it. Cork had trained hardly anywhere else but the Park; what was wrong with it? Joe Desmond though was able to iron that one out, telling them that we had to vary the routine.

I've often told people that if I had been involved with Cork again, Joe would be the first selector I'd have asked for. He was a huge asset to me in '84. He was very organised, very straight and very honest. Father O'Brien, Tom Monaghan and Denis Hurley also played their role. Between them, they exuded a sense of authority and experience and most importantly for me, they could court some favour from the county board.

Every training session that season counted. We could not afford to waste one. Cork's hurling hadn't been as sharp as it should have been the previous two years and that had to be redressed. I told Noel that I respected him but that he wouldn't be given the scope he had enjoyed the previous two years. There had been too much of an emphasis on physical fitness in those years, just as there had been in '72, and the players hadn't been fresh enough as a result. I said that while he would still be the man putting the lads through their paces, I would be watching it all. There would be nights that if I felt the players were going well and didn't need any more physical training, I would call a halt to proceedings. Noel, in fairness, took it on board. I would come to regard him as a good friend as well as an excellent trainer.

We couldn't afford to wait for the evenings to get longer to start our hurling programme. Early in February I told the players to bring their hurleys with them for our next session up in the college. Jimmy Barry-Murphy was amazed. 'Bring our hurleys along, Justin? Aren't we training at half-seven?'

'Jimmy, we'll bring the hurleys and work with them indoors.'

'What can we do indoors?'

'Plenty.'

And there was. We could work on our solo running, hand passing, doubling, goal taking, ball contact, eye contact; in other words, our hurling fitness. So what if it was indoors? By using tennis balls or rubber sliotars, Ger Cunningham's health would remain intact. It might have been a first for Cork teams to train indoors but it was also about time.

It was also important that we win games; to this day, I know of no better confidence-building measure. A pivotal fixture was a league game in mid-February against Galway up in Ballinasloe. It was a real test for our lads, playing a strong, physical team on a good but tight pitch in front of 10,000 people. But we passed it, winning 2-7 to 2-6. We had stood up physically to Galway, a sign that we were turning the corner. Another pleasing development was that Kevin Hennessy, who had previously played most of his hurling with Cork in the inside forward line, had thrived at wing forward against as durable a player as Sylvie Linnane.

It had been a stressful day for me though. At half-time the rest of the selection committee were adamant that Jimmy Barry-Murphy and Seanie O'Leary weren't putting it in and that either one or both of them should be taken off. I was against any move. Shortly after we had come to power, I said to Jimmy that he had overtrained the previous two years and that we needed him to be fresh for the summer. But I also added that it was crucial for team morale that he'd be there for all the RTC training sessions and league games. He had duly obliged. For that alone, he didn't deserve to be taken off. His confidence would also suffer if he was substituted. He just had to stay on.

I got my way on that one, which proved to be no bad thing. In the second half, Pat Horgan flicked a ball into the inside forward line and in the twinkle of an eye Jimmy had finished to the net. O'Leary was not so fortunate. At one stage in the second half, Ger Cunningham got injured and I ran down to enquire about his welfare. When I came back, O'Leary was making his way to the line. I was livid with the other selectors; O'Leary's confidence was as fragile as Jimmy's. When I told him before Christmas that he was a big part of my plans he said, 'Christ, Justin, I can't even run, and I'm overweight. Ye'll all be

PICKING UP THE PIECES 157

running up there and I'll be left behind.' I pointed out that while we did have better sprinters and runners, there was nobody as cute or as quick to a ball breaking around the square. That was where I wanted him to be come summer. Now he was in the dugout in February. After the game he came over and said, 'Well, there you are. I did my best and they took me off. That's my fucking lot with Cork.' I was eventually able to talk him into staying on but I wasn't so persuasive in getting the other selectors to start him for the following game against Kilkenny. O'Leary would have to wait to prove them wrong.

That game against Kilkenny in the Park was another defining moment. More than a place in the later stages of the league was at stake that day. We simply had to beat Kilkenny; otherwise old ghosts would re-emerge. We also knew they would be trying to keep Cork down. But again we passed a real test of our character, winning 0-13 to 0-11. Kilkenny had overpowered Cork in the previous two All-Ireland finals but we more than matched them physically that day.

We were still some way from being the complete package though. Wexford beat us in the league semi-final, 4-9 to 1-14, on the first day of April. It was a setback. We had wanted to remain unbeaten in Thurles all year and to win some silverware heading into the championship.

Thankfully, we had another opportunity to do that. The GAA ran an open-draw competition that year, the Centenary Cup, and we went all-out to win it. We took it so seriously that we played Kilkenny in a challenge match in Ballygarvan to give some fringe players a chance to stake a claim for that campaign. O'Leary duly took it, scoring two goals. After that, Father O'Brien revised his opinion that the Youghal man was past it.

The following week, O'Leary further emphasised the point, scoring another couple of goals in our first-round game against Roscommon. A week later, we rolled over Clare with eight points to spare. O'Leary again starred, scoring four points, but that game will be most remembered for Pat Hartnett making his debut with Cork. Five or six players may not have fallen from the sky for us that year, but one or two from Midleton did. Hartnett in particular was a godsend.

We had tried his brother John at midfield during the league but Pat proved to be more suited to partnering Fenton. While Fenton would do the hurling, Pat would work and forage all day. He was in tremendous physical shape and would die on the field for you. He could be erratic in his striking but he worked on it in the Alley and developed into an incredibly hard puller.

Fenton though was the key to the whole thing. I had always

fancied him as a player but others hadn't. Frank certainly didn't. I remember the first-round game against Tipp in '82 when we were both selectors. The game wasn't ten minutes old and Frank was going, 'Look at Fenton! He's not getting stuck in!' I went, 'Frank, he's hit as much ball as his man. Let him settle!' But Frank persisted and eventually enough of us relented. Fenton was taken off and was a fringe player for the rest of the campaign. Then when it seemed as if he had established himself in '83, he was taken off in the All-Ireland. As soon as I took over, I told him to stop looking to the sideline, that he wasn't going to be taken off under this management team. We wanted him to express himself more, not to rush things. He responded to that.

Fenton was also pivotal because the Midleton players all looked up to him. He was team captain for the year and they were playing for him. Not one of them missed a training session that year and there were a lot of them. Apart from Denis Mulcahy, Fenton, the Hartnetts and Kevin Hennessy, there was Ger Power, who was back-up to Ger Cunningham, while Ger Fitzgerald and Colm O'Neill were on the fringes of the panel. Together they brought a vibrancy to the camp that kept the city players on their toes. Ger Cunningham once said to me, 'Justin, this crowd seems to be taking over. Is it going to be all Midleton on this team?' My answer was that if there were fifteen Midleton players good enough, I'd have them all playing for Cork, just as I'd have fifteen Barrs men if they were up to it. There was a danger that the Barrs–Midleton rivalry would create problems for us, particularly after they had a free-for-all in a championship game that summer, but it didn't. Kevin Hennessy was a ball-hopper *extraordinaire* and would regularly slag off the Barrs lads about the incident. After that, no one could take it that seriously. The lads knew they had to put their differences aside when it came to Cork.

Our two corner backs, Denis Mulcahy and John Hodgins, were proof of that. One was from Midleton, the other a Barrs man, but they were regularly paired together for one drill. Although they were both good strikers of the ball and possessed real cutting, they each had a tendency to misjudge their runs when coming for the ball at speed and leave it behind them. When the evenings got longer, we'd spend at least ten minutes each night rectifying that aspect of their game. I would have the ball, they would be standing thirty-five yards away, and just before I'd hit it, they would take off and run towards the ball.

They had to avoid two common pitfalls – taking their eye off the ball for that critical split second, and having the hurley at the wrong angle. Sometimes they would have the angle too steep and the ball would fly off behind them; they had to work on having the hurley in a more upright position. They also had to ensure that the ball would meet the bas flat on; if it was too much to one side, the ball itself would go to one side. Through sheer practice, they both learned to control a low ball at speed.

Speed. It was a word we kept emphasising in training. Being able to execute a skill in itself was not enough; it had to be done at speed. A regular drill was to have a player start with the ball at his feet and his back to the man out the field. On the whistle, he would have to lift the ball, turn and clear it; go back, lift another ball, turn the other direction and clear it. At speed.

We also wanted our hurling to be hard and direct. We'd have two players in the middle of the field marking each other and two others on either wing. On the whistle, one of the wing players would hit a ball high in the air towards the pair in the middle, who would then have to clash on the ball, watch the break, try to win it and then clear to whichever wing we'd call. After six or eight attempts, they would rotate, the wing men going in the middle and the other pair popping out to the wing. It was a way of showing fellas that they could not hide. Anyone who was shy at pulling in the air was soon exposed. We often paired Tim Crowley and John Fenton together on that one. Tim was stronger; John, more skilful. From it we were able to gauge whether they were competing.

All this was with a pattern of play in mind. We had some exceptional scorers, namely Barry-Murphy and O'Leary, but they could be knocked off their stride if we didn't get the ball in quick enough. The only forward who could push his marker about was Tim Crowley, so the emphasis was on clearing the ball quickly, keeping it moving and spreading it wide if possible. The forwards were told not to crib whether the ball came in high or low. As long as it was fast, they were to have the hurling to deal with it. It was something we stressed throughout April and May. That and the importance of keeping the Centenary Cup run going.

The week after the Clare game, we went to Thurles to play Offaly in the semi-final. We won 1-15 to 3-7, with Barry-Murphy, O'Leary and Fenton scoring all but four of our points. Seven days later, we were in Croke Park for the final to face Laois. That day will last long in the memory. We weren't just hungry for success; we were hungry for food.

The day had started smoothly. The train arrived in Heuston Station bang on time; we got the coach to Croke Park and were there well before the game. Then it emerged we had no dressing room. A few minutes later, we found out there was no place for us to eat. Then we were told there was *nothing* to eat. Between staging the football final the same day and arranging a reception for all four finalists that night in the RDS, the GAA had overlooked the most basic of arrangements for the Cork team. And so you had the comical situation of the Cork hurlers, like primary-school children on a day trip, going into local shops to buy biscuits, chocolate, crisps and 7Up.

The players were not amused. John Fenton, Ger Cunningham, Donal O'Grady and Johnny Crowley were particularly annoyed. Having to tog off and eat junk food in a handball alley was not their idea of getting ready for the final of a national competition. I couldn't have agreed more but there was nothing we could do. I knew it was important to get the players' heads right, so when Frank Murphy said he had a speech to make, I told him to keep it brief because I had a good one of my own to give. I told the players that if they wanted an excuse to lose, they had one. There was only one way to enjoy the day. Win.

I also emphasised that it was time to play championship hurling. The Limerick game was only two weeks away; we needed to show ourselves in a competitive situation that we were ready. Laois had to be respected, having beaten Limerick, Tipperary and Galway within the month. If we were slow and ponderous on the ball, they could make it into a war of attrition.

The players responded, winning 2-21 to 1-9. Tom Cashman, Dermot McCurtain and Hartnett were outstanding, while Tomás Mulcahy did very well when he was moved to centre forward. The post-match meal in the RDS went down well that night. Anything dipped in victory usually does.

The Centenary Cup though was just like the league – winning it would soon be forgotten if we were beaten in the first round of the championship. Many commentators thought that was what would happen to us. Limerick were favourites going into that game. They had been outstanding in the league final against Wexford and were at home; we were seen to be leaking too many goals and still vulnerable after the two All-Ireland defeats.

The way we saw it, Limerick would go at us from the start. Over the years, they had tried to ruffle Cork by getting a few digs in to agitate our better ball players. Our plan was to withstand that, keep with them for the first half and then our superior class would eventually show. That's pretty much how it worked out. Limerick were 1-3 to no score ahead after seven minutes, and by half-time, were still five points in front, but our lads refused to lose their cool. We moved

Pat Hartnett from midfield to stop their wing forward Paddy Kelly, O'Leary got a goal out of nothing, and then Tommy Quaid allowed a Fenton high ball drop over his head. In the end we won emphatically enough, 2-15 to 1-13, to qualify for the Munster final.

There were two significant developments before that memorable game against Tipperary. Kilkenny were beaten by Wexford in the Leinster semi-final. Then we played Kilkenny in a challenge game the week after that defeat. I cannot exaggerate the importance of that game. We needed more than training to sharpen our hurling in the six weeks between the Limerick and Tipp games and I felt Kilkenny were the team who would get the best out of Cork. Pat Henderson, to his credit, agreed to the match on condition all gate receipts would go to a local charity, and his team, to *their* credit, put up a brilliant display considering the disappointment of the previous week. We got a lot out of that night. The two-point win in Nowlan Park further boosted our confidence while the meal and pints in Langton's further boosted team spirit.

Every ounce of that spirit was needed in the Munster final.

There was a real sense of mission about Tipperary in 1984. They hadn't won a Munster title in thirteen years, yet they felt they were in with a realistic chance of winning the All-Ireland. A formidable management team had been assembled, including Pat Stakelum, Liam Hennessy, Len Gaynor and Donie Nealon, a coach I held in high regard. They would be drilling into the players that they were from the home of hurling, that it was Centenary Year and that they would be hosting the final. What better year to end the famine? And what better way than by beating Cork in a Munster final?

But we also had a sense of destiny. It wasn't just that the players needed to banish their double All-Ireland blues; the people of Cork also needed that Centenary All-Ireland. The previous twelve months had been a terrible time for the city and county. Dunlops had closed. Fords and my old workplace, Verolme, were closing. Most of the players knew people who worked in those places and would have passed those plants on their way to the Park. That day in Thurles, I made it very clear. The people of Cork could do with some hope and joy in their lives.

Unfortunately, I wasn't able to make some other points as impressively. The Anner Hotel has been Cork's traditional pre-match meeting spot in Thurles but in 1984 the hotel was being renovated and we were given an area that was separated from the main bar by only a timber partition. It meant it was nearly impossible for me to compete with the mayhem in the background. All week we had been telling the players to play the game, not the occasion, and there they were, in the middle of the singing and shouting. Leaving the hotel that day, I swore things would be different the next day, regardless of tradition.

There almost wasn't a next day. With six minutes to go, Noel O'Dwyer scored a point to put Tipp four points ahead. Anyone who was at Semple Stadium that day will never forget it. O'Dwyer made a little jig of delight. So did a handful of supporters on the roof of the stand, oblivious to the danger of their actions. Hundreds of their county men started to make their way behind the sidelines. They thought it was all over.

It wasn't.

What followed is now part of hurling folklore. Fenton's free. Hartnett's pile-driver which Sheedy could only parry as far as Tony O'Sullivan, who pulled to the net. Doyle's hand-pass and Mulcahy's interception. Sheedy electing to prevent Tony O'Sullivan's effort from going over the bar. O'Leary pouncing on the break. Fenton's insurance point. Our delirium at the final whistle. Tipp's despondency.

Nearly everyone in hurling remembers the score from that day: Cork 4-15, Tipperary 3-14. Nearly everyone has also hailed it as a classic. That's a fair assessment. When you're a former player on the line, you're playing every stroke and judging whether a given decision should or shouldn't have been taken by a player. That day, I could tell a lot of players played exceptional hurling.

Looking back on that roller-coaster ride, several factors decided the outcome. Jimmy Barry-Murphy had his best Munster final up to that point, scoring two first-half goals. Kevin Hennessy made the most of the news we picked up earlier that week that Pat Fitzell was carrying a foot injury and duly ran his man around the field and into the dugout. Tony O'Sullivan had a big impact upon his introduction. Tomás Mulcahy did well when he went to centre forward. And Dermot McCurtain was outstanding; Tipp had to move Nicky English off him and into the corner.

We actually were worried that Tipp might move English to centre forward because he was the kind of player who would trouble Johnny Crowley. They never did. It wasn't the only move they got wrong. Seamus Power had us so concerned we took off Donal O'Grady, but they then moved him back into the defence when Bobby Ryan had to go off injured. We were delighted to see Power further back the field.

Ultimately though it boiled down to us having two things – luck and character. Tipp should not have lost. We snatched it. But we also were in a position to benefit from such luck and that was down to our team spirit. The players did not panic when the momentum and match seemed to be Tipp's. They sensed the game was still in the balance, that a goal could sway it Cork's way. While Tipp had counted their chickens, we had kept our cool.

In hindsight, it was the game that won us the All-Ireland. And deep down, we knew it then too.

After Tipp, nobody was going to beat us in Thurles.

20

JUDGMENT DAY

They talk about the pressure of going for a three in a row. Imagine the pressure that losing three in a row creates.

Jimmy Barry-Murphy

We all know now. That Cork won, that it was one-sided, that it was one massive anti-climax. But there was a time when we didn't. Before 3.30 p.m. on Sunday, 2 September 1984, none of my critics were proclaiming as they would years later that 'anybody' would have beaten Offaly. The only thing everybody envisaged was one of the greatest as well as one of the most historic All-Irelands ever. And for a lot of pundits, Offaly were going to win it. The day before the match, the *Irish Press* asked P.J. Molloy, Tony Doran, Mossy Carroll, Nicky Brennan, Johnny Callinan and Joe Hennessy who they thought would prevail. Only Carroll tipped us. The rest felt Offaly were more settled and better balanced, while the pressure of losing three consecutive finals would cause us to implode. 'Offaly are the better team overall,' concluded Brennan. 'They should win by something in the region of five points.'

Nicky hadn't been privy to our preparation in the build-up to that match though. An admirer of Johnny Clifford's was. The day of the game, he was quoted in the *Sunday Press* as saying that Cork were 'better prepared' than the teams of the previous two years and would win 'irrespective of the opposition'.

That man was Frank Murphy.

I don't think I've ever been as determined to win a match as I was to win that Centenary All-Ireland. That Offaly were the opposition only added to that resolve. While I had been glad a few years earlier to see them make the breakthrough and while I respected their coach, Dermot Healy, a student of mine in Gormanston College, I wanted to give his team another lesson. Five years earlier, when I had been coach to Clare, Offaly played in a league game now known as the Battle of Tulla which resulted in Sean Hehir being suspended and both teams having to play all their league games away for a year. It had been a tough match with a lot of flaking, and as the teams walked off the field and through the crowd on the final whistle, a fight broke out. I went in to try to break it up but I ended up getting a belt of a hurley on the back of my head for my troubles. I was told who that player was but I didn't tell Croke Park when they held an inquiry into the row. The way I saw it, I'd get another chance to beat that player. That player was still involved in 1984.

I also knew that if Cork lost, I was gone and Johnny Clifford would be in. When we had played Kilkenny in a challenge game on Easter Sunday, we were trailing in the first few minutes and as I ran down the sideline, one spectator shouted, 'Bring back Johnny Clifford!' We won that game but similar sentiments would be aired again if we lost to Offaly. A few months after I had been 'appointed', Johnny gave a big interview to the *Irish Press* saying how badly he had been treated. I knew that some day Frank would make it up to Johnny. I kept that article in a special place to remind me of that certainty.

If we were to win, we'd also need to pick our best team. I was adamant that our best team included Tony O'Sullivan. After the 1982 All-Ireland final, he had been condemned to the hurling wilderness for nearly two years. In those seventy minutes, he went from being the future of Cork hurling to an outcast, being only a sub for the 1983 campaign and not even a panellist for most of '84. I thought it was a ridiculous sentence. While he was out-muscled and outsmarted that day, the sideline was hardly the best place to work on the lessons Paddy Prendergast had taught him. From coaching Na Piarsaigh in 1983, I could see at close quarters that Tony's stickwork, footwork and sheer craft were still exceptional. The way I saw it, Cork could not afford to discard such a talent.

My fellow selectors disagreed. Even when Tony had recovered from a bout of illness, Father O'Brien did not want him near the panel, claiming he did not have 'The Right Stuff'. I kept forcing the issue though, and two weeks before the Munster final, eventually got my way. The next step was to get him on the field. That opportunity arose midway through the second half of that match. At the time, Tipp were getting on top and we needed to make adjustments to our half-forward line. When I told the others Tony was coming on, there were some objections but I insisted the matter was not open to debate. Tony seized his chance. It was his goal that drew us level and his attempt for a point that Sheedy batted down to O'Leary for the winner. After that, Tony was always going to start for the final. Listing him as a sub for the All-Ireland semi-final against Antrim was only a decoy. Offaly were made for him. Coming from Leinster, they would have perceived him as the young fella who was blown out of it by Prendergast. By underestimating him, they were leaving themselves wide open.

In sport, there is no such thing as little things. Little things add up; you must strive to do the right thing all the time. When someone says, 'Sure, we've always done it like that here', you don't just go along with him. You need to ask, 'Well, *should* you have always done it like that here?'

Press nights weren't the norm in 1984 the way they are now. Back in '82 and '83, different reporters would show up on different nights, some looking to talk to the players as late as the last training session before an All-Ireland final. I didn't think that was right. We held our press night thirteen days before the game.

We also broke with the tradition of Cork teams training on the Tuesday before a final. That didn't please some county board delegates. They had a board meeting that night and were hoping to catch the team going through their final paces after it was over but we didn't think it was fruitful to train on three consecutive nights; the Wednesday night session would be a more productive one for the players having had the previous night off.

Instead that Tuesday we brought the players down to the John Barleycorn Inn in Riverstown for a meal and went through the video of Offaly's fourteen-point win over Galway in the semi-final. Then on the Wednesday we trained in the Park, where the public gave us a standing ovation coming off the pitch before we went upstairs for a team meeting.

There we went through our game plan. From the Galway game, we noticed that Offaly's goalkeeper, Damien Martin, had a tendency to come out Seanie O'Leary's side every time; Seanie's job was to put Martin under pressure and either hook, block or delay his deliveries. We also decided that Pat Hartnett was going to take up their most pivotal player, Joachim Kelly. After the game, people were amazed Kelly didn't move onto Fenton but we didn't allow it. If all four midfielders ended up on one side of the field that was fine with us but we weren't going to shift Hartnett off Kelly. If they switched, we'd switch. After the 1978 Munster final, no team of mine was going to be the first to give in on that count.

Another key factor would be how Tim Crowley would play Pat Delaney. The Offaly centre back was a hugely influential player who loved to come out with the ball. To beat Offaly, we would have to stop him. I had played against Tim in a club game a few months earlier and noticed that he was inclined to stand sideways to his opponent under a high ball. Against Delaney, he would have to stand in close and whip on the ball as hard and as fast as possible.

In the days leading up to the game, I could sense we were going to win. In one of our last training sessions, Fenton whipped on a ball around midfield, sending it head high into Jimmy Barry-Murphy. Jimmy didn't even bother to catch it; instead he just flicked it into the hand of O'Leary, who drilled it to the net. It made my hair stand; no other team in the country could have reproduced hurling of that vintage. I also knew we had the character. I had seen it in the mud in Ballinasloe and in the Park in that league game against Kilkenny. I had seen it in the Centenary Cup when we had played with nothing but chocolate and fire in our bellies. I had seen it in the way we had come back against Limerick and Tipperary. The only thing that could stop us was if we weren't focused on the day. Our match-day preparations would have to be spot on.

As it turned out, they were. They've gone on to become the stuff of folklore.

There was no way we were going back to the Anner Hotel after the Munster final. We needed some place quiet, far away from the madding crowd. Thurles would be even more hectic this time. The Team of the Century was going to be honoured before the game. Every Sunday paper had produced a final supplement, a rarity back then. Never before had an All-Ireland final been the subject of so much hype. I asked Father O'Brien, with his educational contacts, whether he could get us any school in the area. He came back a few days later and said they were all booked out for various corporate receptions. But then he added, 'I have somewhere else.' His religious contacts had been more fruitful. There were some nuns from Cork he knew based in the local Ursuline Convent that would allow us the use of it for those crucial few hours before throw-in. I said, 'That's great, Father. Well done.' He then asked, 'Will we let the county board know?' I said we wouldn't. I hadn't forgotten '82 when so many people had tried to get in on the act and Derry Gowen's speech had been twice as long as Gerald McCarthy's. The convent would be our secret.

Everything was arranged like clockwork. After our train arrived in Thurles, a coach brought us to the convent. The only county board officer on that bus was Frank Murphy and he had to leave early to referee the minor final. The players didn't know what was happening. A few minutes after Frank had hopped off, the bus arrived at the convent. Two nuns were there to open the gates. Once we were in, they closed them again. The bus was then parked behind the convent so it couldn't be seen from the road.

When we were inside, the nuns gave us a great welcome. We then went into the church where Father O'Brien said Mass and Seanie O'Leary was the stand-in altar boy. Father O'Brien's sermon was very soothing and reassuring, telling us this was our day, while his few words of thanks to Seanie also helped create the right mood. The Reverend Mother though was the star of the show. The last hymn was 'Faith of Our Fathers' and she was marching up and down the aisle, giving it everything like a preacher from the deep south of America, before ending with a loud plea, 'And on this day, Lord, we pray that Cork will WIN!' It was inspiring stuff. After that, to paraphrase another powerful preacher, we were going to get to the Promised Land.

When Mass was over, we went back into the convent where we were served tea and sandwiches. The nuns had planned everything to a T; all the napkins and tablecloths were red and white. Then the players went out for a light puck-around on the green and took some photographs with the nuns, while the five of us selectors sat down on a bench to talk and admire the surrounding shrubberies and overhanging trees. It was all very relaxing, far away from the mayhem that was the Anner Hotel.

Offaly, meanwhile, were in the middle of it. They had stayed in the Anner the previous night. 'It was very unsettling,' Damien Martin would later recall. 'Every man, woman and child in Offaly seemed to be down pucking around with us outside the hotel that morning. We came down to go to the stadium and were greeted by drunken fans wishing us well and spilling beer on us at the same time. Not exactly the ideal preparation for the match.'

John Fenton would later claim that ours was. At the convent the players could relax, eat and – unlike the Munster final – hear my pre-match talk clearly. After the puck-around and stroll around the gardens, we went back into the church and up to the choir section for the talk. Some of the language used had never been aired there before. It was important though for the players to be reminded forcefully what their jobs were. This was the day to do them.

While we were saying all this, another Corkman would have had reason to use abusive language himself. Somehow Derry Gowen had got word that we were staying at the convent and had knocked on the hall doors demanding to get in. The nun who answered said she knew nothing of any Cork team. Derry insisted they were there. The nun then went in and asked one of her colleagues whether Derry was right. The second nun said he was but that no one was to know. The first nun then went back and told Derry that he must have been misinformed.

Fifteen minutes later, Derry called back and reminded the nuns that he was the chairman of the Cork County Board. Again, the nuns denied everything. And so poor Derry had to turn back. When the players discovered his torment after the game, Johnny Buckley in particular gave him an awful slagging. 'Derry, that nun will never get to heaven now because of you! Sure, she told you a lie! That's serious stuff, boy!'

We got a more favourable send-off than Derry. As we were leaving, one nun lit candles for us, another drowned us with holy water, and another drowned us with good-wish kisses. It was a very relaxed team getting onto that coach. The lads even burst into 'The Banks' on their way to Semple Stadium. It was like '66 all over again.

There was little in it in the first half. We had elected to play against the wind and in the early stages Offaly exerted a lot of pressure on our backs. Dermot McCurtain in particular was finding it hard to contain Mark Corrigan, while Delaney and Kelly were also making an early impact. But gradually we improved. After about twenty minutes you could tell that Tony O'Sullivan was at the top of his game, Pat Hartnett was starting to get the better of Kelly, while Johnny Crowley was lording it at centre back. If we could get our noses in front, the game was ours for the taking.

Every game has a turning-point. This game's one came in the twenty-sixth minute. Jimmy Barry-Murphy was pushed as he challenged for a high ball, but Tomás Mulcahy was able to place him back in with a neat flick. Jimmy in turn then put the ball into Seanie O'Leary. Seanie took one quick touch on his right-hand side to set himself up for the shot. Now, any other player would have taken that shot off his right side and tried to shoot across Damien Martin and into the far corner. Damien had anticipated that and had positioned himself well for that shot. But O'Leary had other ideas. Somehow he had the presence to make a half-turn and then shoot on that half-turn off his left side and inside the near post. It was a fantastic finish. The kind of goal only a great player could get. The kind of goal that encapsulated why I had talked him out of retirement.

That goal meant we were 1-5 to 0-7 up at half-time. It was a narrow lead but we knew the momentum was with us. Tim Crowley had started to get the better of Delaney while Donal O'Grady had come to grips with Padraig Horan. Besides, we had a habit of saving our best hurling for the second half.

That's how it panned out. Within minutes of the resumption, we were dominating in every sector of the pitch. At the back, McCurtain and Cashman in particular lifted their game, while between them, Crowley was having the game of his life. The midfield and attack, meanwhile, were really motoring, scoring the first six points of the half. Then in the forty-ninth minute, a Kevin Hennessy goal put us ten points up. The game was essentially over. A few minutes later, O'Leary scored another goal to make sure it was. After that, it was exhibition stuff. Fenton in particular let loose and banged over a couple of long-range points. When Offaly scored a goal with three minutes to go, it hardly raised a cheer.

Offaly froze. They weren't mentally tuned in. John Motherway, a friend of mine who drives lorries, had been in Offaly the week prior to the game and said he had never seen a place so decorated with flags and bunting. The locals were assuming they would win. That attitude might have rubbed off on the players. That said, Offaly were simply outclassed. A scoreline of 3-16 to 1-12 suggests they were.

Winning an All-Ireland as a coach is different to winning one as a player. You're happy but not euphoric; the most dominant sensation is that lovely, understated sense of a job well done. It is a lovely feeling. Every week since that meeting in the RTC in November 1983 we had talked about Thurles, 2 September 1984. Now the mission had been accomplished. What's more, we had done it in style.

When we got back to the dressing room, it was smiles all round. For the team to make such a journey, all the players had undergone their own trials and tribulations; now they had been vindicated. I was particularly delighted for Jimmy Barry-Murphy after the disappointment of the previous two finals. John Fenton had also proven himself to all the doubters; the only time he had looked to the line in '84 was to locate the next cup he was collecting.

They weren't the only ones. Three days after the game, I received a lovely letter from Father Harry Bohan which read, 'I am absolutely thrilled for you and more especially because, as I saw it, the three that you personally placed your faith in made the biggest contribution to the game, namely Tony O'Sullivan, Johnny Crowley and Seanie Leary.'

Those three players certainly had made enormous contributions against the odds. Only two months before the game, Tony was seen as someone with a great future behind him; he scored six points in the final. The morning of the game, Kevin Cashman of *The Sunday Tribune* questioned why Johnny Crowley had been selected ahead of John Blake after his subdued performance in the 1983 All-Ireland final; against Offaly, Crowley was the undisputed Man of the Match.

O'Leary though was the story that gave me most satisfaction. Ten months earlier even he had thought he was washed up. Now he had scored a goal in every championship game. Not bad for the smallest *and* heaviest man on the panel. The point was not lost on Eamon Dunphy. 'The day was a celebration of what we really are, not what we are supposed to be,' he wrote in *The Sunday Tribune* the following week. 'Nothing illustrated this more than the game, the hero of which was a small, fat – yes, fat – Corkman, Seanie O'Leary. Hurling is a great game because it can accommodate his sort of genius, allows for the non-conformist. There are no Official Hurlers.'

Official Cork was even delighted to be proved wrong about O'Leary and me. The day after the final, Frank Murphy was all smiles and congratulations on the train home, giving a great rendition of 'My Old Fenian Gun.'

I knew though that it was all just a reprieve. The previous night I had told Father O'Brien in our hotel bedroom that even though we had won probably the most prestigious All-Ireland ever, '75 and the Clare connection would neither be forgiven nor forgotten. The day we'd lose our championship would be the day I'd lose my job.

21

GLORY DAYS

Ye're going well, boy. But we'll be back with the cuckoo.

Christy Ring

19 May 1985, 2.20 a.m. Corkman's Association Centre, Greenpoint Avenue, Queens, New York.

The moment simply had to be recorded on camera. All of us smiling while joining in with the team's legendary masseur and ball-hopper, John 'Kid' Cronin, singing 'Beautiful City', the players, with their loosened ties and rolled-up sleeves, dancing and drinking as if they were at a wedding, arms linked around each other. It was a night of celebration, a night to be cherished, a night when it was great to be alive.

Yet as the delighted emigrants clicked their cameras to capture the scene for posterity, it seemed as if another button was simultaneously being pressed. That of the self-destruct variety. Our first championship match was only five weeks away. Our opponents in that game, Limerick, had just retained their national league title; did we want to help them add a Munster title to that? Why were people still drinking out of the Liam McCarthy Cup? Why the trip to New York? Why the victory lap so close to the championship?

The reality is we had little choice. Ever since the scheme started in 1971, the annual All-Star trip invariably took place a month or so before the start of the championship. We also felt that the players had earned the right to enjoy themselves. A few months earlier, the county board informed us that Croke Park would not be making any financial contribution towards the two-week trip and that the board itself would be giving little to us; in fact, we'd have to not only raise the money to pay our own way but also fund the cost of some county board officers. It was, of course, a ludicrous arrangement, considering this team had won the Centenary All-Ireland. But this was 1985, a time when everyone in Irish society pretty much accepted their place in the scheme of things. We were no different and went about raising the money.

A committee was formed, headed by John Fenton, Doctor Con Murphy and myself. A bash was held in the Beamish and Crawford brewery at which members of the public could mix with the team. Team photographs were sold for £50 a go. Local businesses were asked to support our cause. I asked a lot of customers in the oil business for contributions ranging from £100 to £500. One of our most generous supporters was Kerry Group chairman Denis Brosnan. I had noticed that CMP, who traditionally supplied milk to the team, had donated only £100 towards our holiday fund, so I approached Denis, whose company owned the Cork-based Ballinahina Dairies. I said that if he wanted a picture of the team drinking their milk, we'd gladly do it for a few quid. So we met the manager up there and had a photo taken; it appeared in the paper and a cheque for £500 was sent to us.

Enough was raised to pay everyone's way but it was hardly a luxurious trip. No wives or girlfriends went. Only our air tickets and accommodation were covered. There was a function laid on for us nearly every night but everything during the day – be it breakfast, lunch or sightseeing tours – came out of the fellas' own pockets. The least they deserved was the opportunity to enjoy themselves. And that they did. From the banter they had with the Kerry footballers on the plane over, to that singsong on the last night in New York, it was a trip to remember.

I'll never forget it for some of the escapades my room-mate Noel Collins and I experienced. Every morning we'd set out at half-seven from the hotel, around the same time that some of our lads were still coming in. One day in San Francisco, the two of us caught the boat to Alcatraz Island. After returning from the Rock, I suggested to Noel that we catch a bite to eat in one of the bars on Fisherman's Wharf. Noel wondered could we not wait, as he had lost a contact lens and had a second pair back at the hotel, but I said that by the time we'd get back there, it would be time to head off again to the function we'd be attending that night. Noel noted my logic so we went into a bar on the wharf and ordered a drink and sandwich each. A few minutes later, two men sat down beside us and asked what we were doing in San Francisco. Without thinking, I innocently replied, 'We're here playing games.'

'Really?' one of them grinned. 'We'd be very interested in that!'

Now, Noel mightn't have had a contact lens in his eye but he knew well enough that there was a glint in the other guy's. The next thing I got this massive kick in the shin, dropped my sandwich and followed Collins out the door.

There was a serious side to the trip though. I was determined that we'd win both games against the All-Stars. We had taken a casual approach to the league after winning the All-Ireland; Jimmy was given the winter off. We also had relinquished the Ford Open Draw Cup. Although training had been going well in the months leading up to the trip, we needed some wins to gather momentum leading into the championship. If we were to beat a team with talents like Joe Hennessy, Sean Stack, Nicky English and Joachim Kelly on board, it would send out a signal to the hurling world – that Cork were still the team to beat.

We won the opening game in San Francisco, 6-9 to 3-17, Tomás Mulcahy scoring three goals. A week later, the second match was played in Gaelic Park. I had never been there before and was initially taken aback by how rundown it appeared, surrounded by the railways and the graffiti-littered walls. I soon appreciated though that it was still a special place, a place where the Irish could meet and keep their games alive. It was all the more special when there were some old acquaintances to greet us. My brothers Barry and Noel were there, as was Dinny John Daly, who had played with me on the Verolme team that won the 1963 inter-firm final. And so was another man who had played that night. Bernie Aherne had been living out in New York for some time and was still looking well. He and Dinny John had sponges and buckets of water for our lads to use in the sweltering heat. Beating the All-Stars with old friends like that on our line made the win even sweeter.

And so that's why we were in such carefree form at the great reception the Corkman's Association threw for us that night at their centre in Queens. The All-Stars had been beaten; we were back on track. It was also a celebration of being from Cork; no, of being *alive*. While the emigrants were thrilled to see us, we were moved to see them. I met Billy Twomey, an old neighbour after whom an annual match between Carrigaline and Passage is named. Seeing my old clubmate Eddie O'Brien also brought back a lot of memories. Eddie was now a security officer in the Rockefeller Centre and seemed to be doing well, yet it was obvious he badly missed home and the glory days when we were kings. Eddie went to see us off at John F. Kennedy Airport the following day. He was crying. 'Don't bother going. Can't ye stay here?' But we couldn't. We had an All-Ireland to defend back home.

Eddie wasn't the only old colleague who parted ways with us in the States. Seanie O'Leary confirmed that at thirty-three, he was getting out at the top and wouldn't be playing in the championship.

Donal O'Grady likewise had made the trip but was calling it a day because of a recurring back injury. Those were two men who had played key parts in the Centenary final. And yet, I wasn't that concerned. Tim Crowley was staying on. Johnny Crowley could shift to full back; he was a strong man with the ability to hurl his way out of trouble. Pat Horgan, a stylish, versatile player, could fill in at centre back, while there was a string of players contending for that vacant forward spot. I could also sense that collectively there was a greater maturity in the side. Winning the All-Ireland had brought the team closer and given the players greater confidence. Fenton was now hurling without fear. Tony O'Sullivan had shaken off the ghost of '82. Hartnett and Mulcahy were blossoming into personality players. Shortly after we returned from the All-Star trip, we beat Offaly well in a challenge game. Then we hammered Kilkenny, 5-22 to 1-12. If anyone was going to beat us in '85, they'd have to be a special team.

Limerick were confident that they were that team. They had run us close in '84, were just after winning the league for the second year in a row and had persuaded Joe McKenna to come out of retirement. By half-time at a packed Páirc Uí Chaoimh, Joe was wishing they hadn't. Limerick were two goals down, having played with the wind. The second half wouldn't have changed Joe's mind. It took a last-minute goal to make the score look respectable, 2-13 to 1-9.

Our next game was hardly a lark in the park though. At times it was more like a war.

We knew the moment we won the All-Ireland was the moment Tipp would have vowed to take it off us. A month before the '85 championship, they signalled their intentions by beating Galway in the Ford Open Draw Cup final. I was also impressed by their display in the Munster semi-final replay against Clare. They won that game 5-14 to 4-6. Leaving Thurles that day, I said to myself that they were considerably better than they had been twelve months earlier.

I also saw some weaknesses that could be exploited. When Cork trained the following evening, I told the other selectors that we'd be moving Jimmy Barry-Murphy back to full forward. They were initially reluctant. Jimmy was thriving that year at right corner forward while Tomás was doing well on the edge of the square, but I convinced them that we'd be presented with two mismatches if we made the switch. The Clare game confirmed to me that Peter Brennan was vulnerable at full back. He was slow, cumbersome, made for someone like Jimmy to take to the cleaners. Tipp's left corner back was also ready to be taken. Under Babs Keating, Pat Fox would later go on to become one of the best corner forwards in the history of hurling, but in 1985, he was just another Tipperary defender one game from oblivion. If we moved Tomás to the corner, he would be too strong, robust and awkward for Fox, whereas if Jimmy went in there, Fox's cuteness and tenacity could trouble him.

When I told Jimmy he'd be lining up in a different spot to the one the programme would be saying, he went, 'But I'm going well in the corner, Justin. I'm enjoying it.'

'Yeah, Jimmy, but you'll be on this fella Brennan. And I'm telling you, you'll round this fella and get goals.'

Jimmy was happy with that.

A few days before the match, there was an interesting development. A friend of mine working in Tipperary tipped me off that Tipp would be going out to cut strips out of us. To this day, I won't disclose who that source was. All I'll say is that some people close to the Tipp team spoke too loudly about how they were going to approach that game.

We had initially planned to meet in the Park at half-one on the day of the match. When I received the tip-off though I felt we needed to be meeting earlier and somewhere else. Father O'Brien suggested the Blackrock club grounds so we met there at noon. After we had a light puck-around and some tea and sandwiches, I addressed the players. I first told them about the switch between Jimmy and Tomás and that whenever they could, they were to get the ball to Jimmy. Then I let them in on Deep Throat's story; Tipp would be reverting to Hell's Kitchen Rules. 'So lads, I'm telling ye now – be prepared. They'll pull hard, they'll walk on top of you if you let them. Steel yourself. Don't start a fight but don't walk away from one. Stand your ground, stand up for yourselves. If the ball is in close quarters, don't be tipping around; let it move. Stay cool but stay strong. Expect anything.'

If it was war we'd be facing, then we'd be needing one of our greatest warriors. Any coach, if he's honest, will tell you there are days when some players have to play even though they shouldn't. Loughnane will admit that Liam Doyle played on one leg against Offaly in 1998 when Brian Lohan and Colin Lynch were suspended. I once went against medical advice when I was involved with Clare. We were playing Tipp in the championship and at half-time Colum Flynn told me that Pat O'Connor's shoulder was gone. I said, 'Where is he?'

Then I went over to Pat. 'What's wrong?'

'My shoulder. It hurts. Colum says it's gone.'

'Don't mind Colum! I'm telling you now, if you don't play this second half, they'll only be laughing at you in Clare tomorrow, boy. They'll say, "O'Connor? He's soft." Now get out there and show them what you're made of!' Pat scored two points in that second half.

It was the same with Tim Crowley in that Munster final in '85. John McIntyre was the cornerstone of that Tipp team. Tim was the man to curb him. He had to play. Problem was, his toe bone was cracked.

When we got to the Park, Doctor Con Murphy came along to me and said, 'Tim's not looking good.'

'Is there anything you can do?'

'Well,' Con sighed, 'we could give him a painkiller.'

I went over to Tim. 'Tim, we might have to give you an injection.'

'Well, I want to play!' Tim said with unmistakable conviction. The next thing, the three of us and Ger Cunningham went into the gym in Páirc Uí Chaoimh. And as I took shots at Ger to warm him up, Tim took a shot of Con's injection. Nothing was stopping him playing in this one.

Then the moment of truth came. The dressing-room door was knocked, I gave my last few words to the team and Tim put on his boot. Just as the team were running out into the light, Jimmy Barry-Murphy ran over to me, obviously looking for some reassurance. 'Justin!' he said excitedly.

'Round your man,' I nodded, patting him on the back. 'You know what to do.'

'Yeah, but if I'm going through and he hooks me, what do I do then?'

Now at this stage I was completely talked out, so I said the first thing that came into my mind. Thankfully it was a better retort than the one I gave in the bar in San Francisco. 'Jimmy,' I said, 'for Christ's sake, aren't you a footballer? Can't you kick the shagging thing?'

Jimmy nodded and then out he sprinted, into the arena.

It was obvious in the opening few minutes that Deep Throat was right: Tipp *were* lowering the blade. Handles were thrown into ribcages, toes were trampled on, heads were butted; on one occasion, one of their backs kicked one of our players in the face as he was on the ground. Nicky English would later accept in his autobiography, *Beyond the Tunnel*, that some of his team-mates got carried away. 'The backs just seemed desperate to hit someone, anyone,' he wrote. 'They wanted to hammer into Cork, soften them up any way they could.'

And as Nicky would point out, such tactics didn't work. While they lost their heads, we kept ours. Jimmy Barry-Murphy in particular wasn't bothered by their antics. After fifteen minutes, he set up Tomás Mulcahy for a goal. Then two minutes later, Tipp's goalkeeper, John Sheedy, let a ball drop out of his hands; Jimmy ran onto it and kicked it in. When I told him 'Well done' at half-time, he grinned that he thought of me when that ball broke loose.

We were only two points ahead at the interval though. While the switch of Tomás and Jimmy was working even better than we had hoped for, Nicky English and Ger O'Neill were wreaking havoc at the other end. Pat Hartnett was being beaten at midfield. Ten minutes after the break, a Liam Maher goal put Tipp level at 3-9 each. The Park quaked. The momentum was now with Tipp. Our Munster and All-Ireland titles appeared to be slipping away.

Then came the game's turning-point. Jimmy, for the second time that day, was pulled to the ground, out in the corner. The referee let play on but then belatedly awarded us a free in. I ran down the line. Fenton looked over. I pointed down. The previous week in training Fenton had been hitting penalties so well that I was worried that our goal-line team of Ger Cunningham, Denis Mulcahy and John Crowley would lose their confidence. When Fenton stepped up to take that free, everyone on our team knew he was going to cling it. And so he did.

Tipp didn't cave in. With seventeen minutes to go, English scored his second goal to leave only two points in it. But the Fenton goal had turned the tide in our favour. In the closing ten minutes, there was only one team in it. Cashman and McCurtain cleared a rake of ball, while Denis Walsh, Pat Horgan and Jimmy scored some excellent long-range points. In the end, we won 4-17 to 4-11.

It was one of the sweetest victories of my career. The '84 Munster final had been more exhilarating but this was more satisfying. We hadn't stolen this one; we had won it playing some fantastic, crisp, fast hurling. I was particularly delighted for some of the players. It is universally accepted that that was Jimmy Barry-Murphy's finest hour for Cork. He scored a goal and three points from play that day, including one amazing effort over by the left-hand touchline near the end. He set up two other goals, while he won three frees which Fenton scored 1-2 from.

Fenton had also been immense, his ground striking as immaculate as his free taking. And then there was Tim Crowley. The previous year, he had been roasted by John McIntyre; now it was he who had burned McIntyre. Remarkable, considering Tim's pre-match condition.

There were other talking points. Like Tony O'Sullivan's three nice quiet points. Like Cashman and McCurtain's sterling displays in the last quarter of an hour. And like Tipp's tactics. It was little wonder that Val Dorgan called the following day asking if we could meet to look back on the match.

I said no problem. I'd meet him at the Imperial Hotel that Tuesday morning at eleven.

22

ON THE RECORD

A little sincerity is a dangerous thing. And a great deal of it is fatal.
Oscar Wilde, *The Critic as Artist*

Cork Examiner, *Thursday, 11 July 1985, page 11*

'In his playing days, Justin McCarthy was known as a great stylist; the kind of hurler whom sidelined fathers offered as a model for their star-struck sons. Now he is regarded as one of the gurus of the modern game. In this Q&A session with Val Dorgan, he gives a remarkably forthright assessment of individual and team performances in last Sunday's Munster hurling final.

Why do we need coaches now when we never did in the old days?

People have the idea that when you become an inter-county player you can't go any further; skill-wise, fitness-wise, mental approach, motivation – the whole lot. They say, "He's a Cork hurler." He's then supposed to be able to do everything. I have seen so many average players coming into county teams and never going a stage further. Some players only go so far because either they do not work hard enough at it, or they don't realise what they can do. There was only one player who really reached his full potential – Christy Ring.

Skill-wise, the Cork team are improving. I have tried to develop a lot of the hurling side of it. The good thing is players with genuine talent are always prepared to learn.

Be critical of the team.

Well, you can be critical of any player, so I'm just picking names at random.

Ger Cunningham is slow to get off his line. He is not at his best with a low ball hopping in front of him. We have spent hours correcting this. Johnny Crowley going up, at one time, might have been just thinking of batting the ball and would have kept his head down. Now he varies his overhead play, batting one, catching another or blocking off another. He had to realise he had three options up there. He probably did not appreciate that a year ago. We have chats with the players and sometimes sessions on an individual basis with them in the Rochestown ball alley or the monastery field.

Give us another example.

If you looked at Tony O'Sullivan, you'd say, "What could you tell him? He's a gifted player." But there are aspects of his play which do not suit him. He picks up a ball, say on the left wing, and turns well. Then he shoots the ball up into the air and lets it fall down into the square and it's killed. Skill-wise, he is very good. But in a game, his pattern of play might not suit the Cork forwards inside him. There are times when he cannot always think about a point, when he has an impossible angle or is under pressure. Then he should cut the ball across – that's teamwork. It is part of Tony's game which he can develop.

Tom Cashman has accepted he must put in more work on his left hand. Jimmy Barry-Murphy is a fine player, a finisher, but you wouldn't expect to see him cutting touches like John Fenton. His overall hurling has improved with constant ball practice.

Tomás Mulcahy has an awful lot of good hurling, tough and hard, but I say to him in training, "Tom, hit the next ten balls over the bar" and he might score with four. As a young hurler, he knows he has to improve his balance and striking.

Timmy Crowley is the workhorse of the team. He is basically a midfielder but we are converting him into a centre forward. He likes to get the ball, round his man and make a bit of room before trying for a point. But we have been asking him to whip on the ball, break it, get it through. That is a different kind of game for him.

It is trying to get the best out of players. Timmy would be the first to admit he hasn't Tony O'Sullivan's skill but he can still develop his all-round hurling. He can learn to connect on a ball in training, otherwise there is no point in trying it in a game. Hurling is such a fast game it has to be a reactionary thing.

John Fenton is a tremendous striker, tremendous pair of wrists. Going back three or four years, he was slow on the pull; he wanted to give a whole swing, man-to-man, shoulder-to-shoulder. But you must be smart on your whip. Nine out of ten times in a clash ball he would be beaten. He had to lighten his hurley. There is no point in having a heavy stick for line balls if you only hit three or four in a match when you could hit thirty shots.

Sometimes he is inclined to hit too many balls on the ground. He is the one player I would advise to pick the ball and then check a small bit, then have a look before hitting it. He is doing that in training. He's a tremendously important player to the team. But he has a bad history with Cork selection committees which probably made him over-anxious.

Kevin Hennessy wants to rattle the net every time he gets the ball. He has banged in a lot of goals for Midleton. But you cannot do that all the time. When you are playing inter-county, you won't get the same time or the same opportunities. He has to remember the old adage – take the points and the goals will come. We want to get him to score more points. He has to develop his left side a bit more.

Pat Horgan is a player who loves to catch the ball. You can't catch every ball unless you want to do without your hand. You have to bat it down, pull on the odd one, vary your play. You have to do it in training and we have set pieces to work it out.

I was watching the Tipperary centre back, McIntyre, playing against Clare and he broke their hearts. I thought Tim Crowley would have his work cut out to beat him. What we decided was that Timmy would go out to meet the puck-out from Ger Cunningham. I played myself on Timmy for seven or eight puck-outs in the Park and we worked it out there. Ger had two options. If Timmy ran out he could hit it to him or if McIntyre followed, Ger could drop it over him into the full-forward line. On a lot of puck-outs, the ball went through to Jimmy Barry-Murphy.

What's your bottom line as a coach?

Hurling is basically a simple game. People don't differ between a great player and a great hurler. It's like there's a difference between a boxer and fighter. You can get fit in eight to ten weeks, you can get motivated in a week, a day or a night. But you have to develop hurling over a long period. You must keep it simple and be able to do the simple things well.

Every practice down the Park, we have a ten-minute period hitting on the run off the hand and the hurley. I say to someone like Denis Walsh when he stops before striking, "You won't get that chance in a match; you must be hitting on the run." There's balance and footwork involved.

We have the three full forwards in front of goal. I hit out six balls to Jimmy Barry-Murphy and he must hit the six of them over the bar. It seems like a simple exercise for a player like Jimmy or Tomás Mulcahy but they must do it. Then we have them running in with the ball, picking on the run or hitting it on the ground.

You must develop hurling first and that is why we are winning matches ahead of other counties – because we have better hurlers. On top of that comes the training, the motivation, the commitment. I think too many teams are too motivated, too committed and are so beaten after training that they forget what to do with the hurley and the ball. This happens to Clare and Limerick and it happened to a certain extent to Tipperary last Sunday. Down through the years we were killed with training. You must have freshness. It is more important than fitness. We will go on winning if we can stay fresh and sharpen up our hurling and our thoughts but don't kill players with training.

What happened to Tipp?
We have better hurlers than Tipperary. But they have good hurlers. Kealy, the right half back, is potentially a great player. Their full-back line was trying to make up for a lack of talent in hardness and toughness.

Did you think Tipperary overdid the toughness?
I did. I thought their tactics were a bit ridiculous at times. We expected this and in the talk before the game I spoke about the fifties, which I barely remember, and the sixties. I think 70 per cent of Tipperary's wins back then were physical. The aim was getting the man out of the game, hitting him, putting him off, jolting him. And the other 30 per cent was hurling. They are trying to go back to this a bit again and I think it is going to be their downfall. You have to have toughness and I think the Cork team has developed an amount of toughness as well as hurling. They are not a shy team. They will get dug in and work hard. But Tipperary too much of the time tried to play the man last Sunday. And if they are going along those lines, I can't see them making too much progress. I think you must develop an amount of toughness and hardness, combined with the hurling skill, team play and fitness.

You cannot go out and try to play the type of game which they played last Sunday; putting fellas out of their stride by giving them a jolt here and a handle there, hitting off the ball. I thought that was gone twenty years ago. If they are going back to that again, I can't see them winning.

Were you satisfied the way Cork coped?
There were times when Cork teams lay down to that kind of challenge. In the last two years at least, we have always emphasised that if a fella cannot stand his ground, then he has no business playing

with Cork. We had them with old hurleys in the Park, clashing and pulling, making sure they have to hunt and work. They can't stand back. We have to say this to some players more than others.

Tipp upset themselves on Sunday because they were not getting any change out of Cork. I was a selector in Croke Park in '82 and thought Cork were roughed out of it that day by Kilkenny in the first twenty minutes. From that day on, I said if I had anything to do with a Cork team, they would give as good as they got; they would never be cowed again.

I maintain most of the stick is given in the first quarter of an hour of any game. When you get over that, the game then takes a pattern. You must be prepared to sacrifice yourself out there for that ten, twenty minutes, to give and take it, as you must realise that it is not going to be happening for the whole game. But you must go a bit deeper in motivating players to win games other than taking and giving stick.

I am not criticising robust play; that's part of hurling. I'm talking about hitting off the ball, giving a fella a poke or a kick when the ball is down the other end of the field. When the ball is around, go for it 100 per cent and if your opponent gets in the way, that's too bad for him.

On Sunday, there was needling off the ball, handles of the hurley and kicks. As well as that, Tipp were mouthing off at Cork and trying to get to them. I think we do not mouth as much; we keep our cool.

Tipp are the team that can take over very easily from us in Munster, no doubt about that. But I advised the Cork players that they must stand up against Tipp. At the end of the day, they should realise that Cork had the better hurlers. We have the skill that they haven't. I would say Tipperary were very highly motivated. You can only go so far with motivation.

Was Tipp's "toughness" a deliberate tactic?

Tipperary must have looked into it fairly deeply, I imagine, because they have not been successful since 1971. I think they have come up with a formula that you have a certain amount of hurlers and a certain amount of hardmen. Sunday hadn't to do with toughness; it was smartness, cuteness, fitness and better hurling. The game has become more open since the sixties, more fluid. People are allowed hurl more. It is a more attractive game. Cork played in All-Irelands and scored 1-6 and 1-7. Look at the score last Sunday.

Maybe defences are less tough?

When you have so much up-and-down play, there are bound to

be scores. You'll only have low scoring when it's the league and either the pitch or day is bad. Fellas are now striking quicker and more smartly. You are bound to have scores – and mistakes.

Standards are higher?

I would say the present Cork team would beat the team we had in '66. There are better hurlers and there is quicker movement today. I also think we are better organised now.

I think one of the main advantages with the present Cork set-up is that we have our house in order. I have seen Tipperary teams going to matches and not have a drink of water. We have a doctor and masseur. We have endless meetings among the selectors and with the players.

We went up to the All-Ireland in '72 hardly knowing who we were playing or where we were going; we just hoped for the best. Cork won matches through the years not knowing how they won them or how they lost them. And there was never a bit of thought put into it, a bit of organisation or professionalism. There is more thinking about the game now and we are doing that. Each player has three hurleys going to a match, two pairs of boots, three pairs of shorts. We are lucky with the players we have.

Tipp selectors were accused of mistakes.

I thought their midfield was adequate. I would not have taken off Ian Conroy. I think Tipperary made some blunders on the line. They could have switched McIntyre off Tim Crowley and put Bobby Ryan in. We were relieved to see Conroy come off; he had done an awful lot of damage. I was going down the line and I said to Len Gaynor, "Len, ye're gone now."

Even though Nicholas English contributed two goals and three points, I still think they're not getting enough out of him. He is a glorious player to watch. I would give him more freedom. He would play really well with Cork, the way they are going now. He won't play as well with Tipp the way they are playing.

Galway?

It is a cliché that every game is different. You can learn something from the last game but the next one has a new challenge. Galway are physically stronger than Tipperary; they might not be as robust or tough but they are stronger. You cannot knock them over as easily. They have beaten us when we were supposed to have won. I see Galway as being on the up and up; they are winning underage titles. Cork will have a job on their hands to beat them.'

23

FEAR AND LOATHING IN THE PARK

Some managers are only interested in keeping their job, sucking up to directors, yes sir, no sir, three bags full, sir. They should be drummed out of the game. You've got to be your own man, be in charge of the whole affair. If you haven't got the guts to do that, get out.

Bill Shankly

The first hint that it wasn't your standard interview was when I called into Kevin O'Leary's garage in Douglas to collect the car after a service.

'Jesus, boy, you're after making headlines!' said Billa Connell, a popular local comedian and hurling supporter, who was also getting his car looked after.

'How do you mean?' I smiled.

'Did you see de paper?'

'I didn't.'

'Christ, you're all over it!'

'Is that right?'

'Yeah! I'm telling ya! A whole page, boy! Fair play to ya; when you do things, you do them in style! Nice piece though. Good reading, like.'

After I got the car, I pulled in to get a paper. Billa was right. The *Examiner* had a small piece on the front page about my views that Tipp were 'too physical', while inside a whole page was devoted to the interview. I had a quick glance at it and then drove back into work, thinking no more about it.

I was in the door ten minutes when the chairman of the county board, Con Murphy, was on the phone. He hadn't enjoyed the interview as much as Billa. 'Justin, I'm very concerned about the article. I think you went way overboard on your comments about Tipperary. I've already had the Tipperary County Board onto me. They say they're on the point of pulling out of our home-and-away arrangement and won't be coming back to Cork. I'm asking you to make some kind of statement, some kind of retraction about your comments.'

Now I liked and respected Con. I still do; he is a man of dignity, sincerity and conviction. He was especially good to me around the time of my accident. He regularly called in to see how I was doing; he arranged a personal television for me when I was up in the Orthopaedic hospital; he was even prepared to speak on my behalf in court before the case was settled. That Thursday morning though I told him politely but sternly that I wouldn't be granting his wish. 'Con, I'm sorry but I said what I said. You were at the game on Sunday; you saw what happened. Things went on in that game that as a hurling man I wasn't happy with. I'm not apologising to anyone.'

And after that, the shit really hit the fan. Over the following fortnight, the papers devoted hundreds of column inches to the controversy, including a spate of letters from irate readers. Páirc Uí Chaoimh and my own house in Rochestown were flooded with mail. Not until Loughnane gave that State of the Nation address on Clare FM in 1998 did an interview by a GAA personality provoke such reaction.

Eudie Coughlan's daughter wrote from London to say that I was disrespectful to Cork teams of the past, including the ones her father played for in the twenties and thirties. 'Hurling,' she reminded me, 'did not start in 1985.'

The main thing that rankled though was what I had said about the Tipperary teams of the fifties and sixties. The Tipperary County Board were particularly upset and confirmed they were threatening never to play in Cork again. Now, I knew their secretary, Tommy Barrett, well. Thirteen years earlier we had sat beside each other on the plane to San Francisco on the All-Stars tour and he was the first man to suggest that I would make a great salesman. In 2001, he would congratulate me on becoming the new manager of Waterford. In the aftermath of that Val Dorgan interview though, Tommy couldn't even bring himself to mention my name, referring to me as 'that man'. 'I abhor what he said,' Tommy was quoted as saying. 'There was no Cork player badly hurt.'

John Doyle felt much the same. 'He mustn't have been around when Christy Ring and Josie Hartnett were playing. This season's Munster final was only a tea party compared to the games we played against Cork. How dare he criticise our players. Let him mind his own business and look after his own players. I hope he doesn't have the sanction of the Cork County Board. Otherwise there will be a big reprisal.' Tipperary County Board chairman Michael Lowry confirmed he would also be looking for an apology.

Lowry got what he wanted. The Cork County Board did distance themselves from my comments and did offer an apology; they would

THE FIRST OF THE HIGH KINGS: Coaching Cashel King Cormacs was an absolute privilege. Cormac 'The Viking' Bonnar was one of the main reasons why. (*Irish Examiner*)

The Cork Examiner

ICL

CDS Computing Ltd.

Price 43p (inc. VAT) WEDNESDAY MORNING, JULY 17, 1985 No. 50,954

Tipperary ultimatum to Cork Co. Board

Who Will Guide Cork For Coming Season?

Will McCarthy be dropped?

Evening Echo

Tipp May Never Play In Cork Again

A Cork clean-out

by Jim O'Sullivan

IN AGAIN: Johnny Clifford (right) and new face Donal O'Grady.

NEW SELECTORS: Pat McDonnell (right) and Jimmy Brohan.

CORK EXAMINER SPORTS 4:

Tipp. man says 'Come off it, Mr. McCarthy'

JUSTIN'S PLACE IN JEOPARDY

The McCarthy affair again

McCarthy a rare breed

By DAVID WALSH

If the County Board apologises it will be hypocrisy unless . . .

CONTROVERSY: There was some fall-out following the 1985 Munster final. The media supported me but the county board didn't.

LOOKING AHEAD: Whenever one door has closed, another has opened. There's always another mission.

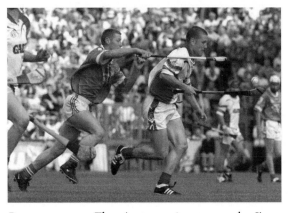

BREAKTHROUGH: There's one main reason why I've taken on the Waterford job. I want to help players like Ken McGrath win something. *(Inpho)*

TOOLS OF THE TRADE: The hurley is everything to me. You can't just say a hurley is 'fine'. All of them need some doctoring.

'I TOLD YE WE'D DO IT!': The Cashel dressing room after winning the 1991 Munster title. Eighteen months earlier, the club had yet to win its first county.

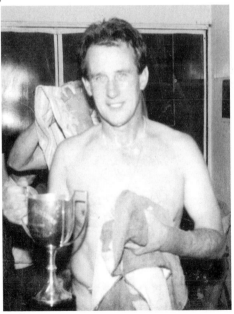

CLOSING TIME: My last game for Passage was the 1991 junior league final. We won it. I was forty-six.

ON THE LINE: Coaching Na Piarsaigh in 2001 with Tony O'Sullivan. (*Irish Examiner*)

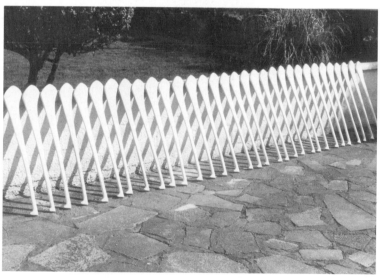

TOUGHENING UP: Hurleys tend to be very fresh when you get them from the hurley-maker. I leave mine out for a few days to weather the timber. Then I reshape them.

FACING THE MUSIC: The Alley should be to the hurler what the driving range is to the golfer. A hurler can't bluff the Alley. The Alley is truth.

STILL HURLING: Some fellas say, 'I stopped playing with the club two years ago. I've retired.' I've played my last game for the club but I haven't retired.

STILL HOOKED: Outside my house in Rochestown, yards from where I posed for that photo heading off to play in the 1963 Munster minor semi-final. A lot has changed in that time but one thing hasn't. I still love this game.

even go so far later in the year as to remove the coach who made those comments. And of course, it made no difference. Tipp didn't renew their home-and-away arrangement with Cork when it expired upon the counties' next clash in 1987, and didn't enter into another until 1990, by which time they had finally won another All-Ireland.

Tipp's reaction was understandable, of course. Before that 1985 Munster final, their county board had come in for stinging criticism from supporters for agreeing to bring their young team to Páirc Uí Chaoimh for such a crucial game. The Tipp board themselves had been split on the matter; the final vote was 18–17 in favour of maintaining the home-and-away arrangement. When Tipp lost, the criticism of the county board executive intensified. Then came my interview with Val Dorgan. A new scapegoat had presented itself.

I will admit one thing. I was wrong in my percentages. That Tipp team of the sixties was the best I've ever seen. To say that 70 per cent of their wins were based on their physical approach and the other 30 could be attributed to their hurling was a hasty, top-of-the-head remark. But the interview was published in a question-and-answer format; Val Dorgan, as was his right, chose not to clean up the quote. And I had no problem with that. Because the thrust of my argument remained valid. As skilled as those Tipp teams of the fifties and sixties were, they were of an era when manhandling was a prerequisite to success. Whether Tipp won or lost, you could be sure that they'd impose themselves physically on you.

The Tipperary County Board also conveniently overlooked the reason why I raised the Hell's Kitchen era in the first place. I did so to put the Tipp tactics of '85 in context. The Tipp management that year would have left no stone unturned to win and in doing so would have asked an obvious question, 'How did we beat Cork in the old days?' And they would have concluded that while there were many factors which contributed to those successes, Hell's Kitchen had been one of them. Years later, Nicky English would point out in his autobiography that there was 'a return to the traditional Tipp style of fire and brimstone' that day. No such candour was forthcoming from his countymen at the time though. Losing another championship game to Cork had wounded them but at least they had the wins of the past. When the Cork coach referred to those past glories in unromantic terms, it was like salt had been poured into those wounds.

I had no agenda against Tipp when talking to Dorgan. I was speaking candidly, a few days after the dust had settled. Tipp's tactics hadn't angered me; if anything, they *helped* me in that they upset Tipp themselves. I was just disappointed as a hurling man with their carry-on. It had been a tremendous, high-scoring game but Tipp's antics deprived it of the classic status it otherwise merited.

The media could see the discourse for what it was. David Walsh, generally considered one of the greatest Irish sportswriters ever, pointed out in the *Sunday Press* that I gave the '85 Tipp team a lot of credit and (correctly) predicted that they would succeed us as the dominant county in Munster. 'One cannot but have admiration for Justin McCarthy,' he wrote. 'For once, a GAA person said things publicly that are generally confined to dark rooms. For once, somebody involved at a high level of activity treated the public with some respect. The public is mostly served with far more diplomacy than honesty. The impression given throughout the interview is of a forthright individual who is not given to small-mindedness. The piece was enlightening, provocative and very readable. And so, three cheers for Justin McCarthy.'

Val Dorgan agreed, saying that no other GAA coach had been so candid in the media before, bar Eugene McGee, himself a journalist.

Kevin Cashman, a long-time observer of hurling, described the piece as 'lucid and pleasantly provocative'. More tellingly, he considered my comments on Tipp's tactics as 'incontestably correct'. 'The so-called "mercilessly hard", "dust flying in the square" games of the early fifties are instanced as vindication of Tipp's recent thuggery,' he wrote in *The Sunday Tribune*. 'The fact is, even if those games were as "hard" (meaning "dirty") as Tipp's apologists and the poor peddlers of nostalgic flummery keep asserting, dirt was as much against the rules then as it is now. But those games, though not notably clean, were not as dirty as the '85 edition. Cork and Tipp men long ago were no better fitted to withstand beating with hurleys than they are now … Cork today are a clean hurling team. Tipp are not. Gibbering on about an illusory past won't change that. Tipp themselves can – if they set about it.'

Cashman wasn't totally enamoured by the interview though. He felt there was 'an objectionable streak of self-advertisement' running through it. He was particularly puzzled by how I could discuss the team's progress without mentioning Johnny Clifford and 'sideline chief' Father O'Brien 'who created most of it'. Now, whether the side progressed from '82 under Johnny is hard to tell but I do know that the side did improve considerably in '84 and '85. And if Kevin had been privy to our training sessions and dressing-room talks, he'd have known that Father O'Brien, for all his previous and later achievements, was merely a selector in '84 and '85, just as I was a selector to Gerald McCarthy in '82. So, if I'm to be totally honest, there *was* a streak of self-advertisement in that interview. There wasn't a lie in it and I used the term 'we' a lot, but I suppose I wanted it known that Cork team was being run my way. Was that 'objectionable'? Well, surely the charade imposed by the county board was immeasurably more objectionable?

For it was a charade. Father O'Brien was joint coach only in name. Now, it has to be said that his commanding, authoritative presence meant he was a good man to have by my shoulder on the line and in the dressing room. I'd discuss the team with him, he'd argue his case well when it came to team selections and he was particularly useful in organising our match-day preparations for the '84 All-Ireland and '85 Munster finals. But not once in those two years did he say, 'Justin, we should try this in training tonight.' We might be down in the Park and he'd say, 'Johnny Crowley is going well tonight, Justin,' and I'd nod, 'You're right there, Father; he is.' And to his credit, Father O'Brien never tried to be anything more than a selector. When it came to a training session on the field or a talk before a big match in the dressing room, he let me do my thing. He was a very good motivator himself long before he famously used Babs's 'You don't win derbies with donkeys' remark to rile Cork in 1990 but I think he recognised that the Cork team of the mid-eighties needed a consistent approach. His hands-off approach suggests that he must have felt his senior inter-county apprenticeship was not complete; that it would be more productive for him at that point to observe and learn.

The joint-coaches façade suited a lot of people though. It suited the county board, they were so desperate to play down my role, they had handed the 'bainisteoir' bib to Noel Collins on All-Ireland final day in Thurles. It did no harm to Father O'Brien, while the players would hardly have been put out by it either; Dermot McCurtain and Tom Cashman especially would have been closer to Father O'Brien than to me through the Blackrock connection. The charade would even have suited John Fenton, who I had a very good coach–player relationship with and would want as a selector if I were Cork coach today. Back then, John was working with a rival oil company to me so he wasn't going to give me an unnecessary competitive advantage. When we were bringing the Liam McCarthy Cup around the county, John would refer to me as one of 'our joint coaches' when he knew I was more than that. Not that it bothered me. I knew it was nothing personal, strictly business.

I could sense some tension at our first training session after the interview. Father O'Brien and the selectors didn't say a word but their body language portrayed a coolness that had never been there before.

I could also tell that some of the players were uneasy that I had spoken openly about their game. Again though my answers to Dorgan stemmed from innocence. I was just having a chat with someone who was asking very good questions; I mean, how many journalists ask you to be critical of your team? I hadn't said anything I hadn't told the players already, I had given those same players a lot of credit and more importantly, I had worked to improve their weaknesses.

If I had to do it again, I would not be so candid in the interview. The timing of it was all wrong. It would have been grand after an All-Ireland but that interview was in July. I don't regret doing it – I learned a long time before this controversy to handle what fate throws at you – but it caused more aggravation than it was worth.

With Tipp threatening not to play in Cork again, the county board would not forget the affair. Within a week or two though it had died amongst the team itself. Training went well in the build-up to the Galway game. The spirit was good, the hurling sharp, the desire to win another All-Ireland very evident. I knew though that Galway would be very hard to beat. Back in March of that year, I was coach to the Munster team which had been lucky to beat Connacht by a point.

To many, that cold, wet, windy day in Thurles is best remembered not as the day we won the Railway Cup but as the day I substituted Nicky English after he had scored two goals. Nicky himself made it clear in his autobiography that he was upset by the decision, saying he couldn't help thinking I was trying to tell him something. I wasn't. English was a player I greatly admired. But we were 1-7 to 0-2 behind at half-time. A few minutes after the break, Galway extended their lead to ten. If we were to have any chance of saving the game, we would have to dig deep. And the reality is Nicky and another favourite player of mine, Tony O'Sullivan, were standing up and letting their men out with the ball. English himself would accept in his book that he felt terribly weak in that match and fell asleep in the car on the way to it. Even when he scored those two goals, I felt his body language wasn't that of a man who could dig deep to ensure we won. Nicky would have been pushing his luck to score a third goal; he just didn't have the zest for it that day. Meanwhile, I had two players on the bench, Johnny Callinan and Bobby Ryan, who were mad for road. So in came Johnny for Tony while Bobby took over from English. Their spirit transmitted itself throughout the field. In the last minute, we went ahead for the first time. We held on. I don't think we'd have won only for the jolt those two players gave us; we were still four points down when Nicky came off. I can understand if he thought it was a bizarre substitution but I'm sure in recent years some of his own players will feel he's made one or two himself. As a coach himself, Nicky will now know you live and die by results. And that day the scoreboard said I got it right.

We just about won though. Galway impressed me. They were a committed, forceful and physical side with a nice mixture of veterans and youngsters. I was also conscious in the lead-up to that All-Ireland semi-final that they had beaten Cork at the same stage in '75 and '79. Everything would have to go right to beat them.

Something went wrong the week before the match. Jimmy Barry-Murphy, who was playing the best hurling of his career, broke his ribs playing football for the Barrs. The following night, Doctor Con said that it was doubtful Jimmy would be able to play. At least now there was no danger of complacency.

It was a miserable wet day, that Sunday in August. Incredibly, conditions were even worse than the last time I had faced Galway. At least the surface in Thurles had been respectable; the Croke Park pitch was an absolute disgrace. The previous month, it had staged a U2 concert; now there were square sods of grass floating above the surface while players were trying to play an All-Ireland semi-final. It didn't help either that the Games Administration Committee had in their wisdom decided to play two games earlier that day on that same pitch. There was no way we could move the ball along the ground and spread the play. What was meant to be primarily a test of skill instead came down to a dogfight.

Only 8,000 people went to the bother of seeing Galway win that dogfight, 4-12 to 5-5. Fenton was outstanding, scoring three goals and two points, but elsewhere, we were beaten. Their half-back line of Peter Finnerty, Tony Keady and Tony Kilkenny were outstanding, while upfront, Joe Cooney gave the nation its first glimpse of a rare talent. In truth, they were that bit hungrier than us although Father O'Brien was right in saying the slow ball suited them more. We brought Jimmy on towards the end but it was an El Cid job. Except this time El Cid's side lost.

A photograph was taken of me when that final whistle sounded. In it, I'm looking out into the distance while putting out a hand of congratulations to the Galway coach, Cyril Farrell. You can tell from my expression that I know the show is over. But then, I always knew the day we lost was the day I'd lose my job. When Ger Canning of RTÉ asked me on the air what was Justin McCarthy's future as Cork coach, I told him it wasn't good. The day that Canning's old colleague, Mícheál O'Hehir, gave his last live commentary proved to be the day Justin McCarthy coached his last championship match with Cork.

When you lose a game like that, most people want to go home and lie low. Ger Cunningham and myself couldn't. We were down to participate in the long-puck competition in the Cooley mountains the following day. An hour after losing that All-Ireland semi-final, the two of us and his younger brother, Brian, were in my car on the way to Dundalk. Even for hurling enthusiasts like us that wasn't easy, driving through the rain, absorbing that defeat, knowing we were hurling again the next day. But then, what could we do?

I got by with a little help from some friends. When I arrived for the competition the following morning, Martin O'Donoghue was already there. Together, we went round the course with its heather and ravines, Martin directing me where to hit the shots. I also availed of some other assistance. I had brought water-repellant spray for my shoes, so when I saw the windy and wet conditions, I sprayed some of the spray on my sliotars to make them lighter. It worked. I came third overall and myself and Dessie Donnelly of Antrim won the team award. Ger won the main competition. Later that evening we headed back to Cork with a massive trophy each. That helped make the 200-mile journey back more bearable than the one we had endured the previous evening.

The Poc Fada may have improved my spirits but not my plight. About ten days later, I got a call at work from Frank Murphy asking me to pop down to Páirc Uí Chaoimh. I said I'd be down after lunch. I was shown into his office and we made some small talk about the game, like how bad the conditions were and how Jimmy had been a massive loss. Then he said, 'What about yourself?'

'Well, Frank, really and truly, we both know that my days are numbered. I think I'll move on.'

'Well, wait,' he said. 'You still have some role to play in Cork hurling.'

But even as he said it, we both knew that role couldn't include being coach of the senior team. So I just replied, 'Ah, Frank, I know where I stand. There are other fields to plough.'

Seconds later, the conversation changed. Frank hadn't called me down to talk about my future with Cork. 'Listen, there's a small problem,' he said. 'This has come down from Croke Park.' And with that, he produced a ten-by-eight-inch envelope, and then, the photograph which had been inside it. There I was, my hair and face dripping wet on the day of the Galway game, in my red adidas raingear. According to some bureaucrat in Croke Park, wearing such gear was contrary to some official ruling; Cork had a case to answer for it.

I was stunned. This was the same Croke Park which, a few months earlier, couldn't fund a trip for its All-Ireland hurling champions and left us to scrounge around from supporters, friends and customers. This was the same Croke Park which was responsible for allowing the second most important match of the year be played on floating sods. Now here they were, asking *me* to answer a case to them. It was the last straw as far as I was concerned.

'Frank,' I said as I reached over to his side of the desk, 'give me that fucking photograph.'

'Steady now, Justin. I'll keep that.'

'Seriously, Frank … I mean, Jesus. This is the lowest of the low. It's bad enough that we lost the game but this … What are they trying to do to me? Is that all they have to be worried about up there, what I wore that day?'

'Well, what is the story?'

'Frank, it was one of the worst days of the year! I bought that raingear three years ago! No one supplied it to me; sure, ye provided us with none. What was I to do? Get fucking soaking wet? That was my own gear I put on.'

'Okay, fair enough, leave it with me. It's just that when something comes down from Croke Park, the county board has to refer to it.'

And in fairness to Frank, he was only doing his job that day. He also accepted my word. The matter died a death.

Another one didn't. There was plenty more speculation about my future over the following two months. Val Dorgan wrote in the *Cork Examiner* that county board delegates were being asked not to re-elect Justin McCarthy as a Cork selector. When another *Examiner* reporter, Tim Ryan, contacted Frank Murphy about the matter, the reply was, 'No comment. Good day to you.' Every day it seemed there was a report about whether I'd be dropped or kept on.

I found it all academic by that stage. There was the night of the failed General Purposes Committee coup, the joint coaches façade, the Tipp controversy, the photograph. I had had enough. I had achieved what I set out to do – to ensure Cork won that Centenary All-Ireland. It would have been great if we had won it all again in '85 because we had an even better team, but it just wasn't to be. When I met Ger Cunningham at a match down in the Park when speculation was at its height, he told me to hang in and stay involved. 'Ger,' I replied, 'it'll be a long time before you see me involved with a Cork team again.'

'Ah, don't say that.'

'Ger, I know where I'm wanted and where I'm not. There are other places where I can enjoy the game.'

And so it proved. The executive were able to persuade the delegates to revert to the old formula of the county champions picking the county senior selectors. Blackrock beat Midleton in the county final. They, predictably, kicked the old committee out and ensured the Big Three all had a selector each. And, of course, Johnny Clifford was brought back in as team coach.

The following September, Cork finally got the opportunity to play Galway on a decent day and decent pitch and won. Credit where credit is due, Johnny delivered.

I was especially pleased that day for Ger Cunningham and Pat Hartnett. I knew how hard they worked for that All-Ireland in '86. Ger and I would often go to the pitch of a local school at lunch-time to work on his game, while Hartnett also regularly called up to get his hurleys fixed or go for a session in the Alley. Eight days before that All-Ireland final, they both came down to the field in Passage. Ger wanted to make sure his eye was in, while Hartnett wanted me to test out his injured shoulder. That same shoulder hit Brendan Lynskey a few times the following Sunday. Pat also asked me to show him how to take a sideline cut. Within an hour, he was hitting some over the bar himself. Hartnett was a player who always wanted to improve. A player I'd like to have worked with more in an official capacity.

But by then, the message had clearly registered. While Frank would like me to have 'some role' in Cork hurling, that could never be coach of the senior team. If I were ever to go for it again, it would end up like it did in '75 and '85.

I'd be hooked.

24

REBEL

Cork is no place for sensitive folk. To succeed you have to have the skin of a rhinoceros, the dissimulation of a crocodile, the quality of a hare, the speed of a hawk. Otherwise, the word for every Corkman is to get out and get out quick.

Sean O'Faolain

It's a scene that has been re-enacted over and over again anywhere in Cork where they talk about hurling.

The topic could be the vacant Cork senior coach's post, or maybe how the team isn't going well, when someone will say, 'Lads, wouldn't Justin be the man for that job?'

And as soon as the suggestion is offered, so is the rebuttal.

'Justin? Sure, Cork couldn't afford Justin!'

And with that, the discussion moves on to the next candidate. The Mercenary Man is dismissed, and with him, the truth.

I'm genuinely not bothered by that kind of talk. For one, it often works to my advantage; opposing teams can be intimidated thinking my team has 'hired Justin'. It is also a form of flattery; money has undoubtedly crept into coaching in the last ten years, so when people hear about some coach on £50 a night, they instantly start thinking, 'Well, can you imagine what Justin McCarthy is on?' Certain people, especially those from the Big Three, cannot be seen to give me credit. They can never say, 'Justin is really good.' They'll say, 'Justin is really expensive.' It's a dig but it's also a compliment because they know the only way someone could be expensive was if they were good. Which is the other reason why such talk doesn't bother me. I realise that it's touted by two kinds of people. Those who don't know the real story, and those who don't *want* to know the real story.

Strange, I can't remember anyone accusing me of going to Antrim in 1970 for the money. The Cork County Board were delighted that I went up there. When they honoured the Cork team that had won that year's All-Ireland at a function, I was a special guest and was congratulated by one and all for 'helping spread the word'. No one objected to me coaching Ballymartle two years later either. They knew that there was little money in the GAA in those days, and what little there was certainly wasn't in Ballymartle.

I haven't changed. I'm still a hurling missionary, not a mercenary, trying to help teams who want help. What changed was that I spread the word in Clare. No Cork County Board officers stood on podiums thanking me for that. After that, my motives were questioned.

I lost money coaching Clare. When I'd clock out early from work to go up to Moloney's, I'd have £15 with me from the Clare County Board for the hire of the car. Often though, all the £15 cars would be taken and I'd have to use a £20 car. That extra five pounds would come out of my own pocket. The only perk I got from coaching Clare was in 1979. That was when there was an oil shortage and everyone was put on a quota of petrol per week. Enda O'Connor was afraid I might have to stop coaching Clare, so he'd fill the car from the petrol storage at his work in Tubber. That way I could still coach Clare without breaking the quota I had been given in Cork.

I didn't make money out of coaching Cashel either. After two years, the committee finally decided we should come to a formal arrangement because I wasn't claiming for expenses and was financially losing out. We agreed on £35 a night. That works out at roughly 25 pence a mile.

I could give a breakdown of all my expenses with every team but I don't see the point. The cynics still won't believe me because they don't want to. Recently someone said, 'Look at Justin going around in that big car. That fella's taking clubs for a ride.' That car is a company car. And when I think of where Tedcastles Oil were when I started out with them in 1978, I know I've earned that car. I'll never be able to repay the GAA enough; so many of my contacts in the oil business came through my GAA connections. But the GAA will never be able to repay me either for the number of teams I've helped.

Mind, I believe the day has come for coaches to get some form of payment. It's fine for the GAA to talk about expenses but expenses for what? We go on about expenses for petrol and meals but what about expenses for expertise? Say your next-door neighbour is a teacher and your son is struggling in maths. If you were to ask your neighbour to help your son, he gladly would as a favour, but you'd still pay him as a form of respect and as a token of his expertise. The GAA should have some guidelines on the matter. Players would much rather have a good coach receiving forty or fifty pounds a night for training them than to have a mediocre one doing it for nothing.

Money is not what is stopping me coaching Cork. The cynics conveniently overlook that I've coached Cork before. And that I would coach my county for free again. But the mercenary myth suits people; otherwise what valid reason have they for freezing me out? I don't know how many times over the years people within and outside the county board have come up to me at matches or on the street and said, 'Justin, you're the man who should be there but sure we all know why you're not.' Yet those same people can't go into the county board and say, 'Listen, don't mind this crap about Justin and whether he's on money or not; we don't know. He's a hurling man and we should be seeing how we can fit him into our plans.' Because if you want to get on in the Cork GAA and keep getting your All-Ireland tickets, you learn to play the Game. You keep your head down. You play dumb. And above all, you don't cross the county board.

Frank Murphy actually was the one man since 1985 to sound me out about whether I was interested in becoming involved with a Cork team again. It was over ten years ago when he enquired would I go forward as an Under-21 selector. When I asked him whether that was a firm offer or merely an invite to put my name forward for nomination, Frank said it was the latter.

'So you're not guaranteeing I'll be a selector,' I said.

'No, the procedure is you put your name forward first.'

I didn't put my name forward. I didn't see why Frank couldn't just have said, 'Justin, there's a job there for you if you want it. We'd love to have you on board.' I haven't been approached to coach any Cork team since. When Frank and myself were seen talking at the 2001 Munster final, people were wondering were we sounding out each other about the vacant Cork coaching job. We just talked about how the heat would affect the players.

Frank and myself have had plenty of civil conversations like that since '85. It would be wrong to think we dislike each other; we don't. Frank can be a charming man and I'd like to think I can be too. It's not an issue of respect either. After I was voted 1966 Player of the Year, he approached me on behalf of Blackrock to join them. Then, shortly before he was appointed full-time secretary to the county board, he wrote a very flattering piece in a GAA magazine about my comeback from injury. I would respect him too. He was a good referee and is an excellent administrator; I've been coaching on the local Cork scene for a long time and my hat goes off to his ability to get so many fixtures run off in time. But Frank likes to be in control. And I don't like to be controlled. I believe everything should revolve around a coach's vision.

Now, if I had played the Game, I could have been in there for life. I wouldn't have said anything about the bumpy pitch in the Farm in '75. I would have invited the county board to the Ursuline Convent in '84 and let Derry Gowen talk for another twenty minutes to the players. I would have apologised to Tipperary for pointing out they used timber in the '85 Munster final. In other words, I could have been someone else other than Justin McCarthy.

I would have a lot of respect for Billy Morgan. Billy did it his way as much as any Cork coach can – and even he found out in 1991 that you make enemies while making champions. Billy ended up surviving that crisis but then, he had a few things working for him that I never could. There wouldn't be as many people lining up to take the Cork football job as there would be for the hurling job; Billy didn't have a Johnny Clifford waiting in the wings. Billy also came from a powerful club. Nemo might be small but it is traditionally powerful. If I had been from one of the Big Three, the Clare factor would have been tolerated. I would have been one of the boys. But I was from Passage. If you're from a smaller club and you don't play the Game, you'll struggle. Bernie O'Connor of Newtownshandrum is finding that out at the moment.

Cork appointed a very good coach to succeed Tom Cashman though. Bertie Óg Murphy came in for unfair criticism as a selector in 2000 when he broke one of the rules of the Game by having his family holiday clash with the All-Ireland semi-final against Offaly. How could anyone doubt his commitment to Cork? The man has coached county vocational schools and Under-21 teams to All-Ireland titles. Thankfully, you can't keep a good man down forever. He knows the game and what's more, he's a good hurling man. He comes from a well-respected club, Sarsfields, where they play in the spirit of the game. He also comes from a great hurling family; Bertie Senior was a selector with Cork in the fifties and was a lovely man. Bertie Óg's brother, Tadhgie, is another great GAA man who I get on well with. I have nothing but respect for Bertie Óg. He was a pleasure to coach; he'd often come up to the Alley with Ger Cunningham for some extra coaching. I sincerely hope he gets a proper chance to do the job.

Cork hurling isn't just about the senior coach's job though. I think as a county we're not fulfilling our potential. The county board is like the government. It can say, 'We're doing this, we're doing that; what's your argument?' But you can just as easily say back to them, 'Yeah, but look what's happening on the ground. You could be doing so much more.' In a strong dual county like Cork, there'll nearly always be at least one captain holding an All-Ireland title for the cover of the Cork GAA Yearbook. The county board can point to that and say, 'We did it again, boy.' But I'm thinking of the titles we haven't won. I'm talking about the whole scene. It has gone stale. Apathy has set in. Good, decent men are going through the motions. The whole thing needs to be freshened up with new faces and new ideas.

Compare us to Kilkenny. In 2000, they didn't win the Leinster minor title for the first time in ten years. Their response to that defeat was to write to forty former county players asking them to get involved in a coaching programme. Twenty-eight of the players wrote back to say they'd help out. Then they divided the county into different areas and assigned different fellas to different age groups.

In Cork, we have no one to think like that. You go into the Park and fellas are looking at you sideways, as if to say, 'What are you doing here?' If we were hell-bent on developing our games, we'd have someone saying, 'Right, I want an elite group of people here who can fashion the future of Cork hurling and football with their ideas and enthusiasm.' Then when we'd have those people on board, we'd say, 'Lads, it's great to have ye. Enjoy it, good luck and thanks again.'

They should be going on their knees to Billy Morgan asking him to set up some football school of excellence. They should be asking Gerald or Jimmy to be a director of hurling and co-ordinate the overall hurling coaching structure in Cork. People are afraid to give power to a man in a tracksuit, yet they have no problem giving power to a man in a suit. Why not give Gerald and Morgan the benefit of the doubt? This is about expertise, not power. I'm the regional manager of a company with a multimillion pound annual turnover and if there's one thing I know, it's that people are your greatest resource.

Every Saturday morning, there should be coaching sessions in Páirc Uí Rinn for underage development squads. We should have Charlie McCarthy and Jimmy going up there a few times a year showing young fellas different shots to use in tight situations. We should have Fenton putting on clinics on how to take a sideline ball. At the moment though, we don't even have coaching seminars. I'm glad to see so many clubs around the county putting up alleys but an alley is only as good as you allow it to be. Surely the county board could say, 'Look, whatever else you say about Justin, he's some operator in an alley. Let's ask him to give a clinic for our coaches.' But in Cork, we can't do that. That would be putting a fella on a pedestal. The only time the county board have been onto me in recent years was to thank me for an article I wrote in the *Irish Examiner* agreeing with their stance on not allowing other sports to be played in Croke Park. They'd never get in touch with me to show players and coaches how to fix hurleys properly.

I love Cork. I love watching the sun going down on that city; I love heading down to west Cork and taking photographs for the day; I love its people. I also love Cork hurling, its tradition, the brilliant players it has produced and its men of the quiet fields. But I hate its GAA politics. That's why I'm glad to be going to Waterford and getting away from the local scene, just as it was refreshing to coach Antrim, Clare and Cashel. I've never felt, 'I should have been let do a Mick O'Dwyer and win loads of All-Irelands coaching Cork.' Nor did I feel at any stage, 'Here I am coaching a club when I should be coaching Cork.' Hurling is still hurling wherever you coach it. I coached Cork to one of the most prestigious All-Irelands ever but guiding Ballygarvan to the 1977 South East Cork junior championship was probably a greater achievement. We put people in boxes. We see a fella walking down the street and say, 'He was some man; he has four All-Ireland medals.' But I might know the fella walking behind him and I'll say, 'Hey, that man there won two South East titles with Tracton. He was a great man too.'

I've been lucky. I got to coach Cork for three summers. I've had the big days in Croke Park, the Limerick Gaelic Grounds and Thurles. I've also seen the bonfires in Ballygarvan and Ballymartle and Ballycastle. The fellas up in the Barrs and the Glen mightn't see that as proper hurling but they don't know what they're missing. Denis Coughlan was one Glen man who broadened his horizons and coached Father O'Neill's to an East Cork junior title. I met him afterwards and he said he couldn't get over how much the game meant to the people there. This game is for everybody. But it's difficult for small clubs to make it on their own. They're crying out for some advice, direction and motivation and I feel I can give it to them. In the GAA we have this notion that you must serve only one club and one county. That's fine for a lot of people but I don't think everyone should have to conform to it. I find it strange that it's only players and coaches who get a hard time if they deviate from the norm. Few people ever say to an administrator, 'Hey, why aren't you back helping your club?' That administrator can quite rightly say that the road he has taken is how he can best serve the GAA. Well, I'm serving hurling best by spreading the word to those who want to hear the word. After Cork kicked me out in '75, it would have been a disservice to hurling if I had said to Father Harry Bohan, 'Sorry, I can't help you. I can't coach another county but Cork.'

You can stay in a place for only so long of course, but that doesn't mean you're a quick fix. You can create a legacy. I always say, 'Lads, I'm only passing through. I'm just hoping what I know and how I feel about this game will inspire you.' Coaching should be about spreading ideas. I learned so much in Gormanston College from men like Father Maher, Donie Nealon, Ned Power, Des Ferguson and Sean Hanley, and I've always felt I should be passing on ideas to others. It's up to the clubs and counties themselves then to build on the ideas you've helped put in place. I found it ironic to hear some Cork people talking about how delighted they were when Clare won the All-Ireland in '95. Those same people were saying years earlier that I was a disgrace coaching Clare! By coaching Clare, I was coaching Loughnane. I'm not claiming I made him but at least I was a model he could look at and say, 'I remember Justin doing that; I must do that too. He did this too though; I'm not sure if I will.'

Unfortunately, I can't be everywhere all the time. That means helping out might only be giving a talk or a coaching session for a day. I remember going down to a place called Kealkil, near Bantry in west Cork, in 1972 where a Father McCarthy had started a juvenile club called St Colum's. There was little tradition of hurling there and their field was close to the woods. One day Father McCarthy had them pulling in pairs when two young fellas dropped their hurleys and ran; the sound of the clash of the ash coming back off the woods sounded more like a peal of thunder to them. But in their naivety was enthusiasm and we had a wonderful day. Later that year for my wedding the club gave me a mantel clock. Ten years later I was down there again to give an all-day coaching course to a vibrant club.

I've given talks and coaching courses to plenty of other teams. Aghada and Castlelyons in east Cork. Clarecastle, Wolfe Tones, Scariff, Tulla and Ruan in Clare. Ballybrown in Limerick. O'Donovan Rossa and Dunloy in Antrim. And Thurles Sarsfields in Tipp. That was some honour, talking to the same club that produced Jimmy Doyle.

Some teams I've been able to help out on a more constant basis. I've coached Na Piarsaigh several times over the years. I've coached Blarney to a Mid Cork title. I took Castlemartyr for a few sessions on their way to an East Cork final. I coached Carbery, the west Cork divisional team, for a season. I helped Kilworth on their way to a North Cork final. I coached Tracton and Carrigaline in the South East division for a few seasons. In all, I've coached sixteen different club or divisional teams in Cork at one stage or another. Even a cynic would have to admit that you need to be an enthusiast to do all that.

One of my most enjoyable coaching jobs was with Ballincollig in the late nineties. They were a superbly organised hurling club based a few miles to the west of Cork city but were struggling to get to the next level. I knew Frank Daly, one of their mentors, from coaching him with a Cork underage team back in the seventies and so I agreed to help them out. We were beaten in the second round of the 1998 county intermediate championship but the following year we reached the final, when we played Mid Cork rivals Blarney. The Thursday before the match, we had a team meeting in the clubroom. Along one of its walls, there were a series of framed photographs but there was one noticeable gap. I pointed to it and I said, 'Lads, I want that gap filled by this team.' Today, it is. Páirc Uí Chaoimh hardly had a blade of grass on it on that dreadfully wet November day but we managed to come from two goals behind early in the second half to win by two points in front of 7,000 people. There were incredible scenes afterwards, scenes which brought back memories of nights in Ballymartle and Ballygarvan over twenty years earlier.

But like Ballymartle and Ballygarvan, there was more to Ballincollig than winning and bringing back the cup. I saw Jeff O'Connell, Podsie O'Mahony and the Beale brothers score goals doubling on the ball first time, shots many inter-county coaches have not had the privilege of seeing their players do. And the people there, from mentors like Dan Murphy, Jack Sexton and Frank Daly, to the ladies' committee, were so helpful. Their path had a heart, so they will forever be in a piece of my heart.

Looking back, Ballincollig was a lot like the Cashel mission.

But not quite.

There will never be another Cashel.

25

WHEN WE WERE HIGH KINGS

There came a McCarthy, high clan of the Rock;
They were scattered by warfare, took refuge in Cork.
We sought one of their number, they gave us the best:
He guided our stalwarts with skill and with zest.
Father Bernie Moloney, 'The Kings from The Rock,' 1991

It began like the other missions, with a plea from the heart. A Seamus King phoned in the early spring of 1990 saying he was chairman of Cashel King Cormacs. They wanted me to be their coach or to at least go up and give a talk. I said no. I had heard of Seamus from his work as a GAA historian and knew of the club from the Bonnar brothers playing for Tipperary, but I told him I couldn't help out because of the travel and time. Seamus though was persistent. The following week he called again. Would I at least give them that talk?

I relented. First though Seamus would have to send me a CV of every player. I wanted to know what they had done, what positions they played, whether they were shoving on or just breaking on. I needed to know I was talking to.

A week later, an envelope came through the door. Its contents made impressive reading. Virtually the whole team had represented Tipperary at underage. When Seamus called back, I asked was he sure they needed me. 'By God, we do,' he said. 'We're not getting it out of them.'

They weren't. The club had never won a senior county title. It had been fifty years since it had contested a county final. For all its underage success in the seventies, it had won only two senior West division titles in the eighties. It had started to win minor titles again and had some talented players like Raymie Ryan coming through, but six of the regular starting fifteen were over thirty-two. Only four of the starters were in that crucial 22–30 age group, a staggering statistic for a club team. If the club was ever to win something, it would have to be soon.

On the first Friday of April, I walked in the door of the Rock Club at quarter to eight. Twenty-five senior players and seven other clubmen were in the room. I didn't stop talking until half-ten. Cormac Bonnar would later say that he never heard a man speak so much sense for so long. Tommy Grogan felt the wonder of it was that I never repeated myself. But then, there was a lot to be said.

I made a particular appeal to the older players to stay on. I reminded them that they hadn't lost their ability and that while they weren't as fast as they once were, their anticipation and maturity were at their peak. If the club was to win anything, it would be with players like them staying on and showing leadership in the close, nitty-gritty games.

I also tried to sell a point to Cormac, Colm and Conal Bonnar. I told them that when you have your name made at inter-county level, subconsciously you tend to take shortcuts with the club. I reminded them that when the county wouldn't want them any more the club still would, but by then they could regret not doing more for it when they were in their prime. There was no reason why they shouldn't be able to take club *and* county on board, starting from 1990.

Then I asked why hadn't Cashel achieved more. I soon found that they weren't ambitious enough. When I asked what would they like to win, the answer was, 'Christ, it'd be great to win the West [division] this year.'

I said, 'Lads, winning the West Tipperary title means nothing to me. If I was your coach, I'd want to be going around the Rock of Cashel with a cup after a county final. But you have to be looking for it yourselves. History shouldn't be a deterrent. I'm a member of the McCarthy clan. So was Cormac who ruled that Rock up there. We have a family motto, "Nothing is impossible to the faithful and the brave." There's enough talent in this room to win that Dan Breen Cup. It's a question of whether there's enough commitment and ambition, whether you are faithful and brave.'

When I finished, Cormac Bonnar stood up to thank me for my 'inspiring words'. Later lads told me they wanted to hurl there and then. My own adrenalin was racing too. Minutes after leaving the Rock Club, a garda flash-lamp was shining at me as I drove past Rockwell College. I pulled over. The officer ran across the road.

'Do you realise you were doing 93 miles an hour?' he asked in astonishment.

I couldn't believe it. I had a nice car and it was a nice night but there was no way I would chance driving that fast.

'Look,' I pleaded, 'I'm sorry. It's just that I was giving a talk to this hurling team up in Cashel, I was speaking for nearly three hours, my head was spinning ...'

'What's your name?'

'Justin McCarthy.'

'Justin McCarthy?' He looked at me closely. He recognised the face. 'And you're saying you were talking to Cashel?'

'I was.'

'Go pull the other one, will ya! I'm sure you were in Tipperary telling them how to play hurling!'

He took my details and said I'd be hearing from him.

A few days later I called Seamus King to tell him about it. He said he didn't want to talk about that. 'Listen, the reaction to your talk was unbelievable. Will you come and coach us? Will you at least consider it?'

I did consider it. I thought back to that night in the Rock Club and the enthusiasm that came from the floor. The potential in Cashel was big. So was the challenge. I called Seamus to say I'd go up and coach them once a week. He said that was great. So was the bit of news he had for me. The word was that there would be no summons. There wasn't either.

Later that week I went up for our first training session. Straight away I knew Cashel and myself were compatible. The first thing that impressed me was the field. It wasn't a GAA pitch; it was a *hurling* pitch with its grass cut beautifully. They had the nets up and plenty of sliotars. That showed they cared. Right then, I knew I'd be coming up to Cashel more than once a week. Just as I was walking off the field exhilarated after that first session though, an old-timer who had been watching had a few words.

'I don't envy you your job,' he said.

'Why's that?'

'I've been watching those fellas since they were kids. I've seen them when they were in their prime. They'll break your heart. You won't be able to keep them out of the pub. Most of them are too old. I'm telling you now, you're wasting your time with them.'

I smiled all the way home, thinking how those words would motivate me. A month later in Cappawhite, I wasn't smiling. It was half-time in the first round of the West Tipperary championship and we were three points down to a combination of junior clubs who had Nicky English among their ranks. When the whistle went, I walked straight for the dressing room, passing some of the players on the way. When they were all in, I sat them down. 'Right, I want every fella in here to listen closely to what I have to say,' I said, calmly but sternly. 'For the past five weeks, I've been driving 130 miles two nights a week to train ye; I've spent hours fixing your hurleys. And for what? For ye to hurl like that? For ye to go through the motions? Are ye taking me for a ride? Have ye been listening to anything I've been saying this past five weeks? Because I'll tell you something. Unless there's a massive fucking improvement in this second half, you won't be hearing much from Justin McCarthy again.' We won pulling up. Two months later we won the West divisional final, beating defending county champions Clonoulty–Rossmore with their county stars Declan Ryan, John Kennedy and Joe Hayes. By October, we were in our first county final in fifty years.

The team had improved beyond all recognition. Every aspect of their hurling was better from the sessions. That all stemmed from their spirit and attitude. In the past, attending training had been governed by whim; now they all wanted to be there. The older lads were especially enthusiastic. When I took over, I had told them that they'd really enjoy it; now they could experience it for themselves. Joe Minogue, our lion-hearted 33-year-old left corner back, was having a new lease of life. In front of him was 32-year-old Tony Slattery, who hadn't enjoyed his hurling so much since he won minor and Under-21 All-Irelands with Tipp. At centre back, 33-year-old Pat Fitzell was playing as well as he had in his prime with the county senior team. Then there were the Grogans, John and Tommy. They were both over thirty-two but they could see that didn't stop them being fantastic strikers of the ball. Meanwhile, Raymie looked as if he'd be joining the Bonnars on the senior county panel. I was also getting great assistance from my selectors, John Dermody, Aengus Ryan and especially Brendan Bonnar, brother to the three inter-county stars. The whole thing was coming together.

Getting to a county final and winning one though were two different things. Our opponents were Holycross–Ballycahill. It was a real clash of opposites. Holycross was home to John Doyle, they had three county titles to their name and were from the traditional stronghold of Tipp hurling, the Mid division; Cashel had no such tradition. Holycross were from the country; Cashel, while only nine miles away, was a town. Historically Holycross would be seen as hardy and serious when it came to hurling; Cashel, as a party town with soft and casual hurlers.

There was another ironic dimension to the match. Former Tipp star Paddy Kenny was coach to Holycross. When I was a kid, my brother Barry and I would often go, 'And it's Paddy Kenny with the ball!' But to Paddy, I would have been the fella who insulted past Tipp teams in that interview; his brother Sean, captain of the 1950 All-Ireland winning team, had a letter in the *Cork Examiner* objecting to my comments. Paddy looked at me when we crossed the field that day in Thurles. It was as if he was saying, 'So you're McCarthy from Cork. Well, we'll show you how we win county titles up here.' And Holycross did give us a lesson on that desperate wet day. They won by only three points but ultimately they were way tougher and cuter than us.

After the match, the team landed back in Grant's Castle Hotel. Everyone was wearing long faces. A cavalcade around the Rock and the town had been planned; now the truck was outside, redundant. I saw it as the perfect opportunity to make a point though. While they were feeling sorry for themselves at that moment, that pain would subside. Over the winter they might start to look back at '90 as a great year, the year they got to a county final. The older players could retire feeling they had given it one last glorious blast. They needed something to tattoo that feeling of being so close and yet so far. So I said to them, 'Lads, outside.'

'Why?' one of them asked.

'We're getting on top of that truck and we're going around Cashel in it.'

'Justin, what are you at? It's a bad night. We've lost.'

'Come on. We're going onto that truck.'

I walked out. They reluctantly followed. When we got outside, I jumped onto the truck and started pulling fellas onto it. I told the driver to go the route we were supposed to go. So out we went around the Rock and the town in the wind and the rain. There were no bonfires, no flags, no singing, no cheering; just some polite clapping from some bemused locals.

As we were arriving back at the hotel, I spoke up. 'Lads, can you imagine what that trip would have been like if we had a cup with us? But fellas, the cup is with Declan Carr in Holycross tonight. Don't ever forget how empty this felt.'

I paused. They all looked even more dejected than they had been inside the hotel. I raised my voice again.

'Now if you think I'm going to be remembered as a loser in this town, you're mistaken. I want to be here next year on this truck with the Dan Breen Cup. Everyone here is to redouble his efforts to make sure that becomes a reality. Because otherwise, lads, tonight will stay with you forever.'

Not one player from that 1990 panel retired.

We freshened things up for '91. The previous year I had often passed Rockwell College and its wide open pitches and wondered what it would be like to have a few pucks in there. Seamus King, a teacher at the college, was able to arrange for us to train there a few times a month. It worked a treat. Having several pitches together gave me great scope in devising sessions, while having to tog off underneath the trees gave the lads great scope for some crack.

We also decided that we'd have team meetings before championship matches up in the Cashel Palace Hotel. When we touted the idea, the lads laughed; the Cashel Palace to them was the preserve of Vincent O'Brien and other rich folk. But Brendan Bonnar reminded them that they were as good as anyone. We had plenty of productive team meetings and banter there.

We also felt the team would benefit from getting out of Tipperary and broadening its horizons. We played in the All-Ireland Elevens in Carlow, winning the plate competition after we had been beaten in the first round proper. We also played Clarecastle of Clare in Cratloe, my old team, Na Piarsaigh, in Cork, and Willie and Eddie O'Connor's club, Glenmore. Probably the most important trip though was a weekend away in west Clare a month before the start of the championship. Looking back, it was to Cashel in '91 what Wembley was to Cork in '66.

We booked into a Lisdoonvarna hotel on the Friday night. Most of the fellas hit the pubs before arriving back at midnight where we all enjoyed a session, listening to the Slatterys playing on the accordion. When I looked out the window the following morning though, it seemed that session was going to be the climax of the weekend. Outside it was foggy, windy and wet; you couldn't see your hand in that weather, let alone puck around on the beach and go for a run in the sand dunes. How were twenty-five grown men going to kill time in a desolate spot like this? When the selectors called in, asking what the programme was, I told them I hadn't a clue. We decided that after breakfast the players should go away and pick a captain while I made some phone calls.

The first call was to St Flannan's College to find out if their ball alleys were open. They were. My next task was to get some racquetballs. I phoned Tommy O'Donnell, who had been the sub goalkeeper to Durack when I had coached Clare. Tommy ran a sportshop in Ennis. He had no racquetballs but would be able to get me some. A few hours in the ball alley wouldn't be enough though. I rang the swimming pool in Ennis. The girl said it was booked out. I pleaded, telling her of my predicament and that I had trained Clare when she was just a kid. 'Okay,' she laughed, 'if you're here at two o'clock we'll let you in.' By the time the lads had come back with Colm Bonnar as their captain, we let them in on the programme. As far as they knew, Plan B was Plan A.

The two hours in Flannan's went well. There were six alleys, so everyone got to hit plenty of shots. First we had a two-versus-two competition. Then we had an individual tournament in which Tommy Grogan and myself made it through to the final. That was the toughest game I've had in an alley. Tommy was a fierce competitor with a hard and accurate shot; next to Fenton, I don't know if I've coached a better free-taker. He also had the crowd with him. Tommy was very popular with the other lads. What's more, he wasn't from Cork. When the game started, so did the slagging and shouting. 'Come on Tipp! Tipp! Tipp! Tipp!' Tommy was inspired by it and went 17–12 up, needing only four more points to win. Then it hit me. This had become a mini-Munster final; the alley in Flannan's, a mini-Semple Stadium. I said to myself, 'You're playing for Cork here, boy! We're not having that Tipp shower singing "Slievenamon".' I clawed it back to 17–16. Tommy dug deep again and soon it was 19–16. I levelled it at 20 all. Then I went 21–20 ahead. The lads watching on couldn't believe it. The shouting grew even louder. 'Come on Tommy!' 'Come on Tipp!' A gasping Tommy scored the next point to level it at 21 all. The shouting grew even louder. But that was all he had. I had little more but enough to win 23–21. When we got to the swimming pool, the others swam and splashed around. Tommy and myself just leaned against the back wall, absolutely exhausted.

By the time we got back to the hotel, the other lads were also spent and immediately went to bed. The most important part of the trip was still in store though. I had arranged a match against Kilmaley at eight o'clock that evening in Ruan. The weekend was about showing as well as developing character. The match would be a test of that character.

At half-time, they were failing it. I knew they were tired but if they were to become Tipperary county champions, they'd have to overcome bigger obstacles than this. At half-time, I laid it on the line. 'This weekend is a disaster if we don't win this match. In fact, the whole season will be. There's my car parked over on that bank. If we lose, I'm getting into that car and driving back to Cork and it'll be the last you'll see of me. If you want it that way, that's fine by me. I won't even think of Cashel on the way home.' They all stood looking at each other, absolutely stunned. They were three points down when I offered that ultimatum. They won by ten. Later that night, some of the wives and girlfriends came up. An even better session was had that night. They had picked a captain, had the crack in the alley and the pool, and had won the match. They had passed the test.

There were other tests for them that year. One Sunday morning it rained so hard, the car in front of me skidded along a surface of water outside Cahir and went across the road. By the time I got to Cashel, it was five to eleven. The players were huddled up in the dressing room, still in their civvies, waiting for me to give the word to go home. I walked past them, made my way to my usual spot in the corner and started togging off. One of the lads asked in amazement, 'Are we going out?' I said, 'Well, lads, I'm going out. I'm not afraid of the rain.' We were out on that pitch for ten past eleven. We didn't come off it until quarter to two. It was one of our best sessions ever.

That resolve was reflected on the field. Again we won the West and again we qualified for the county final, beating Toomevara, 2-10 to 0-13, in a stirring semi-final.

Again though we'd have to play Holycross in the final.

I needed a further sign that we were ready for that test. When we finished our training session the Sunday before the match, a few lads shouted on their way out, 'Right, see you on Tuesday night, Justin.'

'No,' I said, 'we'll go at two o'clock on Tuesday.'

They stopped in their tracks. After a few seconds, one of them offered up the obvious. 'Two o'clock? Sure, we'll all be working!'

'Lads, I'll be working too but I'm getting time off.'

Other lads chipped in, saying they'd be in Dublin, Waterford, Clonmel. I wasn't listening. 'Lads, we need that session in daylight. I want every fella to be there.'

It was bitterly cold that Tuesday. Tipperary's All-Ireland success that year had held up the county championship, so the final had run into November. When I arrived at that field at twenty to two, I looked across and saw snow on the top of the Galtee mountains. Then the cars started to arrive. Conal Bonnar had made it back from college in Dublin. Tony Slattery and Cormac Bonnar had been able to get away from teaching in school. Joe Minogue had been able to swap his shift as a psychiatric nurse. Michael Purdue had managed to persuade the boss at his new job in the bank to give him the time off. By two o'clock, every player was there. That told me what I wanted to know. This team would do anything to win a county.

If we were going to beat Holycross though, we would need more steel in our play. I thought our lads had stood back against Holycross the previous year. I told our lads that Holycross would try to intimidate them in the opening minutes. I repeated the words Cork heard before the 1985 Munster final: 'Don't start a fight but don't walk away from one either.' The game was ten minutes old when there was a mêlée. When it was over, our lads realised that they had stood up to Holycross. It was to be a key moment.

There were others. At half-time we were three points down after playing against the wind. A few seconds after the restart, Tommy Grogan pointed a free. Then Conal Bonnar scored with a long-range effort to bring us within a point. Then with fourteen minutes to go, Jamesie O'Donoghue set Tommy up for a goal. We never looked back after that. All that character, all that hurling and bonding that had been developed in Carlow, Lisdoonvarna, Rockwell and on those wet, cold days in Cashel was reflected on the field. Pat Fitzell, Conal and Raymie were totally dominant in the half-back line, Willie Fitzell and Colm were going just as well at midfield; in truth, it was a wonder Holycross were still in the game. With five minutes to go though they were killed off. Cormac Bonnar won a ball out on the forty and scorched past two defenders before sending a driving shot to the net. That was that. Just to be sure, Jamesie O'Donoghue made it 2-8 to 1-5. Then a whistle went. And a town went absolutely mad.

It stayed that way for the whole night; the party just transferred from Thurles to Cashel. It was lashing rain yet the town was packed; there must have been 3,000 people there. This time, the lads needed no help getting onto the truck. But then, this time they had a cup. We went around the Rock and the town. This time there were flags, buntings and bonfires burning in the distance. And everywhere there were happy faces. The club president, Mick the Thistle, was invited up on the podium. Mick by now was in his eighties and had been unable to attend the match but nothing was going to stop him making the reception. In previous years, Mick had written out his speeches and given them out to younger men to read out. That night, Mick stood up and spoke for himself and sat down to a standing ovation. A few weeks later, a visiting *Sunday Tribune* reporter would hear an emotional supporter tell some of the lads, 'There was fellas on tablets that aren't on them any more because of ye.'

The good news even spread to America. A few minutes after I had addressed the thousands on the podium, I was told there was a phone call for me in Grant's Hotel. It was my brother Barry. He hadn't even called the night of the 1984 All-Ireland.

I was determined that there would be more cause for celebration. That night at dinner I told the players that we should go all out to win the Munster club title to prove we were a real top team. We were back training on the Tuesday night. Five days later, we gave an exhibition in beating Clarecastle 3-11 to 2-4 in atrocious conditions in Cusack Park.

Our opposition in the Munster club final were much more formidable though. Midleton boasted three players – Kevin Hennessy, Ger Fitzgerald and David Quirke – who had featured in the previous year's All-Ireland final, while Pat Hartnett and Denis Mulcahy would win another Munster medal with Cork in 1992. And then they had John Fenton, who had remained arguably the best club free-taker in the country.

This game would be much bigger than a clash between Cashel and Midleton. Earlier in the year, Tipp and Cork had produced two exhilarating but controversial matches in the Munster championship. Cork were sore about how Jim Cashman had sustained a hand injury. Tipp folk, meanwhile, felt that Cork had been fortunate to win the 1990 All-Ireland. Whoever won between Cashel and Midleton would strengthen their county's case.

A few days before the match, I happened to catch John Fenton being interviewed on local radio. When the reporter mentioned that I was coaching Cashel, John shot back that I didn't have a good record against Midleton and that my record wouldn't improve the following Sunday. I thought it was a tenuous argument; I remember a Na Piarsaigh team of mine losing to Midleton in the early eighties but that was about it. When the team met at the Firgrove Hotel before the game I raised the subject of Fenton's comments. 'Lads,' I said, 'today's game is for me. The county final was your day; this is mine. Remember, when this game is over, I have to head back to Cork.' I also reminded them that they were all playing for Tipperary in a Munster final, an opportunity most of them thought they would never be presented with again. For the Bonnars, it was the opportunity to complete the perfect year. This game had to be won.

There was wicked tension in Mitchelstown that Sunday in December; other than the 1978 Munster final, I've never experienced anything like it. People who had never been at a hurling match before were at it; in all, 9,000 people crammed into the venue. And just like Thurles '78, that tension carried onto the field. When I ran onto the pitch after one of our players went down injured, Sean O'Brien, who had been a fringe player with Cork in '84, passed a comment saying I should get back off it. I quipped back that if he had been a better player, he'd have seen more of the pitch with me and with Cork. Sean actually had a very good game that day but deep into injury time, he and Cormac Bonnar were sent off. Both were unlucky to be the ones dismissed, but it was inevitable someone would march. The final score of 0-9 to 0-6 tells you how tense and scrappy it was.

It was also riveting and glorious and sweet. Our backs were outstanding, while Colm Bonnar was even better at midfield. Midleton had no qualms. The first man to congratulate me was their coach and my old friend, Paddy Fitzgerald. The following month, Fenton and myself talked away like long-lost friends when I was honoured at the Jury's Cork Sport Star of the Month awards. But, no, I didn't ask him, 'By the way, John, what was that you were saying on the radio?'

The All-Ireland series turned out to be another adventure. Our opponents in the semi-final were Kiltormer, who had Galway stars Conor Hayes, Justin Campbell and the Kilkenny brothers, Ollie and Tony, among their ranks. Cashel and I had our first and only dispute in the lead-up to that game. The club had been given the choice of where to play the game. The committee felt they owed it to the local community to play the game in Cashel. I wanted the game in Semple Stadium because our style of play was more suited to the open spaces and good fast sod of Thurles than the tight confines of Leahy Park. The committee eventually rejected my recommendation. Twenty minutes into the game, Kiltormer were 1-6 to 0-1 ahead. It was then we brought Cormac Bonnar from full forward to centre forward in a direct switch with T.J. Connolly. Within minutes, T.J. had set up Jamesie O'Donoghue for a goal. Then just before half-time, T.J. soloed through to score a goal himself. The game finished 2-7 to 1-10 in what the *Cork Examiner* described as 'unquestionably one of the greatest games in the history of the club championship'.

There was now a danger that the players might feel we had blown our chance. One interested spectator, Brendan Lynskey, said as much to me when I met him in Grant's Hotel after the match. 'Your record against Galway isn't great either,' he added. The putdown was unmistakable but it helped trigger a fact I might otherwise have overlooked. Before I headed to Cork, I gathered the players in the hotel lobby. 'Listen, we're heading for Ballinasloe next week. Now, I don't want anyone believing this lion's den shit. I've never lost a match in Ballinasloe. I'm not losing there next week either. We're going up to win.'

We *were* entering the lion's den though. Relations between Tipp and Galway were even frostier than they were between Tipp and Cork. When we got off the team bus, a few home supporters greeted us with anti-Tipp jeers. By the throw-in, 10,000 people were in the ground. Another gripping encounter ensued. At the end of normal time, the sides were level. It was the same at the end of extra time: Cashel 2-11, Kiltormer 1-14.

It was now mid-March. The GAA needed some hurling match to precede the club football final on St Patrick's Day. And so the third game was set for Croke Park. It was the least both sides deserved. The hurling world was now gripped by the trilogy; Barry made his way back for it. That third game was as intense as the first two. With twelve minutes to go, we were holding on to a one-point lead. Then Colm Bonnar got a bad blow on the hand. He fell to the ground in writhing pain and looked at his finger which was all cut up. The referee, Dickie Murphy, picked Colm up by the collar. I ran onto the pitch, shouting, 'For Christ's sake, Dickie, can't you see the man is injured?' Dickie smiled and waved me away. Colm ended up having to go off and get a pin put through that dislocated finger.

Colm's absence in those closing minutes was critical. So was another decision. With four minutes to go and the sides level, John Grogan drew hard on a ground ball, sending it to a promising space towards the right corner of the field. Dickie adjudged that John had drawn on Tony Kilkenny's shin first, when he hadn't. Kiltormer scored a goal seconds after the resultant free. It was the last score of the game. Kiltormer clung on to win 2-8 to 1-8.

It proved to be the real All-Ireland final; Kiltormer, to their credit, had enough in the tank to beat Birr 0-15 to 1-8 the following week. It was rough for us, being that close yet that far, but there was no shame in losing to such a dogged, strong team. How many people two years earlier would have foreseen Cashel being one of the top two club teams in the country? Or that Cashel would win the junior, Under-21 and senior county titles in the one year? Croke Park had been a journey, not a destination, and for the people of Cashel, it had been the ride of their lives.

It had also been one of the best of mine. I didn't want to get off. I stayed on as Cashel coach for another four and a half years. In that time, we won another three Wests, three All-Ireland Elevens titles, reached four county semi-finals and contested the 1994 county final. Dan Breen though never got another trip around the Rock. But I have no regrets about staying on. I enjoyed my last two years there as much as my first two. I was at home in Cashel. Every other place I coached, I'd remind them I was passing through but with Cashel, I'd point to the Rock and say, 'Hey, don't forget, I'm not a stranger. My forefathers were here long before any of ye! That's our Rock up there! This is just a case of coming home.'

That's the way Cashel saw it too. A few weeks after the county final when we were honoured with a civic reception thrown by the urban district council, I was presented with a special plaque. The best of the lot though came at the club's annual dinner dance when I was bestowed the title of being the club's first honorary life president. I value that scroll more than my 1966 Caltex Award. For a Corkman to be so honoured by a Tipperary club is the ultimate in my book.

Family counted for a lot in Cashel. Be it a challenge match or a county final, there would always be a strong contingent of loved ones. It was the same at training; in the build-up to the county and Munster finals in 1991, a dozen or so onlookers would clap us off the field every night. Pearse Bonnar, God rest his soul, must have been at every session, making sure we had enough water. Pearse was a character; even his own children called him Pearse. He had another son, Ailbe, who was a very good club player but not quite up to the standard of Conal, Cormac and Colm. One night we had a league game and the three lads were training with Tipp. When we arrived at the field, one of the other team's supporters asked, 'Are the Bonnars here?' 'No,' replied Pearse, 'the Bonnars aren't here.' Ailbe laughed at that. It was as if he didn't qualify as a Bonnar just because he didn't play for Tipp.

There were plenty of other nights when all the Bonnars were there. They took on board what I said that first night in the Rock Club. The Friday night before they played in the 1991 All-Ireland final, they joined in with us for a puck-around. It was the same when Raymie made the county panel; if he wasn't training with Tipp he was training with Cashel.

The other lads were as dedicated. I thought I'd never come across a group as eager and as respectful as I had in Clare, but I did in Cashel. There were nights when training went so well, my head would be hitting the roof on the way home. Now, they loved to party. We arranged to go to the 1995 All-Ireland club final but instead of joining the selectors and myself in Croke Park, they ended up in the pubs after our challenge game in Kilmacud. By the time we rounded them up and headed back to Cashel, it was half-one in the morning. There were plenty of Sunday mornings when they went onto that training field with sore heads. Yet once they hit it, they were mad to train. I'd say, 'Right, that's it' and they'd go 'Come on, Justin, another ten minutes.' I'd often look across and watch the sun going down on the Rock and say, 'This is something special.'

Sometimes my mind goes back to that poky old dressing room. I become emotional thinking of the men and hurlers I shared it with. John Bob Ryan, who used to play out the field but worked so hard to become our goalkeeper. Tony Slattery, a brilliant marker with a delightful first touch and a wonderful ability to read the play. Then there was our resident full back and gentle giant, Pat O'Donoghue. Next to Colm Bonnar, Pat was our most consistent player.

Raymie Ryan was our most gifted. He was a joy to watch and coach, with his stickwork, footwork, balance and style. If he was from Offaly, he'd be a star. He seemed inhibited playing for Tipp, as if he was under instructions to play the perfect ball, instead of expressing himself like he did with Cashel. I never bought that theory that he was too loose for an inter-county wing back; even if he was, the Tipp selectors should then have tried him out as a forward. We were losing this West championship match in New Inn when I ran over and said, 'Raymie, there's five minutes left. Go up to the forwards and get us a goal.' He did both and we won. I don't go along with the notion that he didn't have enough cutting either. I remember one West final when Clonoulty cut lumps out of him and he still managed to score six points from play. John Leahy was the only other player in Tipperary at the time who could have done that.

Pat Fitzell was another player who I'm amazed Tipperary didn't get more out of. He was an incredibly skilful and courageous player. Pat was the kind of fella you had to get to know to get the best out of him. He was his own man, a man of the land, not of the pub. I was like him that way so we'd walk through the fields and talk about dogs and the outdoor life. We'd never have won the county only for him.

I could wax lyrical about them all. The speed and versatility of Michael Purdue. The honesty of Willie Fitzell. The delightful strokes and gentle nature of the Grogans. The flamboyance but reliability of Cormac 'The Viking' Bonnar. The strength and whipping power of T.J. Connolly. The heart of Joe Minogue. The skill of little Declan McGrath. The leadership and consistency of Colm. Then there was Liam Barron, Kevin O'Sullivan, Timmy Moloney …

I was especially fond of James O'Donoghue, our pleasant and plucky young forward. Jamesie worked in Cork for a computer company and we'd travel to training together, more often than not with my son Justin John, who'd pal around with Jamesie's brothers, Ronie and Donie, when we'd get to Cashel. On the way back, the three of us would stop in Cahir and get some chips and 7Up. By the time we'd hit Mitchelstown, Justin John would be asking questions from a quiz book to keep my mind alert, while Jamesie, more often than not, would be sound asleep. Little did I know that he'd have his eyes closed when I would see him for the last time. In 1995, he was killed in a car crash. The town and club were devastated by that tragedy. Jamesie was a week short of his twenty-fifth birthday.

I'm still good friends with his parents, Pat and Una. It's the same with everyone in Cashel. I'm especially close to Seamus King. Like Father Harry, he gave me an opportunity to experience another hurling culture and I'm grateful to him for that. I can now understand why Tipp were so hell-bent on winning in '85. Going to places like Clonoulty, Cappawhite and Bansha taught me hurling is a way of life in Tipperary. The whole scene there reminded me of the fifties and sixties in Cork. When you'd walk into the Cashel dressing room, they'd be talking about the county team or the Under-14s' win over Clonoulty. In Cork, fellas would be chatting about some soccer match on television. Cashel was a throwback to the dockyard days, when hurling consumed us all.

We had great games on those fields of west Tipperary. The intensity was a lot like the South East in Cork. Even the league games were magical. One night we beat Clonoulty by two points in the best club match I've seen. I don't normally go into opposing dressing rooms but I did that night to tell Declan Ryan and his team-mates to forget about the result and thank them for a wonderful game.

I'll also remember our adventures outside the county. Like the all-day tournaments in Carlow. Like the game against Tullaroan which gave me the chance to see where Father Roch and Lory came from. And like when we won the Paddy Grace Memorial Tournament in Dicksboro. We tend to dwell on championship finals and rolls of honour and overlook when teams from different counties get to mix and celebrate this great sport. Every year someone will win a county or divisional title but nights like that are precious.

Cashel haven't been going that well in recent years. Then again, players like the Bonnars, Grogans, Slatterys, Fitzells and O'Donoghues don't come around often. I was privileged to get to coach men like that. I'm glad to say that respect was reciprocated. One time, Pat Fitzell went out of his way to get a terrier for me. That was a great little dog; I was fierce upset when he was knocked down a few years ago. I trained him to go for any stray ball out the back garden. If I hit a few sliotars into the bushes, he'd bring them back for me. It got to the stage that whenever I'd come home from work, he'd be waiting to go out and play ball. One time, my wife Pat and I came home from a function at half-three in the morning. The dog got all excited and ran over to my hurleys in the corner of the utility room. We switched on the big light out the back and went out. We stayed there for half an hour.

What was his name?

Cashel, of course.

26

THE CLUB

If a man does not keep pace with his companions, perhaps it is because he hears a different drummer. Let him step to the music he hears, however measured or far away.

Henry David Thoreau

L ooking back, it was probably the biggest decision of my hurling career.

A lot of people wouldn't have made it.

Even more would have regretted making it.

In 1967, two of the biggest clubs in the country wanted me to join them. In January, Gerald sounded me out on behalf of St Finbarr's. It was awkward for him because he had been to Passage with the Liam McCarthy Cup only a few months earlier and had seen what it meant to the people there to have one of their own on the Cork team. There was nothing improper or unusual about his approach though. It was common at the time for players from the smaller country clubs to join one of the Big Three; Charlie, for instance, was originally from Redmonds, Con Roche was from Bishopstown while Denis Murphy's first club was Grenagh. I was tempted to join. The Barrs would be contending for county titles ever year while Gerald, Charlie and Denis were three of my best friends on the Cork team. One night I decided to go up. Jimmy Goulding, their club chairman, gave me a warm welcome and we trained for an hour and a half. It didn't feel right though. Afterwards I went over to Gerald and said, 'Look, I don't think I can move. I'll stick with the lads below.'

Later that year, Frank Murphy knocked on my parents' door. He pointed out that by joining Blackrock I'd be able to get a good job in either Dunlops or Fords, where the pay was better than it was in Verolme. Another promising player from Passage, John Horgan, had also been approached. John's father, Tim, had played for the Rockies and was anxious that I transfer along with John. Tim said that if I joined, there'd be bonfires from Rochestown to Blackrock all along the old railway line to greet us. But John went alone.

John went on to win five county titles and three All-Ireland club medals. I never won a championship medal of any sort with Passage. Those four Under-15 finals back in 1959? We lost all of them. And the 1966 county senior semi-final when we were favourites against Avondhu. And the 1976 county intermediate final against Newtownshandrum. And ...

We didn't have much luck through the years. Eddie O'Brien was in hospital for one of those Under-15 finals; Father O'Callaghan's only beat us 6-4 to 6-1 and I can't help feeling Eddie would have swayed it our way. Then there was 1970. We had a really good team that year, even though I was out injured from the accident. Wexford's Pat Quigley was living in Passage at the time and had scored two goals in that year's All-Ireland final, while Eddie O'Brien had scored three himself for Cork in the same game. The week after the All-Ireland, we lost to Muskerry in the second round of the county championship. The deadly duo who had scored 5-4 between them in Croke Park had combined for two points in Ballinhassig.

Probably the cruelest twist of luck though came a year later. You're not going to believe this is true.

Babs Keating wrote in his autobiography that Frank Cummins and myself would have been the ultimate midfield pairing. Passage were very close to having that pairing. Frank had being playing for Cobh for a few years where he had been based as a garda before being transferred to the station in Passage. Once I heard about that development, I approached him about joining Passage. He said he would and I organised two new hurleys for him. A few weeks later, we had a league game against UCC in Passage. I introduced Frank to the team in the dressing room and all the lads let him know that they were delighted to have him on board. No sooner were we on the field though than it became very dark. Then snowflakes started to fall. We kept pucking around but then it started to snow and it was impossible to see one end of the field from the other. The referee called the game off. A few weeks later, Frank Cummins was transferred back to the garda station in Cobh, and then a year later, to Shandon Street in the city. The rule is that you've transferred to a team only when you've played for that team. The snow meant Frank never played for our team. It didn't snow on Frank's debut for Blackrock.

It wasn't the last of our bad-luck stories. Two weeks before that 1976 intermediate county final, I got a bad belt on the wrist in a challenge game against Kilworth. I thought it would go away and strapped it up myself but it was still hurting the Wednesday before the game. When I got it x-rayed, there was a cracked bone in my hand. The doctor told me the best he could do was give me an injection before the game, so I took it. I played alright but I was definitely restricted by the injury. We lost by a point.

In truth though, bad luck had only so much to do with it. We weren't organised enough. It was only when we ran onto the pitch for that 1976 intermediate final that we realised we had forgotten to bring any sliotars with us; we ended up using a borrowed one between the twenty-five of us.

We didn't have the necessary commitment or ambition either. In the late sixties, we had some exceptional players but were short another four or five with the ability and commitment required to really threaten the Big Three. I remember reading in 1998 that the players of Doora–Barefield said to themselves at the start of that year, 'Lads, look at the talent we have here. The club will never have a better chance of winning something than now.' Passage should have been saying the same thing back in the late sixties – Joe Murphy, Eddie O'Brien, Bernie Meade, John Barry, Georgie O'Sullivan, Timmy O'Shea, Martin O'Donoghue and myself had all played for Cork at some level – but we didn't have that mentality. The club had been traditionally a junior or intermediate club and it continued to think like one. Growing up, I'd hear the old fellas talk about the '45 team that won a divisional title but as I got older, I found myself asking, 'What did they win?'

The talent we had in the late sixties would probably win a county title now. Back then though, the Big Three were awesome, with their combination of tradition, home-produced talent and outside talent. While we would regularly beat them in the league, we needed everyone to be dedicated to the cause if we were to take them in the championship. That effort wasn't forthcoming. Senior hurling was too serious for too many of our lads. And for someone as dedicated as myself, that was extremely frustrating.

There were some great times and great wins too. One year, we won the league, while in '71, we beat UCC, who were the reigning county champions. And I loved practising on our pitch, Manning Park. I'd often stay on there after training, taking lineballs and frees, and taking shots with some of the other lads. I'd even go down there on Christmas Day for a puck-around with the likes of Bernie Meade, Martin O'Donoghue and Mattie Aherne.

There were also some great characters on those Passage teams. John Connell, or 'Gigli' as he was better known, was one of the most honest, jovial and absent-minded people you could meet. One day we played St Vincent's in a championship match in Douglas. John had played a stormer but at the final whistle he was a disappointed man. He went over to his marker, Christy O'Shea, who had played in the 1956 All-Ireland, shook his hand and said, 'Christy, the best of luck in the next round. At the end of the day, we just weren't good enough.' Christy looked at 'Gigli' as if he had two heads. Passage had won by a point.

Another time, 'Gigli' got a bad belt on his leg and went up to hospital. There he had a great old chat with the doctors and nurses while getting his leg strapped. When he came back, we asked him if we could look at his leg. 'Gigli' rolled up his pants before realising, 'Christ, they're after putting it on the wrong leg!'

Some of the club's mentors and officers were lovely men. Dan O'Mahony was a wonderful advisor and supporter through the years, while another former chairman of the club, Johnny Ryan, was also a dedicated and caring soul. And our team trainer, John 'The Runner' Barry, reminded me a lot of his namesake 'Tough', an absolute gentleman.

I played my last game for Passage in 1991 at the age of forty-six in a junior B league final in Ballinure. It was a very emotional day. I knew it was my last game. I looked around the dressing room, taking everything in, and it hit me that I had played with five of the team's fathers. I scored eight points, including a sideline ball from forty yards. We won by two points. It was a lovely way to go out. Our opponents were Father O'Callaghan's. That was the same club who beat us in three of those four Under-15 finals back in '59.

Today the club is junior. I'm no longer involved with it. I'll often bump into two great clubmen – Kieran Keane and Thomas Harrington – and ask how Passage are going but between coaching other teams and writing about the big matches for the *Examiner*, I haven't been at one of Passage's matches in five years. My relationship with the club had cooled some time before that. Now, you might think, 'How can he not be involved? The club is junior! They need him!' Well, one day the club decided they didn't need me. In the mid eighties, I started coaching this lovely group of young fellas, one of whom was my son, Cormac. I took them when they were Under-12, all the way up to Under-16, at which grade they won the B championship, the first trophy the club had won in fifteen years. A few months later, the club held its annual general meeting but I couldn't make it. The following

March, the chairman of the club called the house. I answered it. 'Is Cormac there?' he said. 'There's a game.'

'The minors have a game? How come I didn't hear about it?'

'Well, there's a new committee for the minors.'

I was taken aback. I had been with these lads for five years and they were flowering into a grand team.

'So do I have any role with this team?'

'Well, I suppose you don't. You weren't at the meeting.'

'I couldn't make the meeting. Listen, I was with those kids for five years.'

'Well, you're not with them now. Sorry.'

'Fine,' I sighed. 'Here's Cormac.'

That was that.

The GAA is full of stories like that. Recently a well-known former Cork player suggested to his club that it should compete in the All-Ireland Sevens tournament. The club threw the motion out on the basis that the player was no longer actively involved in the club. Even Liam Griffin was shafted as a Wexford minor selector a few years after winning the senior All-Ireland. What happened was the norm rather than the exception.

Was I a good clubman? I think I was. I played adult hurling in five different decades for the club and coached many of its teams. Any night I wasn't training with Cork I trained with Passage. True, I played that one game with Shamrocks but it was the only championship medal I ever won and I was back playing with Passage the following year. Even in the late seventies, when I was coaching Clare, I was on the club's juvenile committee.

I suppose though we never had your conventional club–player relationship. I was from Rochestown, two miles from the town, so I wasn't living amongst them. Then as the years went on, a lot of the friends and players that I did know well were no longer involved. By the eighties, more emphasis was being put on football and I felt the club had no real vision or ambition of being a serious force in hurling. I didn't get the same respect or appreciation in my own club that I would command anywhere else. Today, I doubt whether I would have enough ties with the club to galvanise the situation, but who knows, some day I might get involved again. The club probably feels the same. I can understand if there are fellas saying, 'Well, Justin went his own road while we kept the club on the road', but no bridges were actually burnt. We may link up again.

So do I regret not joining either Blackrock or the Barrs? There were times when I did feel sorry that I didn't. I'd watch Gerald or Con Roche have the occasional poor game but the rest of the talent around them would bail them out. With Passage, I never had that support; I had to be everywhere and could never have a bad game. But that was also a good thing. I learned to become a more rounded and consistent player that way. Passage were also the first team that asked me to become involved in coaching, back when I was out injured for a few weeks in '67. I'll forever be grateful for that. And if I had gone to the Barrs or the Rockies, I'd have developed a big-club mentality. I wouldn't have gone to Antrim, Clare, Ballygarvan, Cashel, Ballincollig and all those other underdogs I helped out over the years. Coming from Passage, I was an underdog myself.

So no, I don't regret it. Passage was the road less travelled. And it has made all the difference.

27

IN THE NAME OF THE GAME

This game is for everybody.

Justin McCarthy

Where would we be without the GAA? I often ask myself that and it scares me. I wouldn't have had the job, wife or life I've had only for it; I'd have been in America. Hurling kept me here. Growing up in the country in the fifties, I needed an outlet and the GAA provided it; no other sport was remotely as well organised. It gave me the chance to express my Irishness too. I wish I was a native speaker but I'm not. I wish I could play music but I can't. But as Griffin said, hurling is the Riverdance of sport. Only for it and football, a lot of us wouldn't have danced.

Even for those like my brother Barry who left for the States, the games have been a way of keeping in touch with home and their roots. Imagine the identity crisis northern nationalism would have suffered in the last eighty years without the games. Anybody who knocks the government giving multimillion pound grants to the GAA does not have a true understanding of rural life or of Irish social history. This country will never be able to repay the GAA enough.

That's why what I'm about to say should be taken in the proper spirit. When you criticise the GAA, you tend to be labelled as a critic of the GAA. That's wrong. I'm trying to improve the association, not knock it. The powers-that-be need to appreciate that. I'm not saying that I'm a better GAA man than any of them but I'm as good a GAA man as any of them. We're all meant to be on the same side, part of the same family, and I believe there are ways that team, that family, could be even better.

First, we need to recognise that members of that family are dying. What are we doing about it? Not enough. Back in 1980, I wrote the same thing. We've lost Westmeath hurling since then. Laois could soon follow. Filling Croke Park on All-Ireland final day is fine but there's more to the game than that.

It's not enough to say that counties should be doing it for themselves, that they're doing it for themselves in football. Football is not as specialised a game as hurling. Alan Kerins had been playing club football for only a few months before he started with the Galway senior county team, but there's no way even someone as gifted as Michael Donnellan could take up hurling today and be playing with the county senior hurling team in two years' time. I've told Antrim, 'Go to Croke Park. Tell them your situation, that you have the interest and that you want the money, the support and the ideas. Ask them can they do anything for you.' I'm afraid though what they'll be told. In 2001, Tom Magill, one of the selectors with the Derry senior team, came to Cork to see me a few weeks before his team played Galway in the All-Ireland quarter-final. I've never met a more enthusiastic hurling man. We spent three hours talking in a local hotel and I showed him twenty different drills they could use. He had never seen anything like them. Before he left, he asked, 'Look, can we ever make the breakthrough?'

'You can. What's your trade Tom?'

'I'm a carpenter.'

'Is a carpenter from Derry any worse than a carpenter from Cork?' The problem is we're not sharing the expertise of the trade called hurling.

I know the GAA has set up coaching structures and has full-time underage coaches. That's all fine but we're working too low to come up. A twelve-year-old Roscommon kid is going to opt for football down the line if he sees the senior hurling team being hammered all the time. But imagine if he saw that Loughnane was coming up five times a year to do some coaching with the senior coaches and team? You cannot expect a Roscommon county manager to run a session like a Loughnane until he's seen a Loughnane on the training ground.

We should remember that not so long ago, Ireland was one of the poorer nations in the European Union. France and Germany though didn't say, 'Well, that's too bad for the Irish.' The EU identified us and others as nations that needed financial assistance. The Celtic Tiger was a child of that vision and support. The GAA needs to give a similar leg-up. We have nine counties who are in reasonable health. The GAA should target the next eleven counties below that where hurling is weak but the interest is strong and involve them in a five-year development programme.

I include Dublin in that. I include Laois; we must not lose them. In Connacht, I'd target Roscommon; let's start with them where there's some tradition rather than, say, Sligo. I'd also include Kerry, Carlow,

Westmeath, Kildare, Meath and the three leading Ulster counties in this special programme for Category B counties.

The programme would be threefold and funded by Croke Park.

First, each county would have the option of appointing a full-time manager to coach the Under-21 and senior teams.

Then, above that, there would be a national task force, comprising ten or twelve of the country's top coaches, who would go around to each of these Category B counties and give seminars and coaching sessions throughout the year to the players and the full-time coaches. This task force should have coaches of the calibre of Loughnane, Farrell, Griffin, Babs, Cregan, Gerald, PaJoe Whelehan, John McIntyre and Dermot Healy. I couldn't go up to Tom Magill in Derry but maybe Cyril Farrell could. Why not utilise our expertise? Why let it go to the grave? The GAA hierarchy, unfortunately, does not value managers; an All-Ireland winning coach doesn't even get a medal. The suits have a fear of personality managers, a fear that they wield too much power, but the GAA must realise those managers aren't egotists; they are competitors who push it to the limit in the pursuit of excellence. That desire for excellence could be tapped into by the GAA for the greater good of the game.

Category B counties should also be allowed to use up to four players from outside the county. There are plenty of players in Cork, Kilkenny, Galway and Tipperary that either are just short of the mark or have fallen out with the coach of their own native county. It's a shame talent like that is not being utilised. I'm thinking of Ken O'Shea of Kilkenny; imagine what he'd do for Carlow? Or what Galway's Nigel Shaughnessy would do for Roscommon? Or what Tipp's Kevin Tucker would for Kerry? I'd have it that the Category A counties name thirty players over twenty-two years of age at the start of a season and anyone not on that list and who is over twenty-two could be snapped up by a Category B county for a year. Everyone could win this way, providing it was done in the spirit of developing the game. The Category B counties certainly would benefit. The Category A counties would too, as they'd have the option of recalling such a guest player the following season.

By the end of the five-year plan, several of those counties should have made significant progress. Then other counties could be targeted. Not that we should forget about the Sligos and Tyrones now either. They too should benefit from an elite coaching task force. Then, if they've shown enough interest, they could be promoted onto the Category B list and enjoy the full-time senior coach and transfer privilege that go with such status.

A pipedream? More like a blueprint. The alternative is the status quo. And it's not working.

The GAA could be doing more to develop the game in every county. They have, for instance, yet to really tap into the value of a ball alley. The alley should be to the hurler what the driving range is to the golfer – a place to test and work on your technique. Every golfer will use a driving range but not every hurler uses an alley. Croke Park should be encouraging or inviting someone like me to give talks and demonstrations to coaches and clubs how to use an alley, but then, Croke Park itself doesn't know the value of one.

Liam Griffin wrote a great article saying that we should have indoor hurling tournaments. He pointed out that, as a new sport, Tyrone would be starting off at the same level as Cork, and that it would help close the gap in field hurling itself. Not only that, but having Joe Deane, Paul Flynn and D.J. Carey pucking a plastic sliotar in the Neptune Stadium would promote our sport in the off-season. I couldn't agree more. Why shouldn't we have it with our weather patterns? And why shouldn't we be watching the Deanes, the Flynns and D.J.s playing alley tournaments instead of watching Man United on TV? Imagine the shots they'd come up with. Imagine how it would develop and promote the game.

Think about this too; in the off-season, most of our players throw away the hurley for a few months because they're sick of the whole scene from so much physical training, whereas in every other sport, the off-season is a chance to develop your game. In the sixties and seventies, we didn't train collectively four or five nights a week in February like teams do now, but we'd never leave the hurley out of our hand for more than a week. Not only would an All-Ireland alley competition mean the good player from Mayo would have a chance of being in the national limelight, but it would also encourage established stars to develop their game further in the off-season. That would mean the overall standard of the sport would rise. Think how much fun it would be to see D.J. going against Deane in an All-Ireland alley final. And how much fun it would be for the players, free from the strain and monotony of collective training and matches.

I'd also like to see some changes to the rules of the game itself. Not only are some hurling counties dying; so are certain hurling skills. While the modern game has many attractive features, I'm alarmed at how few players can execute overhead shots. I'd like if we brought in a rule where you couldn't handle the ball from puck-outs. At the moment, we have a crowded half-back line area with every fella jumping on top of the other trying to handle the ball. More often than not, it breaks on the ground and a group of fellas stand over it, trying to pick it up. It's sloppy and unsightly. If players had to connect first time, the game would be speeded up, you'd have less broken fingers and above all, you'd have a great skill being preserved. Don't forget, players would still have plenty of opportunities to catch the ball in general play.

The skill of chipping the ball off the ground also needs to be encouraged more; again, few players can do it well. I remember talking to Donie Nealon a few years back at a championship match and he suggested that a player should get two points for successfully chipping a ground ball over the bar, be it a sideline ball or a free. I think it's a magnificent idea. Other sports have done something similar; basketball, for instance, introduced the three-pointer to reward the art of outside shooting. It would also make our game even more exciting. Imagine a team is a point down with a minute to go and they're awarded a free thirty yards out. Does he go for his point or trust his ground striking and go for 'two'?

I'd love to have been a full-time hurler. Training with the team three hours every morning; then resting; then doing some gym work; then resting; then go taking frees and lineballs for two hours; it would have been heaven. There is nothing morally wrong with professionalism. I find it ironic and indeed hypocritical when GAA officers insist that the association must retain its amateur status above anything else; some of those officers are full-time. If professionalism was feasible and operated in such a way that it would not lead to the movement of players and the breakdown of the county system, then we should have full-time players. The sport cannot realise its full potential until it has. That is fact.

I can't see professionalism happening in my lifetime. I wouldn't want it either if it were unfeasible and led to a situation where a Mark Foley ended up transferring to Cork because the money was better there. I do think players need some reward for the effort they're putting in though. I'm certainly glad to see that they're guaranteed at least two championship matches a year but they should have even more to show for their efforts. Any player who is on a championship panel should get at least 1,500 euro. Any player who reaches a Munster or Leinster final should get at least 4,000. Any player who plays in an All-Ireland final should get at least 7,000. That way, a fella can say to his family or girlfriend, 'There's something to show for all the nights I've been away from you.' A fella will gladly play for free for a few years, but after a while he'll stop because he'll realise that he could be investing that same time into his job. In most other sports, an athlete is only coming into his prime at twenty-eight; in Gaelic games, he's coming towards the end. Why? Because he'll allow his career and family life suffer only so much.

There's another reason why he may opt out. He could be burned out. Some of the training regimes in the past ten years have been ridiculous. A lot of teams wouldn't have a Seanie O'Leary near their set-up. They'd have their bleep tests and their sub-maximal tests before cutting him from the panel. Those tests may measure physical fitness but they can't measure hurling fitness. I'm all for teams using the sports sciences and for players getting the meals, the tracksuits, the blazers, the diets, the session in the swimming pool after the game. But all those things are peripheral to the game itself. I don't want my players to have all that and not be able to execute the shots. We're neglecting the core fundamentals of the game. We say our sport is virtually professional in approach these days but we're only fooling ourselves. We're more *organised* than we were but we're not professional. If you compare us to nearly every other sport in the world, we're still amateurs when it comes to exploring our game.

Look at how few players practise – as oppose to train – in the off-season.

Look at how many 'coaches' are more comfortable telling their players to do forty press-ups than showing them how to take a lineball.

Look at how few players use the alley.

And just look at the most basic thing of all, the thing they're holding in their hands.

28

My Best Friend

Hurling has always been a way of life with me. It was never my ambition to play the game for the sake of winning All-Ireland medals or breaking records. It was to perfect the art as well as possible.

Christy Ring, *The Spirit of The Glen*

The hurley means everything to me. That's the tool of my trade. Most players don't know a good one from a bad one. They'll get a stick from a hurley-maker and say, 'That's fine' when it's almost certain that it's not the finished article. It's crazy. The hurley-maker is unlikely to have played in Croke Park, and extremely unlikely to have played in the hurler's position, yet the player won't even think that it needs some modifying. It's like the fella with the car that has no power steering. He thinks it's fine, it gets him from A to B, no problem. Then he drives in a car with power steering, looks at the old car and says, 'How did I ever settle for that?' You'll never know a good hurley until you have one in your hand. It can add 15 per cent to your game.

One of the first things I do with a team is look at their hurleys. I want my players to appreciate what a good hurley is. Hurleys are mass produced. If someone makes a dozen hurleys, only two or three are likely to be exceptional. Sometimes, I have to tell a player, 'Look, I'm wasting my time fixing that; we'll have to get you another one.' The grain could be too straight or too close, which means the timber is liable to crack quickly. I look for a wide grain running down the shaft and round the bas. If it runs along the back of the heel, that's better still. That tells you the ash comes from a good root, that it's durable.

There's also nice 'give' in a wider grain. The spring of a hurley is important. I don't want too much 'give' in it though. When I was starting out with Cork, I thought that it was great to have a stick which could spring two inches either way; I was one of those fellas who loved to bend a hurley. Then I went up to Ramie Dowling's workshop on Upper Patrick Street in Kilkenny. I was constantly testing the spring of this one hurley. Paddy Grace, the famous player and administrator, was there too and he told me, 'Justin, don't do that. A hurley is made up of fibres. The more you test the spring of a hurley, the more you're weakening its fibres.' I'm no longer the type who gets a kick out of bending a hurley. If a hurley has too much spring in it, you're not going to have the direction and accuracy you want when it connects with the ball. You can throw away that kind of hurley.

The same if a hurley has a knot. I've seen loads of hurleys that had a perfect grain, a lovely bit of ash, and then, halfway down the shaft, there was a knot. A knot means your hurley is likely to give in one good clash. I don't doctor hurleys with knots.

Now, if the hurley has good ash, the right amount of 'give' and no knots, that means I can do something with it. The next thing I look for is if it has the right size and shape. In 1966, I won an All-Ireland medal and the Player of the Year award using a Saint Lua hurley made in Clare. I wouldn't use the same hurley if I had to do it again. It was 37 inches long. It should have been 36. That inch makes a big difference. A 36 is easier to handle. You have more control over it. You can always extend your hands or bring your back down that extra bit to make up for that extra inch, whereas a 37-inch hurley is more difficult to manoeuvre in a tight space. I could get away with a 37 inch back in '66 because the game wasn't as fast then. I couldn't get away with it now.

An extra inch also means extra weight. Most inter-county players these days use 36-inch hurleys (and a smaller player could go for a 35 or 35½ but most young fellas starting out favour a longer and heavier hurley. They think the extra weight will help them when they're clashing on the ball, that it will offer them more protection, that they won't be splashing out on another stick. The reality is they'd break less hurleys using a shorter model because they'd be able to deliver the ball faster. That's why, when an outfield player gives me a 37-inch hurley, I reduce it by an inch.

That Saint Lua hurley also had too much timber on the snout of its bas. Since then, I like the bas of my hurleys to be more compact to give a more consistent, controlled shot. I also make sure the face of the bas is flat. I'll put a straight edge across it and hold both towards the light. If I see any light below the ruler, that tells me that there's a slight curve on the bas. Even the smallest of deviations can cause the ball to veer away, so I'll take a few shavings off the centre of the bas with a spokeshave to eliminate that curve. The same, of course, with the other side if needs be.

I don't want a bas that's too rounded either. That's the problem I have with the traditional Wexford hurley. The ash in it is very good but the bas is too stubby. There's not enough of the hurley on the ground.

That means it's not conducive to ground hurling, even though Liam Griffin and Tony Dempsey in recent years have tried to bring more of it into the county's style of play. Wexford players also tend to struggle more than others at picking the ball up at speed. That has more to do with the standard of hurleys than the standard of skill in the county. The hurleys are that bit too thick at the point where it slips underneath the ball. I'd pair down the bas to make it easier to pick up the ball. Wexford players are obviously used to those hurleys but it would add 15 per cent to their game if they'd take a few shavings off the bas. Those hurleys are too stubby at the moment which means they lack balance.

It's vital that the overall feel of the hurley itself is balanced. The reason I fix hurleys is that the player can pick it up and say, 'That feels great.' When I'm reshaping a hurley for myself, I'll measure its centre of gravity and mark it. Then I'll get out one of my favourite old hurleys and measure and mark *its* centre of gravity. If the new hurley has a different centre from the old one, I'll make some adjustments to get it closer to 'the prototype'. I can take a bit of weight off one side by taking a few shavings, and I can add a bit of weight to the other by putting on an extra band or some more tape. In general, a hurley should weigh 22 or 23 ounces. More importantly though, it should *feel* great. You must be able to feel that hurley. I can pick ten hurleys in my workshop that are roughly the same, close my eyes, and pick out which one I played with in, say, the 1972 league final. A hurler should have that *feel* relationship with a hurley.

It helps if you have a good handle. The handle is very important because you're always catching the hurley there. I don't like a round handle because it can turn in your hand. My handles are oval to flat so that my small finger fits in snugly underneath the grip on top of the hurley. I also put a tape around the very top of the handle six or seven times so that my hand won't slip off the top of the hurley. That could happen on the point of impact if your hands are sweaty.

The tape also helps dress up the hurley. I think any hurler with pride in himself and his hurley should dress it up. It's like putting on a new suit – it makes you feel ready, confident, good about yourself. I'd always write my name clearly on both sides of the hurley; your name is the best thing you have. I hate to see a player going out with a hurley not banded. I think that's a disgrace. I wouldn't play with a hurley that wasn't banded; I'm amazed so many players from Wexford do. A steel band helps protect the hurley. Remember, a hurley is only a little plank of wood, at most an inch at its thickest point. The band tightens up the timber, meaning that if it cracks, it won't just break; it can be repaired. And again, the band helps dress up the very tool of your trade.

That's why I also put some tape slightly above the second band. I never put on colour tape, only black. You must remember, the sliotar is nearly always white. If you're going down to pick a ball at speed, red or green tape could catch your eye ahead of the ball and you won't pick it up cleanly. The white shows up well against black. That's why my tape is black.

You should also study the heel of your hurley. Some say it should be an inch thick but three-quarters of an inch is plenty. True, an inch means you get a better cut off the ground but it leaves the hurley too wedgy and unbalanced. John Fenton used to have heavy hurleys at the start of 1984 because he had a great shot on the ground. But I said to him, 'John, you won't be taking lineballs all day. You won't be hitting every shot on the ground either. You'll have to pick a ball, you'll have to hit out of your hand, you'll have to hit in the air. Right now your hurley is too heavy for those shots.' John had to compromise to get the best hurley for his game. I refined his hurleys down to a more respectable weight to give him a balance between a light and heavy hurley. I also reminded him that it shouldn't affect his sideline cuts. That shot primarily comes down to the speed of your hands, the speed of your hurley and the angle of your shot. I'd make sure that the edge of the heel of my hurley is sharp because that's where you lift the ball when taking a lineball. Sometimes when a fella goes out with a new hurley, he gets great height in his lineballs, but after a week or so, the edge wears down, which hinders the elevation in his ground strokes. I file down the heel to bring back that edge.

I like most of my hurleys to have pretty much the same type of banding, the same tape, the same shape. They can't all have the same weight though. I was a versatile player. When I was playing in the half-back line, I'd have a different hurley to the ones I'd use in the half-forward line. A lot of players don't realise that. That shows how far we have to go before we're really professional. The average inter-county player will dabble with golf. He wouldn't dream of going out onto a golf course with only a putter and one other club because he'd know that you need different clubs for different distances. He mightn't know that you need different hurleys for different positions though; he might think his team's big full back has a similar kind of hurley to his team's big full forward. Goalkeepers tend to be the exception, not just out of necessity but out of personality too. Seamus Durack had to have his hurleys down to the last detail. The same with Ger Cunningham. He once called me at eleven o'clock the night before a Munster final to say he wasn't happy with one of his hurleys. His father came over with it and we were still in my workshop well after midnight. Outfield players don't have that same eye for detail, even the versatile ones. They need to realise that there are different hurleys for different lines of the field. Fenton had slightly more weight at the bottom of his hurleys than had Seanie O'Leary. Fenton was playing further out the field and needed more distance in his shots. O'Leary needed a lighter hurley because inside-forward play is all about the quickness of your stroke.

Every hurler should have at least three or four hurleys. I'd always have a dozen ready to be dressed up and three or four already dressed up. I'd always use at least two different hurleys in training, one maybe for half an hour, the other then for the next half-hour, go back to the first one again and then finish up with the second. I'd also bring a slightly heavier hurley on match days in case it rained. On a wet day, the ball will be that bit heavier and you won't get the same drive as you otherwise would. These little things count.

I think it helps to know how the elements can work for and against your hurley. Hurleys tend to be very fresh when you get them from the hurley-maker. Before I reshape mine, I sometimes leave them on the clothes line for a few days to put a skin on the timber. The wind, sun and rain toughen them up, make them more durable. When I've finished reshaping a hurley, I put two coats of yachting varnish on it. The varnish reduces the chances of the sun cracking the hurley. It also means that if ever the hurley gets wet, the weight won't go out of it. (You should be careful though that the varnish doesn't leave the hurley too shiny; lightly sand the varnish off.) I'm also vigilant after the hurley has been done up. When I've cleaned and dried my hurley after I've come home from training, I make sure to put it in a place that's cool enough, so it won't crack. That's why I never keep my best hurley in the car. I'd always have some hurley there but never my best because the heat in the boot opens cracks in the timber. Remember, a hurley is only three feet of ash.

I'd like to see more players being more familiar with the hurley. Hurley-makers are great but they can't make a tailor-made hurley for a player if the hurler himself isn't aware of the benefits that some modifications can create. I'd also love if each club and each stadium in the country had a special room and special equipment for hurleys. There should be some place where they keep spokeshaves, hammers and pinchers and you can go in and fix your hurley. I coached in Na Piarsaigh recently and they had the vision to have such facilities. Croke Park and Páirc Uí Chaoimh don't.

And we claim our game is virtually professional.

29

RETURN TO THE EDGE

It's lack of faith that makes people afraid of meeting challenges I believed in myself.

Muhammad Ali

A few days before the 1997 Munster final, Ger Loughnane was asked in an interview whether he could see himself coaching hurling after his days as Clare manager were over. He said that he couldn't, be it a minor team, club team or school team. Nothing could compare to the buzz of Championship Day at the highest level. *Nothing.*

I've coached a lot of teams since 1985. I've enjoyed each challenge, because to me, the game is the game, but I can see where Loughnane is coming from. That buzz is the ultimate. First, there's the honour and challenge of preparing the best players in a county to be the best in the country. And then there's Championship Day itself. The sound of that siren as the team coach and escort approach the stadium; the cheers and butterflies as you walk off that coach; the knock on that dressing-room door; that moment when the clatter of studs is drowned out by the roar of the crowd; that explosion of light. That *buzz.*

I've had plenty of offers since 1985 to experience that buzz again. And yet I've repeatedly resisted it. If I was going to do it, I was going to do it properly. And up until 2001, I felt certain factors would militate against me doing it properly.

Two months before the 1992 championship, Wexford asked me to come in as team coach. I felt though that the travel would be too much and that I wouldn't have enough time before their first game. They turned to Cyril Farrell instead.

Then at the end of that year, I was offered the Offaly position. Again, I felt a six-hour round-trip would be too much. Eamonn Cregan filled the post. Four years later when Cregan stepped down, Offaly again sounded me out. Once more I was tempted to work with such a bunch of gifted hurlers but once more I felt the travel would be too taxing, so John McIntyre got the job.

A few months before the 1997 championship, Limerick manager Tom Ryan asked me to become involved, feeling that a new voice and some new hurling ideas would be what his veteran team needed. I liked Tom and would love to have seen his team win an All-Ireland, so I thought seriously about it for a few days. But when Tom called back, I told him to work away. It might have been different if he had called me earlier in the year but just like with Wexford in '92, I felt the championship was too soon. When Limerick were knocked out of that championship, the county board asked me would I be interested in talking to them. I didn't think it was right that Tom should be shafted after bringing the county to two All-Ireland finals, so I didn't put my name forward. Eamonn Cregan ended up being the new manager.

Waterford were another county that sounded me out a few times. They had a better chance than the other counties, with Dungarvan being only an hour away from Cork and the fact that their chairman, Paddy Joe Ryan, is an authorised oil distributor with Tedcastles and a personal friend. But when he asked me after the 1996 championship to become Waterford manager, I declined. I had just been appointed Tedcastles regional manager and felt I wouldn't have the energy and time.

Another Tedcastles' colleague at the time, the dual star Denis Walsh, then recommended Gerald McCarthy after playing under him with Cork in the early nineties. When Paddy Joe asked for my opinion, I agreed that Gerald would be a very good appointment and so it came to pass. After Waterford were beaten in the 2000 championship though, Gerald announced he was stepping down. Paddy Joe asked me to take over but I declined, so he went back and coaxed Gerald in to giving it one more year. After Waterford were beaten by Limerick in 2001, Gerald made it clear that he wouldn't be coming back. And this time, I said 'Yes' to Paddy Joe's plea from the heart. The following week, my appointment was unanimously ratified by the Waterford County Board.

Why did I say 'Yes'? Throughout my life, I've just known when is and when isn't the right time to do something. In 1978, I was a 33-year-old boilermaker when I saw an ad saying that a small Irish-owned oil company was looking for a sales representative. All I had sold prior to that was the game of hurling but I got that job. Something had told me to go for it. The time to leave my old job had never been right until the time *was* right. Anyone who has proposed marriage knows what

I'm talking about. Why didn't you ask six months earlier or later? Because it didn't feel like the right time. When Paddy Joe asked again in 2001, it felt like the right time to experience *the buzz* again.

I've always felt that I'd end up coaching Waterford some day. Over the years I've helped out teams that have needed help. And when you look at hurling over the past fifteen years, every leading county has had their day in the sun except Waterford. That's the main reason why I'm going down there. The best thing that could happen to hurling would be for Waterford to win a major title. As a hurling man, I want the people of Waterford to experience what Clare had in '95 and Wexford had in '96, or even what Limerick felt when winning Munster in '94 and '96. I still have the energy and enthusiasm to help them do it.

I've long had a soft spot for Waterford hurling. The last year they won an All-Ireland was the first year I went to a Munster final. I'll never forget going to see that match in Thurles in '59 with Derry Doody and seeing the likes of John Barron, Austin Flynn, Martin Óg Morrissey, Tom Cheasty, Frankie Walsh, Larry Guinan and the brilliant midfield of Philly Grimes and Seamus Power. They were outstanding stickmen who were blessed with tremendous grit. In later years, I'd be privileged enough to play with some of them for Munster and to this day, I can still name off those Waterford teams that won those Munster titles in '59 and '63.

I've also closely followed this current Waterford team over the years. I was a guest of honour when the 1992 Under-21 team were presented with their All-Ireland medals, Tedcastles have sponsored the county championship for almost ten years, while Gerald's involvement would have been another reason why I'd have been at all their championship games and a lot of their league games over the last five years. And in that time I've formed one conclusion – they're not that far away.

Take the 2001 championship. Tipperary were undoubtedly the best team in it but the best thirty minutes of hurling were produced by Waterford against Limerick. That same championship also underlined that there is only a puck and a break of a ball between the nine top counties. My job is to get Waterford on the right side of that puck or break of a ball. They may not be the perfect team but there is no perfect team out there. If I can get every Waterford player to improve a little bit, then the whole team improves considerably. Waterford have as good a chance as any team of winning the 2002 All-Ireland.

People argue that this team is too old. I don't buy that argument. Wexford had a similar age profile when they won the 1996 All-Ireland. Experience is vital; look at what Wexford did under Griffin or what

Cashel did when I was there. There is a popular theory now that hurling is a young man's game. But why's that? Because there has been an overemphasis on physical fitness. We won't be making that mistake in Waterford. I want our players to have a balanced lifestyle. Nobody is more fanatical about hurling than me but I have a life outside of it. I spend a lot of time with Pat and the children. I walk through the fields. I have a huge interest in photography, and yet I'll find the time to clean my car at least twice a week. We've stressed to our players the importance of time management so that they're fresh enough for hurling. We're focusing on quality rather than quantity. Come the championship, we'll be hurling fit.

I've also inherited a decent set-up. It's not as if I went down there and said, 'This is a mess.' Gerald put a good structure in place. Colm Bonnar is a crucial figure in our set-up. Jim Greene, who was interested in the coaching position after Gerald stepped down, argued quite reasonably that it would take me at least a year to get to know the players, a year he felt they could not afford. Colm though adds that necessary continuity to the set-up. His expertise in the physical preparation of teams is also critical. Some people have argued that I've been out of the inter-county scene for too long, but to that I have four answers. One, it's not as if I'm someone like Kevin Heffernan, who wouldn't have done much coaching at any level since '85; I've been taking serious teams for the last ten years. Two, I've always kept my eye on the inter-county scene from my work as a columnist with the *Irish Examiner*. Three, the core of the game itself hasn't changed. And finally but significantly, Colm knows all about the changes on the periphery of the game.

What are Colm, Seamie Hannon and myself trying to achieve? The goal is to deliver at least one major trophy. If we don't land either a national league, Munster championship or All-Ireland title, our reign couldn't be deemed a success. I would hope that my ideas and enthusiasm would influence them in the long term the way they influenced Loughnane, Honan, Stack and Callinan, but my target is to spread trophies as much as the word.

There's one difference between this chapter and virtually every other one in this book. I don't know the ending. With almost every other team I've coached, I've won something. I don't know if we will. But I'm not afraid to fail. A lot of people would have turned down this job, just like they would have turned down Clare or Cashel, for fear of being seen to fail. Not me. I'm not afraid of it, just like my team won't be afraid of any team or the winning post. And I am as committed to us passing that winning post as I have been to any other mission I've set out on.

30

FOREVER HURLING

To play the game is great
To win the game is greater
But to love the game is the greatest of all.
Plaque in the lobby of the Philadelphia Palestra

25 December 2001, Rochestown, County Cork.

I went down to the Alley this morning. I go down there every Christmas morning, at about half-eleven, after Mass in the monastery. I'll be down there again tomorrow, and on New Year's Day too. I hadn't been down this past few weeks though. Today it showed.

I started off like I always warm up – trying to hit six shots off that front wall, one hop at a time. But for some reason, I couldn't do it. After three or four shots, I was having to step five or six feet inside the endline; the ball was coming back short. And so I had to think. 'God, I'm doing something wrong here. What is it? Am I hitting it hard enough? Are my feet in the right position?' And after a few minutes I realised what it was. I wasn't watching the ball closely enough. See, to get the perfect shot, you have to stare at the ball up until the very last second, until it's a hurley's length from you, at which point you then trust your timing and muscle memory. It's something you can forget when you're a natural striker. It's something you'll forget on the field too because you're hitting the ball anyhow. But if that ball is to keep coming back at you in the Alley, you need the perfect shot. And the reason I wasn't getting it was because I had stopped staring at the ball when it was about halfway back down the Alley. I wasn't concentrating enough; I wasn't staring long enough at it. When Ring was asked what was the most important advice he could give a young hurler, his reply was 'Always keep your eye on the ball, even when it's in the referee's pocket.' And so there I was, at fifty-six, appreciating once more the wisdom of those words.

I rediscovered another good bit of advice today. After a while, I went up closer to the front wall and started practising some shots I'd use in a match in here, shots to kill the ball and win the point. And I found that my shots were too high, and therefore coming back too far out the Alley and allowing my imaginary opponent the chance to return. But then I remembered something Father Roch used to show me. If I wanted to hit a really low hard shot on goal, he told me to turn the bas of the hurley upside down, meaning the heel would be on top. See, the heel is the thickest part of the hurley, so you have more power there and you can bring the shot down. And when I tried that shot today, right enough, I was killing the ball and winning the point against my imaginary opponent. Crazy, isn't it? Fifty-six and still learning.

That's the thing about this game. You're always competing with the hurley and the ball. You'll never master it. They say the same about golf. I love watching golf but I'll play only a round or two a year, on holidays. If I played more of it, I'd be good at it and I'd only want to be better at it and that would mean the enthusiasm, time and energy I have for hurling would be diluted. I don't want that to happen. I still hurl every day. A fella can play golf in his seventies; why can't he have a puck-around in his seventies?

That's one of my biggest fears; that some day I won't be able to puck the ball. Probably my greatest quality as a coach is that I can still demonstrate every skill there is to my players. I'm out there, pucking balls among them; I'd hate to be coaching and not be able to do and show things. But even if I had to stop coaching, I'd hate to stop playing. I've been hurling since I was fourteen months old. Hurling is as natural to me as breathing.

Even on holidays, I bring a hurley and ball with me. I remember one family holiday in Rathdrum, County Wicklow, twenty years ago. I popped down to see the local team training and, not knowing who I was, they let me join in. After a few minutes, they picked teams. They asked what position I played. 'Sure, stick me in there at full forward,' I said. The game started and in the first ten minutes I let on that I was no good. Whenever the ball would come my way, I'd either let it drop or miss it completely, making my man look like Brian Lohan. Then a ball came in and hopped off the ground. I pulled first time and it flew into the roof of the net. A few minutes later, another ball came in high; I pulled first time overhead and it flew into the net. Brian Lohan wasn't feeling like Brian Lohan any more. Afterwards they said, 'God, you can play. Would you play for us? We have a game next week.' I said that I might, that I was thinking of getting a job in the area. The following night, I trained with them again when a man who worked with Tedcastles showed up. 'Holy God, what are you doing here, Justin?'

The lads all said, 'You know him?' He said, 'You mean you don't?' I just smiled, winked and walked away.

I still get a kick out of the game today. It could be going out the back and playing goal-to-goal with our 21-year-old daughter Úna or our 23-year-old son Justin or our 25-year-old son Ciarán.

It could be going out the back with no one but our little highland terrier, Misty Mac, and trying to hit a marker thirty-five yards away before Misty Mac comes back with the ball.

It could be trying to hit the ball from forty yards between these three trees we have out the back (I usually make it with one in every four shots; the key is to hit the ball out from my body).

It could be walking through the field behind us and pucking the ball from one corner to the other; it's about 350 yards long, so the test is to make it in four shots.

It could be going onto the road in front of us, where Barry and I used to play fifty years ago, and trying to get the ball to spin into the side entrance of the house fifty yards away.

Or it could be going back up to the college field and clipping lineballs over the bar from fifty yards.

And to add to the fun, I'll try all these things with different hurleys. I'll get one hurley and find myself saying, 'I'm not as good with this one; I need to practise more with this.' Then after a while, I start to get its feel and I'm going, 'Yeah, it's grand now' and I'm making the shots with it.

I know someone else whose eyes light up when he gets a hold of that hurley. Jamie Daly is the eight-year-old son of my good friend Paddy Daly, who I coached long ago in Ballymartle and was a selector with the Cork minor team that won the 2001 All-Ireland. Jamie is already technically better than most senior county players; he can double in the air, take lineballs, execute drop shots and take frees in the same style as Joe Deane. The other day, he and his brother Paul were pucking around in my back garden. The next thing, Jamie came down towards my end, dribbling the ball along the ground. And you know what he said? 'Come on, Justin. Take it off me.' Imagine that? 'Take it off me.' He's eight! He enthralls me. Like the game enthralls him.

I hope it continues to. I hope he doesn't get weighed down by all the expectations, pressure and disappointments that will be heaped upon him. I hope he doesn't define his career purely on whether he wins county medals or plays with his county. I hope that in fifty years' time, he too will be able to go out into his back garden and get the same buzz out of it as if it were Croke Park. Because to a lot of fellas, hurling is playing for the county or club. People ask them, 'Are you hurling any more?' And they say, 'Na, I stopped playing with the club two years ago.' But I'm still hurling. My last game with the club was ten years ago but I haven't retired. I should never have played after the accident but I didn't want to give up that hurley. And it's the same today. They can fire me, they can suspend me, but they can never take the game away from me. They can even jail me and I'll make an alley out of that cell, boy.

Because I'll be forever hurling.

I'll be forever hooked.

Justin's Roll of Honour

AS A PLAYER
1   All-Ireland senior medal (1966)
1   Caltex Hurler of the Year award (1966)
3   Munster senior medals (1966, 1969, 1972)
3   National League medals (1969, 1972, 1974)
1   All-Ireland Under-21 medal (1966)
2   Railway Cup medals (1968, 1969)
1   *Oireachtas* medal (1974)
2   Poc Fada bronze medals (1984, 1985)
1   Munster intermediate title (1964)

AS A COACH

1   All-Ireland senior title (1984, with Cork)
3   Munster senior titles (1975, 1984, 1985, with Cork)
2   National League titles (1977, 1978, with Clare)
1   Centenary Cup title (1984, with Cork)
1   Railway Cup title (1985, with Munster)
1   Munster club championship title (1991, with Cashel)
3   All-Ireland elevens titles (1993, 1996, 1997, with Cashel)
1   All-Ireland intermediate title (1970, with Antrim)
1   Tipperary senior county championship title (1991, with Cashel)
1   Cork intermediate county championship title (1999, with Ballincollig)
1   Cork Under-21 county championship title (1981, with Na Piarsaigh)
1   Philips Manager of the Month award (December 1991)
1   Jury's Sports Star of the Month award (December 1991)
4   Cork South-East division titles (1972, with Ballymartle; 1977, with Ballygarvan; 1980, 1981, with Shamrocks)
1   Mid-Cork division title (1980, with Blarney)

AS A SELECTOR ONLY
1   Munster senior title (1982, with Cork)

ACKNOWLEDGMENTS

The first time I spoke to Justin McCarthy was in the summer of 1995. I was just out of college, writing a weekly GAA column for the *Evening Echo* in Cork, when its sports editor, John Horgan, asked me to write an article on the state of Cork hurling. Before I did, he advised me to seek the opinion of Justin McCarthy. I hardly knew who Justin McCarthy was, but John informed me that he had been a great player and was probably the most respected coach in Cork. I knew why after making the call. And so, over the following five years, I'd occasionally call Justin if I wanted an insight into some players, especially those involved in those epic clashes between Cork and Clare in the late seventies. We'd also exchange pleasantries when we'd meet at matches. I hardly envisaged writing a book with or about him though.

Then in May 2000, I was researching an article on twentysomething players who had been discarded by their counties. Danny Murphy, who had played a pivotal role in the Cork hurling renaissance by captaining the county to two All-Ireland Under-21 titles, was no longer on the senior panel. Was he travelling or was he still playing with his club, Ballincollig? Justin McCarthy coached that club. He would know. He did. Danny was still playing. We then talked about the upcoming championship before he confided, 'I'm thinking of writing a book. I might need some help.'

I was flattered but hardly ecstatic when the proposal was aired. I was changing jobs within the month; writing a book was well down the list of priorities. Besides, McCarthy was a mysterious figure to most people of my generation, even those of us in Cork. I knew he had previously coached Cork but not in which years. I remembered hearing about the controversial interview he gave the *Examiner* after the Munster final in '85 and that the reason he wasn't coaching Cork was that he didn't see eye to eye with the county board. I also recalled meeting Danny Murphy in the Burlington Hotel the night Cork won the 1999 All-Ireland and him singing the praises of the man who a month later would lead his club to the county intermediate championship, and that Johnny Callinan said in Brendan Fullam's *Hurling Giants* that McCarthy had been easily the best coach he had encountered. A controversial interview, an intermediate county title, two national leagues with Clare and some guru-like statements from the bowels of the Rochestown ball alley though would hardly sustain a book. I told Justin that I'd get back to him when I was settled into my new job.

Three months later Justin wrote an excellent column in the *Irish Examiner*. It reminded me of his proposal. I phoned him and a few days later when I was back in Cork, I called up to his house. It was an education. I soon realised that I had known so little about this man; that so many people's perceptions of him were based on innuendo, ignorance and corner-boy gossip rather than fact. I hadn't known about Ardee and Ballygarvan or those long trips to Tulla. I also hadn't known why he didn't see eye to eye with the county board. It was fascinating to find out why – and to learn about inspiring figures like Father Roch, Father Harry Bohan and Jim 'Tough' Barry. The following day, I called Justin back. I'd never get a chance to write a better first book.

That hunch was reaffirmed every time we met. Justin McCarthy was one of the most obvious GAA books out there; that it wouldn't have been perceived as that was an indictment of how short people's memories can be. Imagine Seán Óg Ó hAilpín coaching Kildare while recovering from his leg injury; Brian Corcoran coaching Cork within a year of playing his last game for them; D.J. Carey in the next few years coaching Laois to two national league trophies; Ger Loughnane, after all those comments and needle matches against Tipperary, going up to coach a club team in that county; Loughnane travelling up to, and lying on, that field in Ardee. McCarthy has done all that – and much more. Yet it has been largely unnoticed or forgotten. When Justin was appointed Waterford manager last summer, thirty-one years after guiding Antrim to that All-Ireland intermediate title, an RTÉ reporter asked him would he find the transition from player to manager difficult. In one sense, it was sad that McCarthy had to approach a journalist, rather than one approach him, for people to either realise or recall the mould-breaking achievements and influence of an extraordinary hurling man.

I feel privileged to have been the one approached. Over the past eighteen months, I've kept our project a secret to most of my friends and acquaintances. In that time, I've heard many comments about Justin McCarthy, ranging from the complimentary ('God, what a player he was,' gushed Liam Griffin; 'The best coach you could have; that is fact,' said Raymie Ryan) to the derisory ('Justin? That junior player? Sure, he's only in it for one thing, boy,' by people who can't even remember he coached Cork, let alone Antrim that day in Ardee). I soon realised that the only people who had a bad word to say about him were confined to Cork. Anyone from anywhere else who knew him only raved about him. I didn't know Justin McCarthy before the summer of 2000. I know him now. That is to know he is probably the most decent, interesting and genuine man you could ever meet. Thanks, Justin, for your time, honesty, courage and friendship.

I will also treasure the hospitality I was given by the rest of the McCarthy family. To Pat for all those sandwiches, pots of tea and kind words; to Úna, Justin John, Cormac and Ciarán, for your interest and feedback; thank you so much.

Paul Howard, Kevin Kimmage and Seán Ryan are three of the keenest and shrewdest observers of sportswriting in this country. I am fortunate that they are also three friends of mine. Their advice, encouragement, honesty and humour were invaluable; again, lads, thanks for the time you gave to this. The vigilant editing of Finbarr O'Shea and the guidance, support and patience of Fergal Tobin at Gill & Macmillan were also deeply appreciated. We owe a debt of gratitude to the *Irish Examiner* too, for giving us permission to use Justin's interview with Val Dorgan which they first published.

There are some other people who influenced me in writing this book through the support, time and advice they gave at various stages of my career. To Tom Wilkinson, Tom Aherne, Tony Leen, John Horgan, Cormac MacConnell, Adhamhnán O'Sullivan, Mark Jones, and especially my parents Brendan and Rosaleen and my brothers Simon and Damien; I don't know if I'll ever get another opportunity to thank you, so I'm taking it now.

Kieran Shannon
March 2002